CAMBRIDGE
Primary Mathematics

Learner's Book 1

Cherri Moseley & Janet Rees

CAMBRIDGE
UNIVERSITY PRESS

University Printing House, Cambridge CB2 8BS, United Kingdom

One Liberty Plaza, 20th Floor, New York, NY 10006, USA

477 Williamstown Road, Port Melbourne, VIC 3207, Australia

314–321, 3rd Floor, Plot 3, Splendor Forum, Jasola District Centre, New Delhi – 110025, India

103 Penang Road, #05-06/07, Visioncrest Commercial, Singapore 238467

Cambridge University Press is part of the University of Cambridge.

It furthers the University's mission by disseminating knowledge in the pursuit of education, learning and research at the highest international levels of excellence.

www.cambridge.org
Information on this title: www.cambridge.org/9781108746410

© Cambridge University Press 2021

This publication is in copyright. Subject to statutory exception and to the provisions of relevant collective licensing agreements, no reproduction of any part may take place without the written permission of Cambridge University Press.

First published 2014
Second edition 2021

20 19 18 17 16 15

Printed in Italy by L.E.G.O. S.p.A.

A catalogue record for this publication is available from the British Library

ISBN 978-1-108-74641-0 Paperback with Digital Access (1 Year)

ISBN 978-1-108-96410-4 Digital Learner's Book (1 Year)

ISBN 978-1-108-96409-8 Learner's Book eBook

Additional resources for this publication at www.cambridge.org/9781108746410

Cambridge University Press has no responsibility for the persistence or accuracy of URLs for external or third-party internet websites referred to in this publication, and does not guarantee that any content on such websites is, or will remain, accurate or appropriate. Information regarding prices, travel timetables, and other factual information given in this work is correct at the time of first printing but Cambridge University Press does not guarantee the accuracy of such information thereafter.

Projects and their accompanying teacher guidance have been written by the NRICH Team. NRICH is an innovative collaboration between the Faculties of Mathematics and Education at the University of Cambridge, which focuses on problem solving and on creating opportunities for students to learn mathematics through exploration and discussion https://nrich.maths.org.

NOTICE TO TEACHERS IN THE UK
It is illegal to reproduce any part of this work in material form (including photocopying and electronic storage) except under the following circumstances:
(i) where you are abiding by a licence granted to your school or institution by the Copyright Licensing Agency;
(ii) where no such licence exists, or where you wish to exceed the terms of a licence, and you have gained the written permission of Cambridge University Press;
(iii) where you are allowed to reproduce without permission under the provisions of Chapter 3 of the Copyright, Designs and Patents Act 1988, which covers, for example, the reproduction of short passages within certain types of educational anthology and reproduction for the purposes of setting examination questions.

Introduction

Welcome to Stage 1 of **Cambridge Primary Mathematics**. We hope this book will show you how interesting and exciting mathematics can be.

Mathematics is everywhere. Everyone uses mathematics every day. Where have you noticed mathematics?

Have you ever wondered about any of these questions?

- Are the numbers we use when measuring the same as the numbers we count with?
- Why are the same 10 digits used to make all numbers (0, 1, 2, 3, 4, 5, 6, 7, 8 and 9)?
- What is the difference between 2D and 3D shapes?
- How do you describe a pattern?
- How do you measure the passage of time?
- How do you solve a mathematics problem?

You will work like a mathematician to find the answers to some of these questions. It is good to talk about mathematics and share ideas as you explore. You will reflect on what you did and how you did it to think about whether you would do the same next time.

You will be able to practise new skills and check how you are doing and also challenge yourself to find out more. You will be able to make connections between what seem to be different areas of mathematics.

We hope you enjoy thinking and working like a mathematician.

Cherri Moseley and Janet Rees

Contents

Page	Unit		Maths strand
6	How to use this book		
8	Thinking and Working Mathematically		
10	1	Numbers to 10 1.1 Counting sets of objects 1.2 Say, read and write numbers to 10 1.3 Comparing numbers 1.4 Number words 1.5 Odd and even numbers	Number
36	2	Geometry 2.1 3D shapes 2.2 2D shapes	Geometry and measure
48	3	Fractions 3.1 Fractions	Number
56	4	Measures 4.1 Length	Geometry and measure
66	Project 1: Snakes		
67	5	Working with numbers to 10 5.1 Addition as combining 5.2 Subtraction as take away	Number
86	Project 2: Compare the rows		
87	6	Position 6.1 Position	Geometry and measure
97	7	Statistics 7.1 Sets 7.2 Venn diagrams	Statistics and probability
110	8	Time 8.1 Time	Geometry and measure
118	9	Numbers to 20 9.1 Counting to 20 9.2 Counting, comparing, ordering and estimating 9.3 Number patterns	Number

Contents

Page	Unit	Maths strand
137	Project 3: Counting fish	

138	10 Geometry (2)
	    10.1 3D shapes
	    10.2 2D shapes
		Geometry and measure

155	Project 4: Which one doesn't belong?	
156	11 Fractions (2) 11.1 Halves	Number
165	Project 5: Fair fruit	

166	12 Measures (2)
	    12.1 Mass and capacity
	    12.2 How do we measure?
		Number

178	13 Working with numbers to 20
	    13.1 Addition by counting on
	    13.2 Subtraction by counting back
	    13.3 Using the number line
	    13.4 Money
		Number

203	14 Statistics (2)
	    14.1 Venn diagrams, Carroll diagrams and pictograms
	    14.2 Lists, tables and block graphs
		Statistics and probability

221	15 Time (2) 15.1 Time	Geometry and measure
230	16 Position, direction and patterns 16.1 Position, direction and patterns	Geometry and measure
241	Project 6: Finding drawers	
242	Glossary	
262	Acknowledgements	

How to use this book

How to use this book

In this book you will find lots of different features to help your learning:

Questions to find out what you know already. ⟶

> **Getting started**
>
> 1 This cookie is a whole.
>
>   How many parts is the cookie cut into?
>
>   Are they the same as each other? _____

What you will learn in the unit. ⟶

> **We are going to . . .**
> • count sets of objects.

Important words that you will use. ⟶

> count   estimate   how many   set   total

Step-by-step examples showing a way to solve a problem. ⟶

> **Worked example 1**
>
> Which domino has 4 spots?
>
>
>
> **Answer:**
>
>
>
>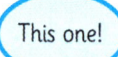
>
> 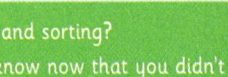 This one!

Questions to help you think about how you learn. ⟶

> What have you learned about sets and sorting?
> Write or draw one thing that you know now that you didn't know before.

There are often many different ways to solve a problem.

How to use this book

These questions will help you develop your skills of thinking and working mathematically.

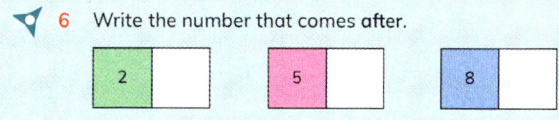

6 Write the number that comes after.

| 2 | | 5 | | 8 | |

An investigation to carry out with a partner or in groups. This will help develop your skills of thinking and working mathematically.

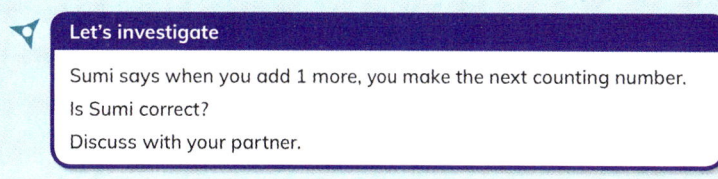

Let's investigate

Sumi says when you add 1 more, you make the next counting number.
Is Sumi correct?
Discuss with your partner.

What you have learned in the unit. Tick the column to show how you feel about each thing.

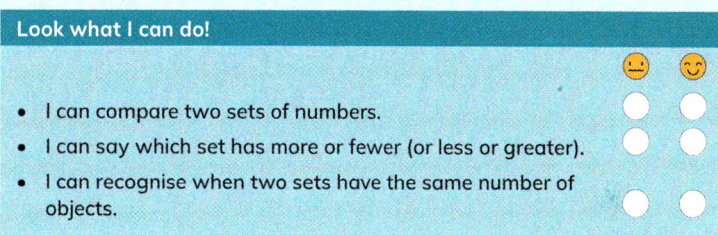

Look what I can do!

- I can compare two sets of numbers.
- I can say which set has more or fewer (or less or greater).
- I can recognise when two sets have the same number of objects.

Questions that cover what you have learned in the unit.

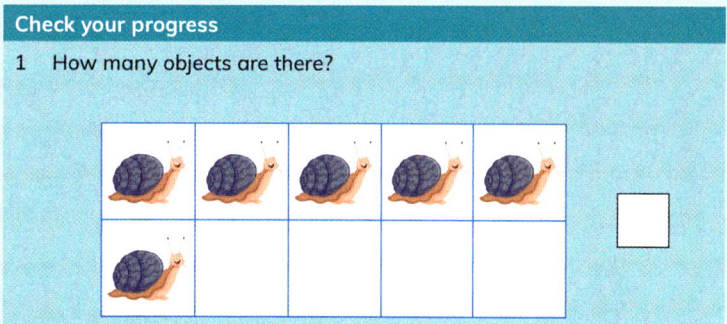

Check your progress

1 How many objects are there?

At the end of some units there is a project for you to carry out, using what you have learned. You might make something or solve a problem.

Snakes

Your first challenge is to make a snake!
You could use card, paper, dough, pipe cleaners, ribbon, glue, tape, cubes, blocks... anything that you can find.

Projects and their accompanying teacher guidance have been written by the NRICH Team. NRICH is an innovative collaboration between the Faculties of Mathematics and Education at the University of Cambridge, which focuses on problem solving and on creating opportunities for students to learn mathematics through exploration and discussion https://nrich.maths.org.

Thinking and Working Mathematically

There are some important skills that you will develop as you learn mathematics.

Specialising is when I test examples to see if they fit a rule or pattern.

Characterising is when I explain how a group of things are the same.

Generalising is when I can explain and use a rule or pattern to find more examples.

Classifying is when I put things into groups and can say what rule I have used.

Thinking and Working Mathematically

Critiquing is when I think about what is good and what could be better in my work or someone else's work.

Improving is when I try to make my maths better.

Conjecturing is when I think of an idea or question linked to my maths.

Convincing is when I explain my thinking to someone else, to help them understand.

1 ▶ Numbers to 10

Getting started

1. How many hippos are there?

   Draw a ⓡⓘⓝⓖ around the number that matches the set.

 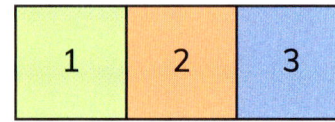

2. Count the toys and write the numbers.

3. Write some numbers you know in the space below.

Tell your partner something about each of the numbers you wrote.

1 Numbers to 10

Numbers are all around us.

Sometimes a number is a label, like the number on a football shirt or the number on a bus.

We count to find out how many there are.

A pack of 2 T-shirts shows 2 on the pack.

1 Numbers to 10

> 1.1 Counting sets of objects

We are going to …
- **count sets of objects.**

You need to say the numbers in the correct order to count.

To count objects, start with 1 and say a number for each object.

The last number you say tells you how many objects there are.

count   estimate   how many   set   total

1.1 Counting sets of objects

Exercise 1.1

1 Count together.

1 Numbers to 10

2   Put some objects in the box.
    Count your set of objects.

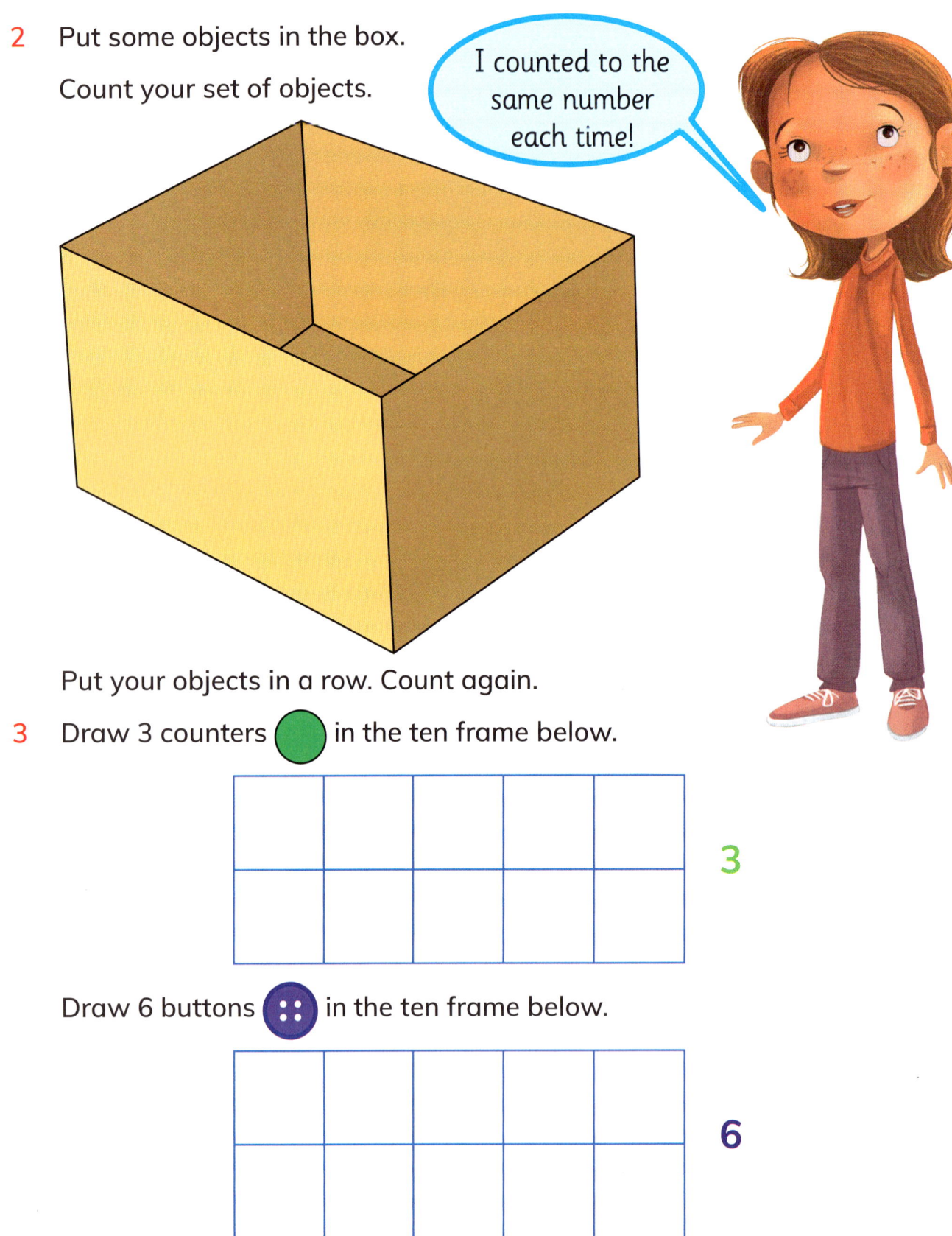

I counted to the same number each time!

Put your objects in a row. Count again.

3   Draw 3 counters ● in the ten frame below.

    3

Draw 6 buttons in the ten frame below.

    6

1.1 Counting sets of objects

Draw 0 counters ● in the ten frame below.

0

Worked example 1

Which domino has 4 spots?

Answer:

This one!

4 Which domino has 5 spots?

Draw a ring around the correct domino.

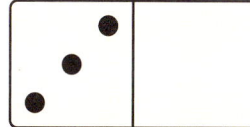 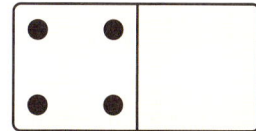 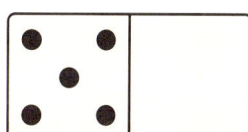

5 Which domino has 9 spots?

Draw a ring around the correct domino.

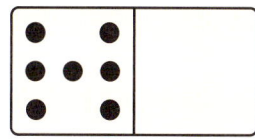 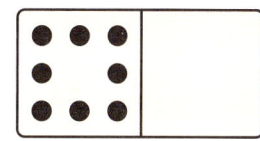 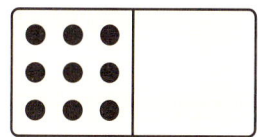

1 Numbers to 10

6 Match each picture to the correct number.

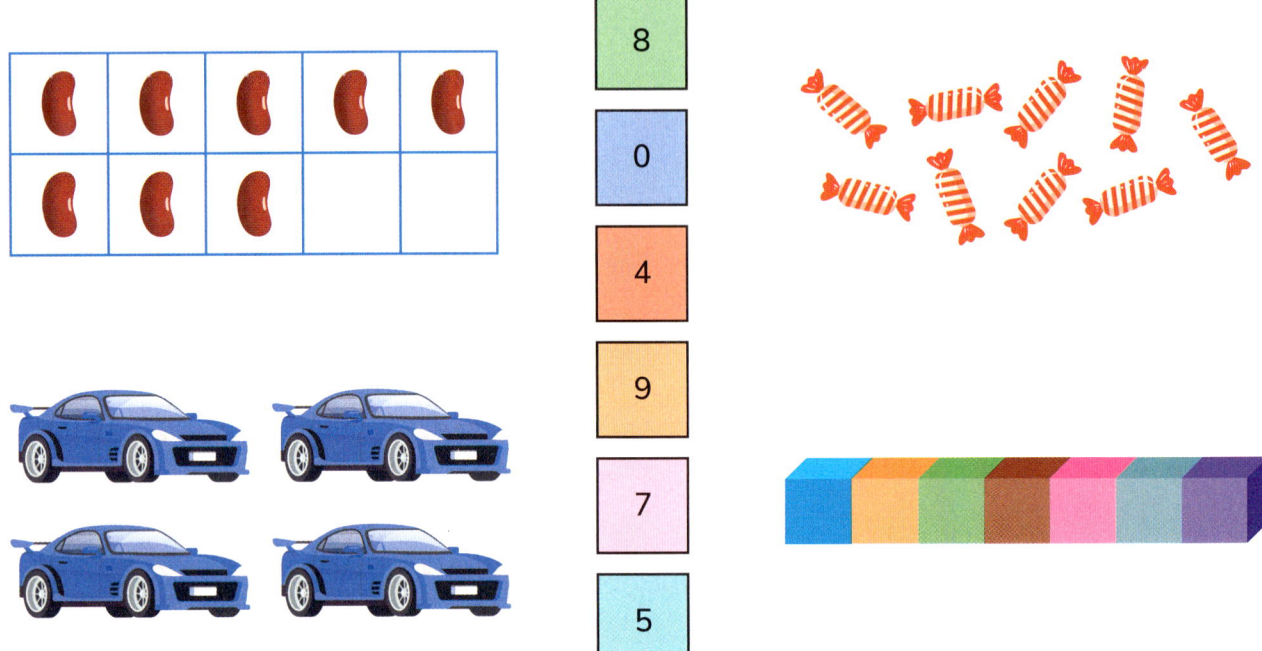

Ask your partner to show you how they got their answer.

 7 Draw 7 bananas.

Make it easy to see how many there are.

Look at your answer to question 7.
How did you make it easy to see how many you drew?

1.1 Counting sets of objects

Worked example 2

How many sunflowers are there? Estimate then count.

Answer:

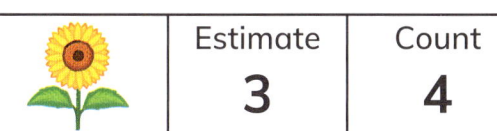

	Estimate	Count
🌻	3	4

An estimate is a good guess. I estimate there are 3 sunflowers.

I am going to count the sunflowers to see if your estimate was close. 1, 2, 3, 4. There are 4. I estimated 3, so I was very close.

17

1 Numbers to 10

 8   Look at the picture on the previous page.
Estimate then count. Write the numbers.

🦋	🐇	🐸	🌳	🦅
Estimate	Estimate	Estimate	Estimate	Estimate
Count	Count	Count	Count	Count

Let's investigate

Work with a partner.

Make a poster all about a number.

Talk about your poster with your class.

Look what I can do!

- I can count objects and write the matching number.
- I can find or draw the correct number of objects.
- I can say how many objects are in some sets without counting.
- I can give a good estimate of how many objects there are.

> 1.2 Say, read and write numbers to 10

We are going to ...

- say, read and write numbers and number words to 10.

Saying the numbers in a number rhyme is a good way to learn the order of the numbers.

between   number
order   point
number track

Exercise 1.2

1   Say this number rhyme together.

> 1, 2, 3, 4, 5,
> Once I caught a fish alive!
> 6, 7, 8, 9, 10,
> Then I let it go again!
> Why did you let it go?
> Because it bit my finger so.
> Which finger did it bite?
> This little finger on the right.

2   Say your favourite number rhyme to a partner.

3   Count to 10. Point to each number as you say it.

1 Numbers to 10

Worked example 3

Which number is missing?

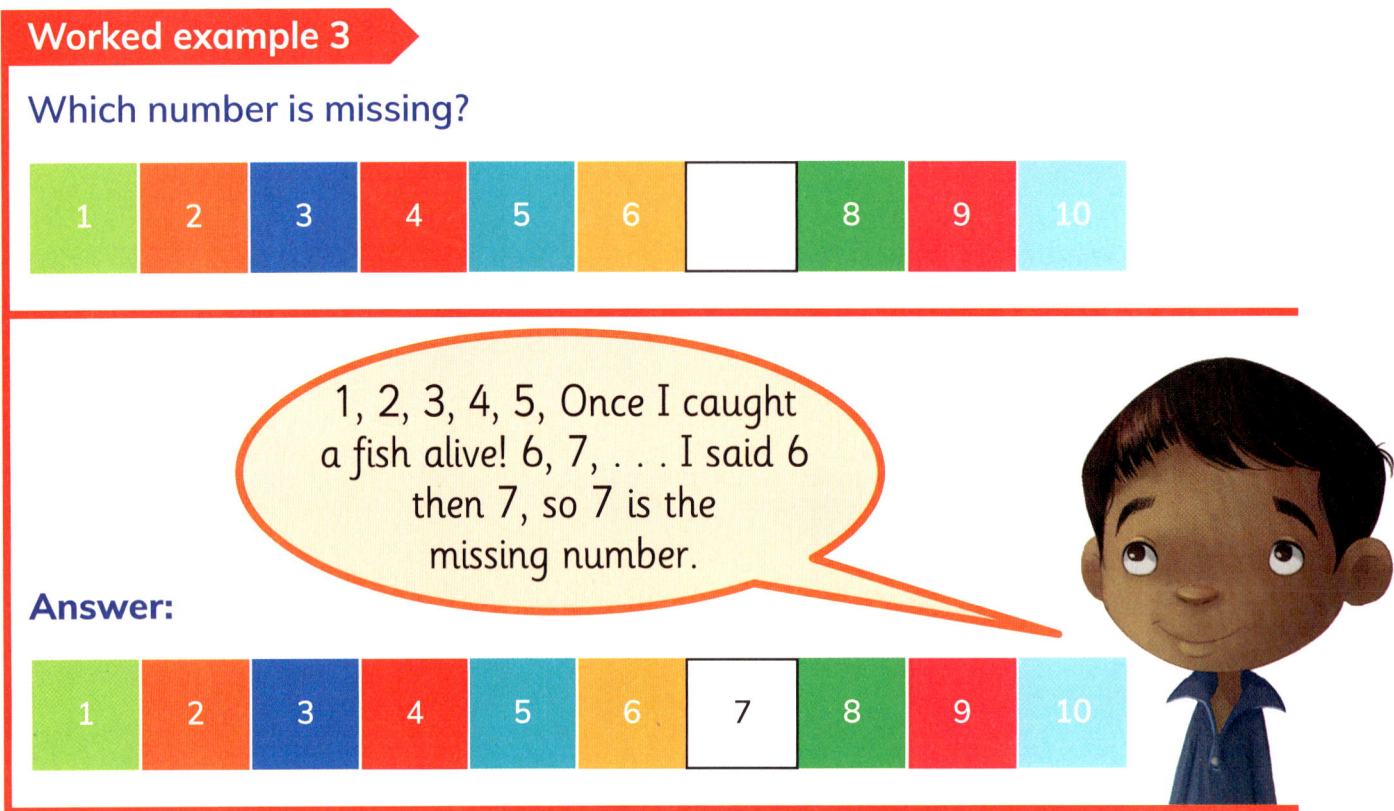

4 Count to 10. Write the missing numbers.

5 Which numbers have been swapped in this number track? Write the numbers in the box.

1.2 Say, read and write numbers to 10

6 Write the number that comes **after**.

| 2 | | | 5 | | | 8 | |

7 Write the number that comes **before**.

| | 2 | | | 5 | | | 8 |

> What do you do if you cannot remember a missing number?
> Ask your partner to tell you what they do.

Look what I can do!

- I can count to 10 and find a missing number.
- I can say some number rhymes.
- I can read and write the numbers 1, 2, 3, 4, 5, 6, 7, 8, 9 and 10.

1 Numbers to 10

> ## 1.3 Comparing numbers

We are going to …
- compare sets of objects and numbers.

You can compare different sets. You can find out which set has more, fewer or the same number of objects as another set.

Fewer means the same as **less**.
More means the same as **greater**.

> compare   equal   fewer
> less   more   same

Exercise 1.3

Worked example 4

Compare the two sets. Look for what is the same or different.
Tick ✓ the set that has more objects.

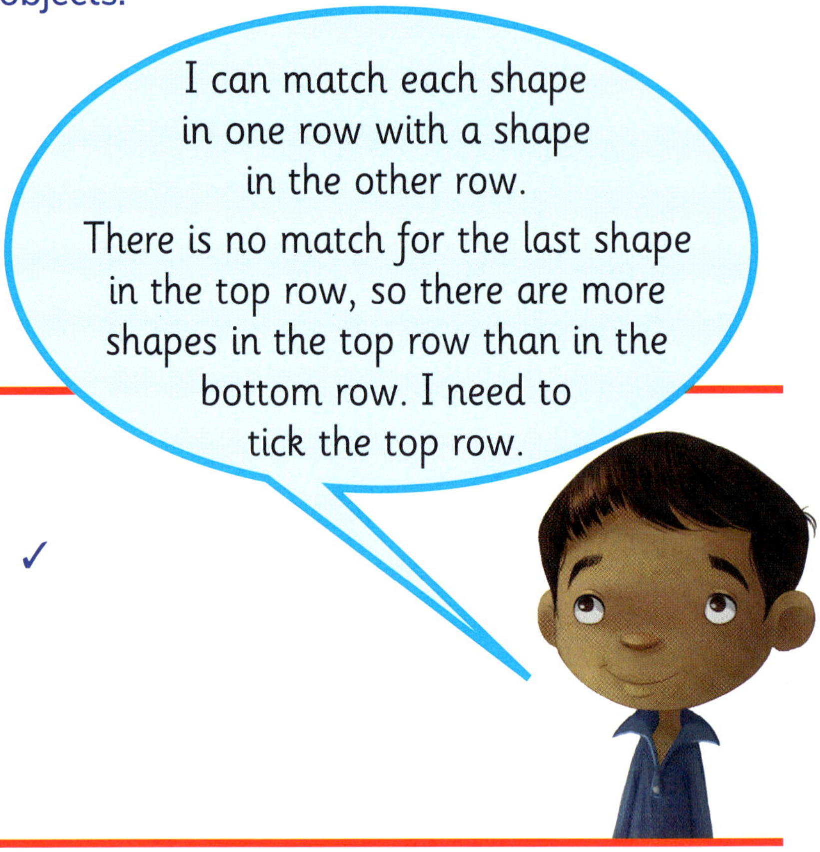

> I can match each shape in one row with a shape in the other row.
> There is no match for the last shape in the top row, so there are more shapes in the top row than in the bottom row. I need to tick the top row.

Answer:

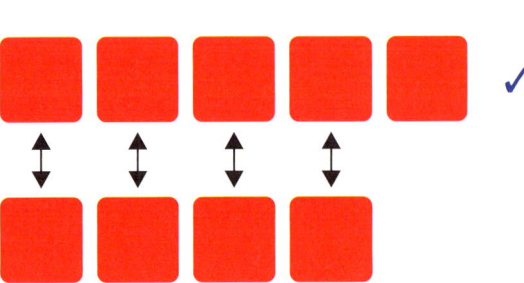 ✓

22

1.3 Comparing numbers

1. Compare the sets.

   Tick ✓ the set that has fewer objects.

   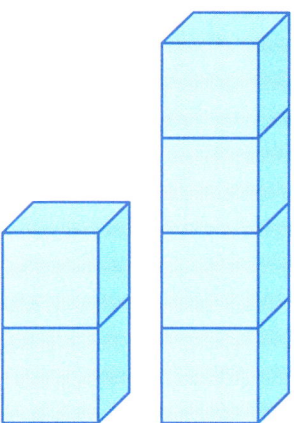

2. Compare the sets.

   Tick ✓ the set that has fewer objects.

3. Compare the sets.

   Tick ✓ the set that has more objects.

1 Numbers to 10

4   Compare the sets.

Tick ✓ the sets that have the same number of objects.

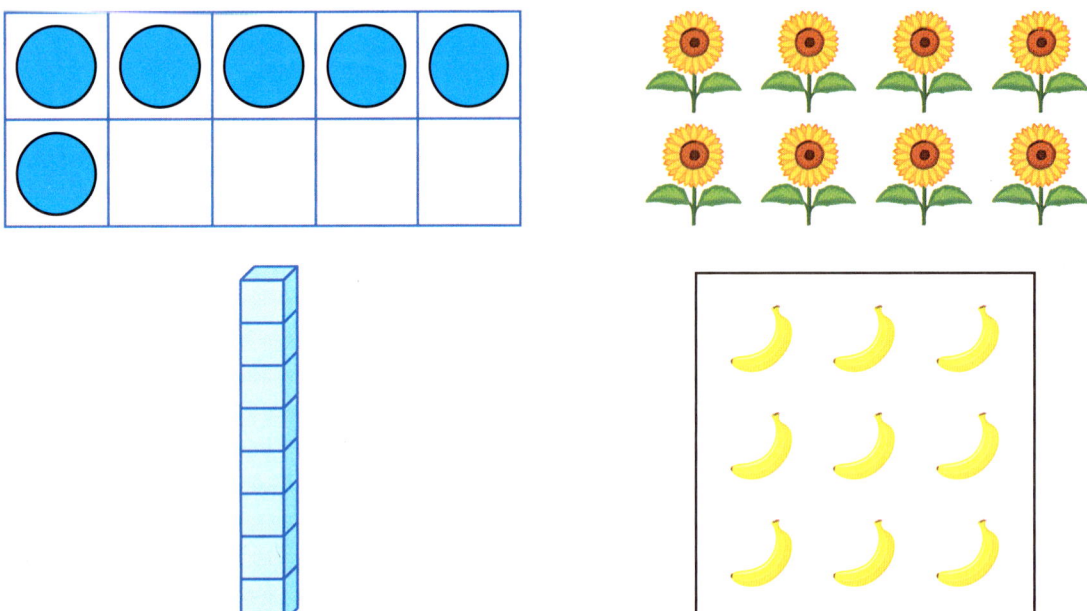

 5   Compare the sets.

Complete the sentences.

There are _____ 🍌.

There are _____ 🍊.

There are more _____ than _____,

so there are fewer _____ than _____.

24

1.3 Comparing numbers

6 Compare the sets.
Complete the sentences.

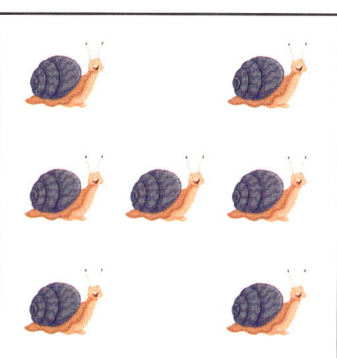

There are _____ 🕷.

There are _____ 🐌.

There are fewer _____ than _____ so there

are more _____ than _____.

7 is less than 9.

7 Look at question 6.

How many more spiders than snails? ☐

How many fewer snails than spiders? ☐

Use the number track to help you answer questions 8 to 10.

| 1 | 2 | 3 | 4 | 5 | 6 | 7 | 8 | 9 | 10 |

8 Write a number that is greater than 4. ☐

 9 Write a number that is less than 5. ☐

1 Numbers to 10

10 Draw a ring around the correct number to complete each sentence.

> To find a number that is **more** than a given number, look along the number track towards the   1 or 10.

> To find a number that is **fewer** than a given number, look along the number track towards the   1 or 10.

Let's investigate

Work with a partner or on your own.

Take 3 objects.

Take 1 more.

How many do you have now? ☐

Take 1 more.

How many do you have now? ☐

Repeat until you have 10 objects. What do you notice?

You have 10 objects.

Put 1 back.

How many do you have now? ☐

Put another 1 back.

How many do you have now? ☐

Repeat until you have 0 objects left. What do you notice?

If you were going to start your investigation again, would you do anything differently?

> 1.4 Number words

Look what I can do!

- I can compare two sets of numbers.
- I can say which set has more or fewer (or greater or less).
- I can recognise when two sets have the same number of objects.

> 1.4 Number words

We are going to ...

- say, read and write numbers and number words to 10.

We can write numbers in words.

Coins often have words instead of numbers on them.

We often use words instead of numbers in a story.

> zero: 0　one: 1　two: 2　three: 3　four: 4　five: 5
> six: 6　seven: 7　eight: 8　nine: 9　ten: 10

1 Numbers to 10

Exercise 1.4

1 Count the spots and read the number words.

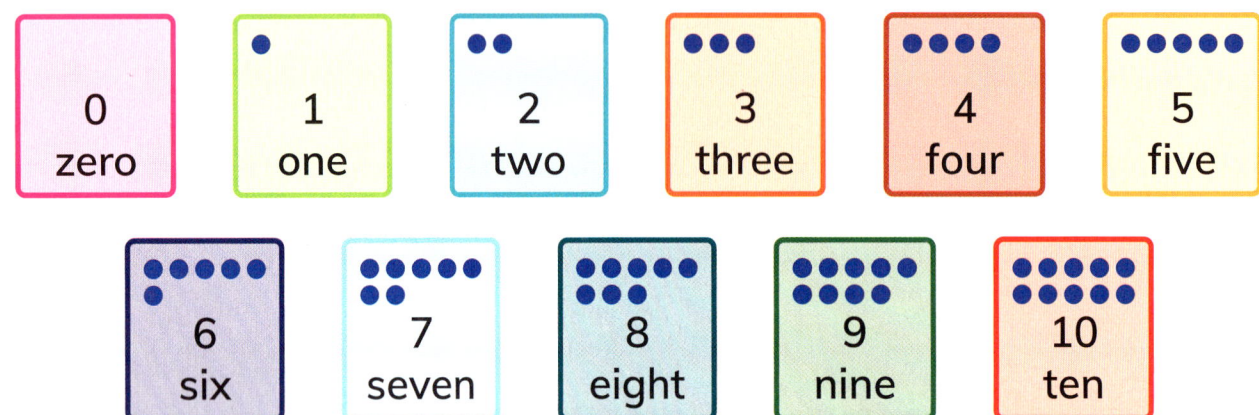

2 Write the missing word or number on each ten frame.
The first one has been done for you.

1 one	2		4	
		three		five
6	7		9	10
		eight		

1.4 Number words

3   Match the sets to the number words.

one · three · five · seven · nine

zero · two · four · six · eight · ten

Which words do not have a matching set of fruit? _____

  4   Draw eight apples.

Make it easy for others to quickly see how many there are.

5 Draw a basket with **zero** fruit in it.

6 Write the number word after.

one		four		eight	

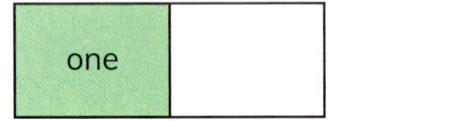

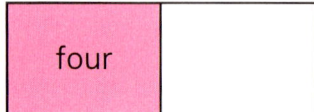

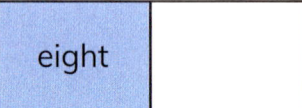

7 Write the number word before.

	one		four		eight

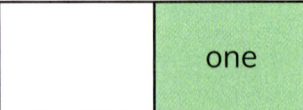

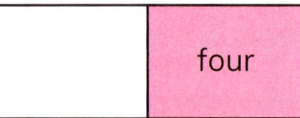

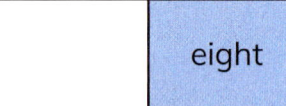

Can you read and write all the number words correctly?

Do you find the word track, word ten frame or domino layouts with number words helpful? Explain why.

Let's investigate

All the number words from zero to ten have either 3, 4 or 5 letters in the word.

Work with a partner to find out which number words have 3 letters, 4 letters or 5 letters.

1.5 Odd and even numbers

> **Continued**
>
> How do you know you have checked all the number words?
>
> Are there any number words that have the same number of letters as that number?

Look what I can do!

- I can read all the number words from zero to ten.
- I can write some number words from zero to ten.

> 1.5 Odd and even numbers

We are going to ...

- **find out about odd and even numbers.**

There are different kinds of numbers.

Some numbers are called even numbers. An even number of objects can be put into pairs with none left over.

> even   odd   pair   pattern

Some numbers are called odd numbers. An odd number of objects always has 1 left over when the objects are put into pairs.

1 Numbers to 10

Exercise 1.5

> **Worked example 5**
>
> Draw a ring around the correct word for 3.
>
> Use some cubes to help you.
>
>    odd / even
>
> ---
>
> **Answer:** 1 pair and 1 left over. 3 is an (odd) number.
>
>

1   Is each number odd or even? Draw a ring around the correct word.

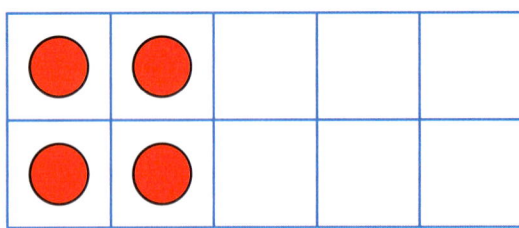   odd / even

8   odd / even

1   odd / even

 2   Draw an odd number of counters on the ten frame.

Make it easy to see that it is odd.

32

1.5 Odd and even numbers

> Do you need counters or other objects to find out if a number is odd or even?
>
> Explain to your partner how you use the counters.

 3 Colour the even numbers on the number track **red**.

Colour the odd numbers on the number track **blue**.

| 0 | 1 | 2 | 3 | 4 | 5 | 6 | 7 | 8 | 9 | 10 |

What pattern have you made?

---

 4 Is each number odd or even?
Use the number track in question 3 to help you.

| 1 | odd / even | 7 | odd / even |
| 4 | odd / even | 10 | odd / even |

Let's investigate

Work in a group of four. You will need a set of ten frames cut into jigsaws.*

Put two numbers together to make ten, so that the ten frames are whole again.

Discuss what you notice about the numbers in each ten frame.

*See the additional teaching idea 'Odd and even on a ten frame' in the Teacher's Resource.

33

1 **Numbers to 10**

Worked example 6

6 is the answer.
What could the question be?

Answer:

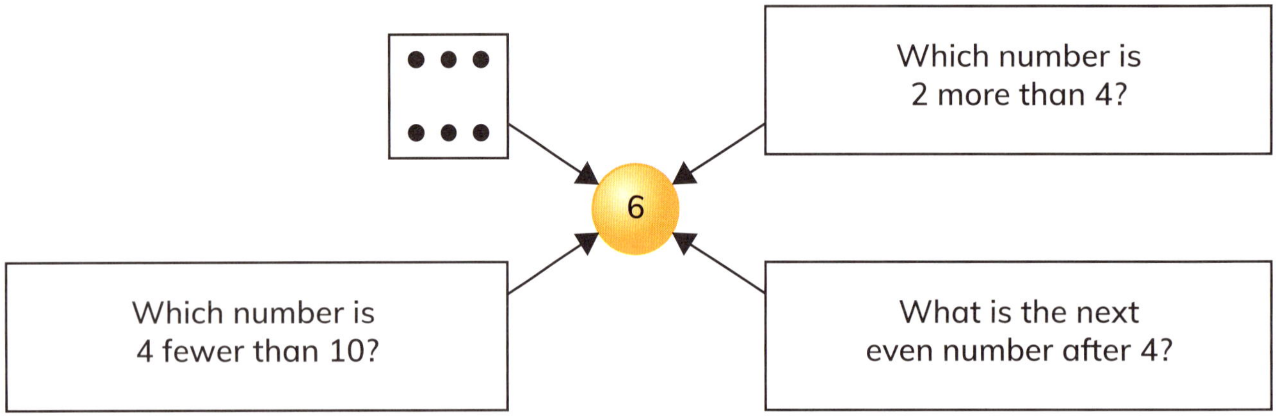

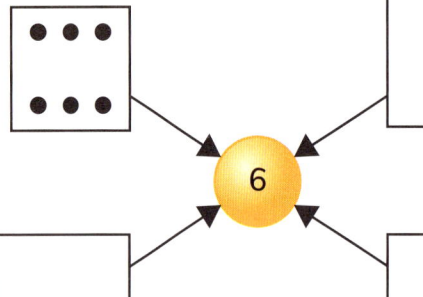

Which number is 2 more than 4?

Which number is 4 fewer than 10?

What is the next even number after 4?

 5   8 is the answer.
What could the question be?

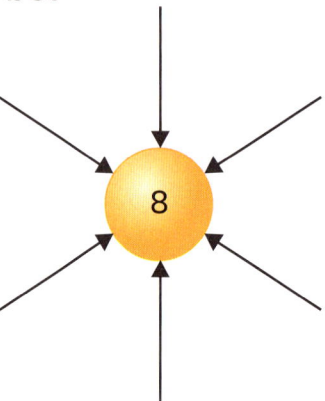

Look what I can do!

- I can find out if a number from one to ten is odd or even.
- I can remember some odd and even numbers.
- I can describe the pattern of odd and even numbers.

1.5 Odd and even numbers

Check your progress

1   How many objects are there?

2   Estimate then count.

   Estimate ☐ Count ☐   Estimate ☐ Count ☐

3   Draw a ring around the odd numbers.

   7   2   6   9   1   8

35

2 Geometry

Getting started

1. Talk to your partner about these shapes.

   What can you see?

   What do you know about these shapes?

   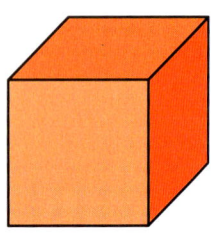  

2. How many?

   There are _____ green shapes.

   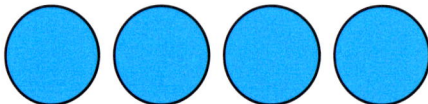

   There are _____ blue shapes.

   There are _____ red shapes.

2 Geometry

You are learning about 2D and 3D shapes so that you can use them in different ways.

We live inside 3D shapes and we fill our homes, villages and towns with 2D and 3D shapes. Making patterns with shapes will help you to learn much more about them.

2 Geometry

> 2.1 3D shapes

We are going to ...
- describe and sort 3D shapes
- find what is the same and what is different about 3D shapes
- learn and use the right words for 3D shapes.

We live inside 3D shapes.

3D cube
cylinder
edge face
sphere

We have 3D shapes all around us.

You can hold a 3D shape in your hand.

3D shapes have faces. Many also have edges.

face

edge

Pick up a 3D shape.

Can you touch an edge?

Can you touch a face?

3D shapes can have flat faces or curved surfaces.

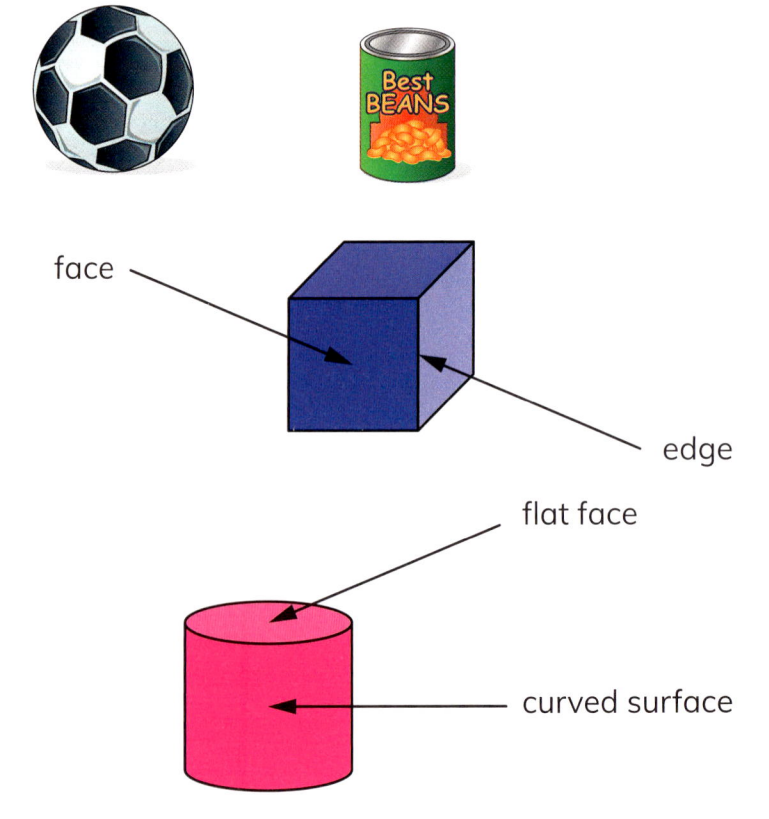

flat face

curved surface

38

2.1 3D shapes

Exercise 2.1

1 Look at the pictures of 3D shapes. Join the shapes that are the same.

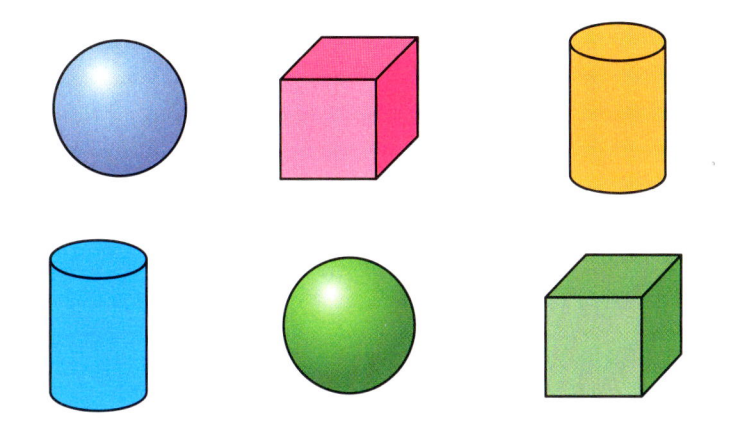

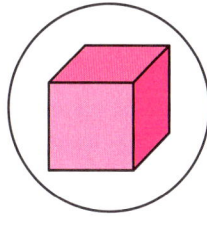

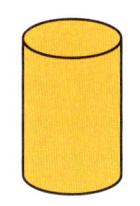

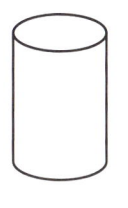

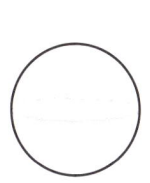

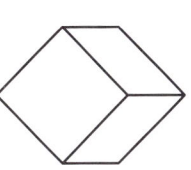

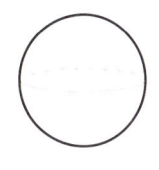

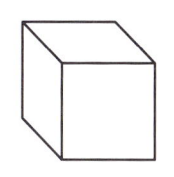

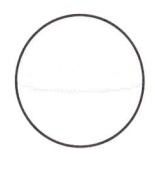

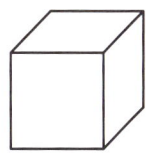

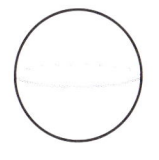

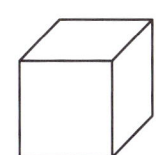

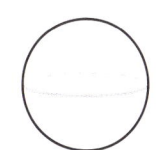

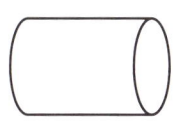

2 Draw a ring around the cubes.   Colour the cylinders yellow.   Colour the spheres blue.

39

2 Geometry

3 Draw a ring around the shapes that will roll.

Draw a ring around the shapes that you can stack.

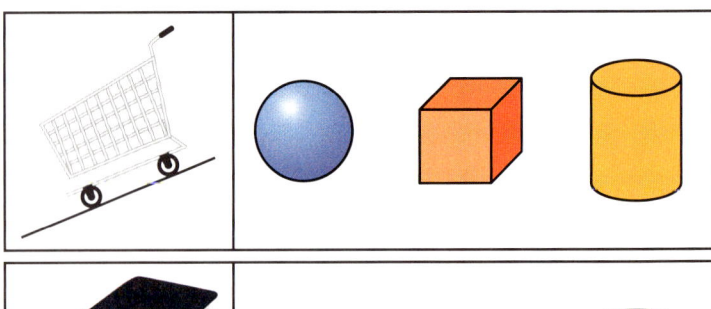

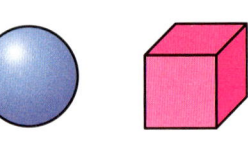

Does it make a difference if you turn the shape?

4 Look at the shapes in question 3.
Which 3D shapes fit onto these 2D shapes?
Which 3D shape is missing?

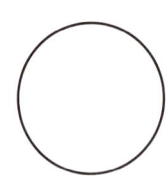

5 Join the name of the shape to the shape itself.
The first one has been done for you.

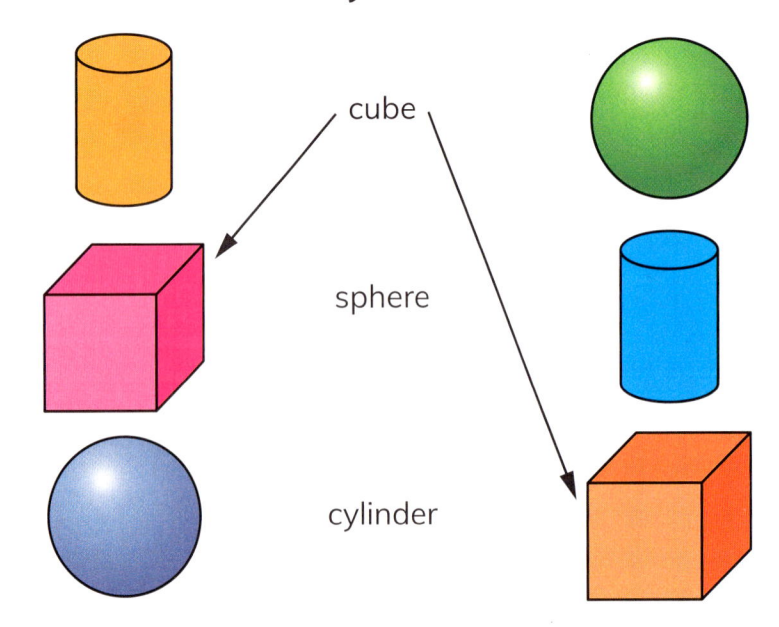

cube

sphere

cylinder

40

2.1 3D shapes

6 How many edges, faces or surfaces does each shape have?

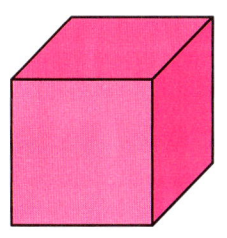

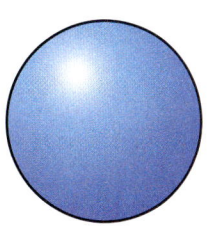

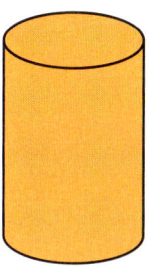

| Edges: | Edges: | Edges: |
| Faces: | Faces: | Surfaces: |

Let's investigate

Work with a partner to build a tower.

You can use more than one of each shape.

Talk about your tower and the shapes you will use.

Use the words edge and face.

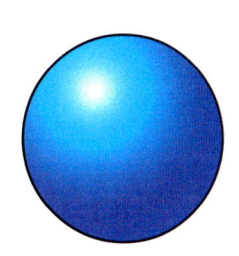

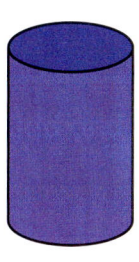

Which shape would be good to start with?

Which shape would be better at the top of the tower?

If you built another tower using the same 3D shapes would you do it the same way or a different way? Why?

41

2 Geometry

Look what I can do!

- I can describe and sort 3D shapes.
- I can find what is the same and what is different about shapes.
- I can use the right words for the parts of 3D shapes.

> 2.2 2D shapes

We are going to ...

- describe and sort 2D shapes using the number of sides
- find out the number of sides that different shapes have
- find what is the same and what is different about shapes
- use the right names for 2D shapes.

2D shapes are flat. This is what makes them different to 3D shapes.

Playing with shapes and making patterns using 2D shapes will help you to learn much more about them.

I can hold a 3D shape in my hand. I can't hold a 2D shape.

2D   circle   curved   rectangle   side   square   straight   triangle

2.2 2D shapes

Exercise 2.2

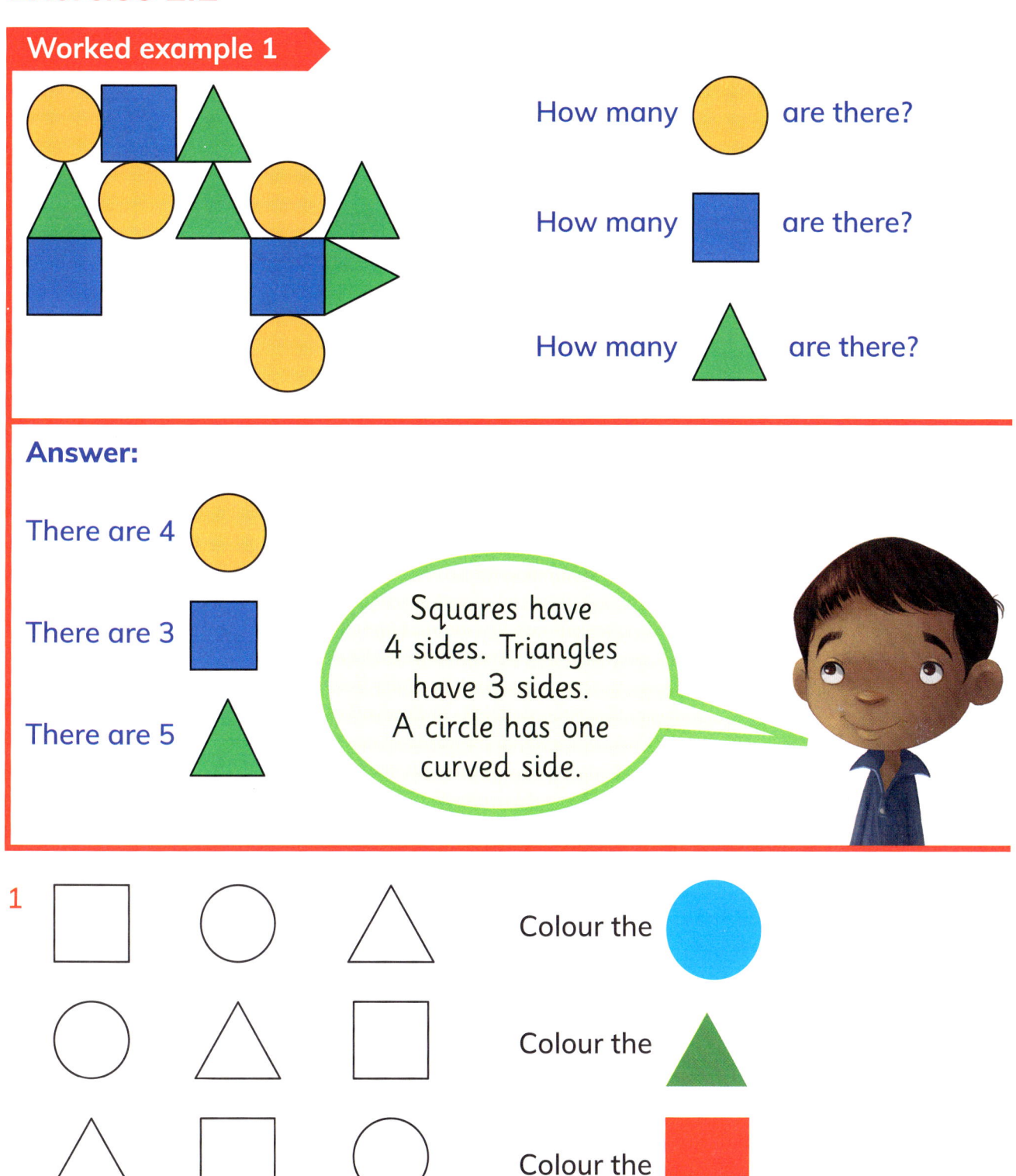

Worked example 1

How many ○ are there?

How many ■ are there?

How many ▲ are there?

Answer:

There are 4 ○

There are 3 ■

There are 5 ▲

Squares have 4 sides. Triangles have 3 sides. A circle has one curved side.

1

Colour the ● (blue)

Colour the ▲ (green)

Colour the ■ (red)

Colour the ■ (yellow)

43

2 Geometry

2 A circle has curved sides.

A square has straight sides.

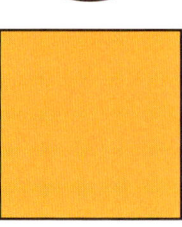

Draw a ring around the correct word in each sentence.

A rectangle has 4 **curved / straight** sides.

A triangle has **1 / 2 / 3 / 4** straight sides.

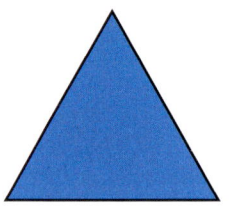

3 Match each shape to the correct clouds.

Are the sides straight or curved?

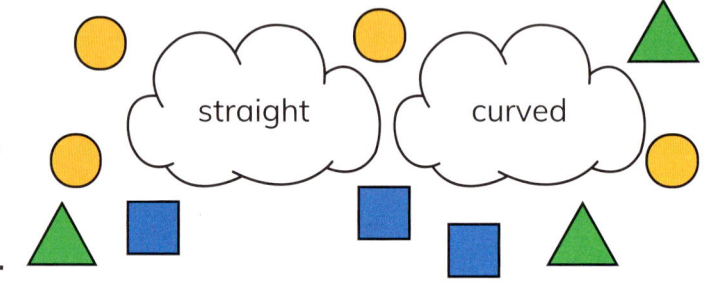

Count the shapes for each cloud.

straight   curved

Work with a partner. Keep asking your partner questions until they work out what each shape is.

Write the number in these boxes.

Straight	**Curved**

2.2 2D shapes

4   Use shape pieces to draw a rocket.

Use as many of each shape
as you want.

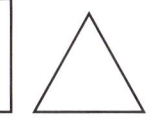

◯ ▢ △

How many shapes did you use?

How is your partner's rocket the same?

How is it different?

Let's investigate

You will need a set of shapes and a partner.

Put your shapes in a bag or a box.

Take turns to pick a shape. Do not show your partner the shape.

Your partner should ask questions to find out what shape it is.

Your partner should say what shape it is.

How many sides does it have?

Are the sides straight or curved?

If they say the correct shape, it is their turn to choose a shape.

You can then ask questions to guess what shape it is.

2 Geometry

What did you find easy about 2D shapes?
What did you find difficult?

Look what I can do!

- I can describe and sort 2D shapes.
- I can find what is the same and what is different about shapes.
- I can use the right names for 2D shapes.

2.2 2D shapes

Check your progress

1. Which shape has 6 faces or surfaces? Draw a ring around the word.

    sphere   cylinder   cube

2. Which shapes will go through this hole?
   Draw a ring around the words.

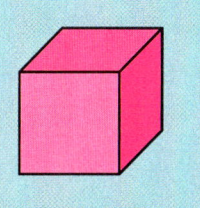

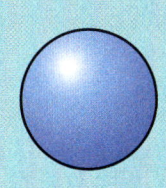

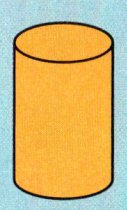

    cube   sphere   cylinder

3. Join these words to the correct shapes.

    All flat faces   Some flat faces   No flat faces

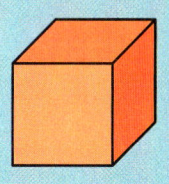

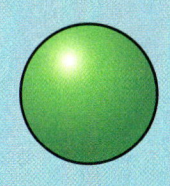

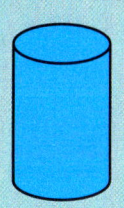

4. Draw a ring round the shape that has 4 sides.

5. Which shapes can fit together with no spaces? Draw your answers in the space below.

    For example,

3 Fractions

Getting started

1   This cookie is a whole.

   How many parts is the cookie cut into?

   Are they the same as each other? _____

2   This bar of chocolate is a whole.

   How many parts is the chocolate cut into?

   Are they the same as each other? _____

You are learning about fractions so that you can use them in different ways.

Each fraction can look different. It depends on the shape you start with.

A fraction is part of a whole.

48

> 3.1 Fractions

We are going to ...
- find half of a shape
- recognise when a shape is not split into halves
- put two halves back together to make the whole.

We use fractions to help us share fairly.

We both get the same, half each.

We use fractions every day.

This is a pair of shoes.

Two shoes make a pair.

One shoe is half of that pair.

fraction   half   part

We need to match our shoes.

3 Fractions

Exercise 3.1

Worked example 1

Find half of a square.

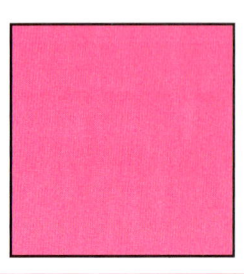

Answer:

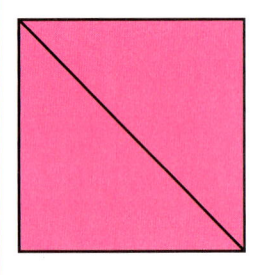

Each part is a half. Both parts are the same size. They are equal.

Worked example 2

Is this shape cut in half?

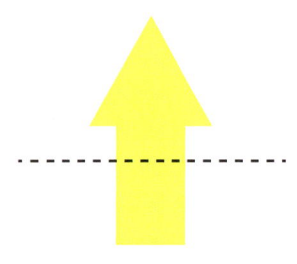

Answer:

I can see a line through this shape. Both parts are different, so this isn't a half.

3.1 Fractions

1   Draw a line on each shape to show two halves.

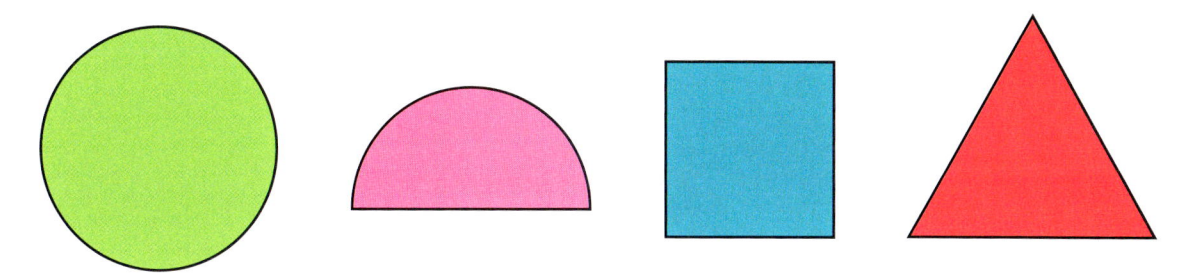

2   Draw a line on each shape to show two pieces that are **not** halves.

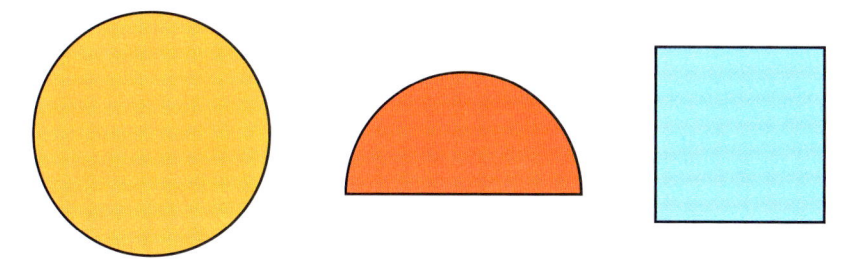

3   Draw a ring around the shapes that have been folded in half.

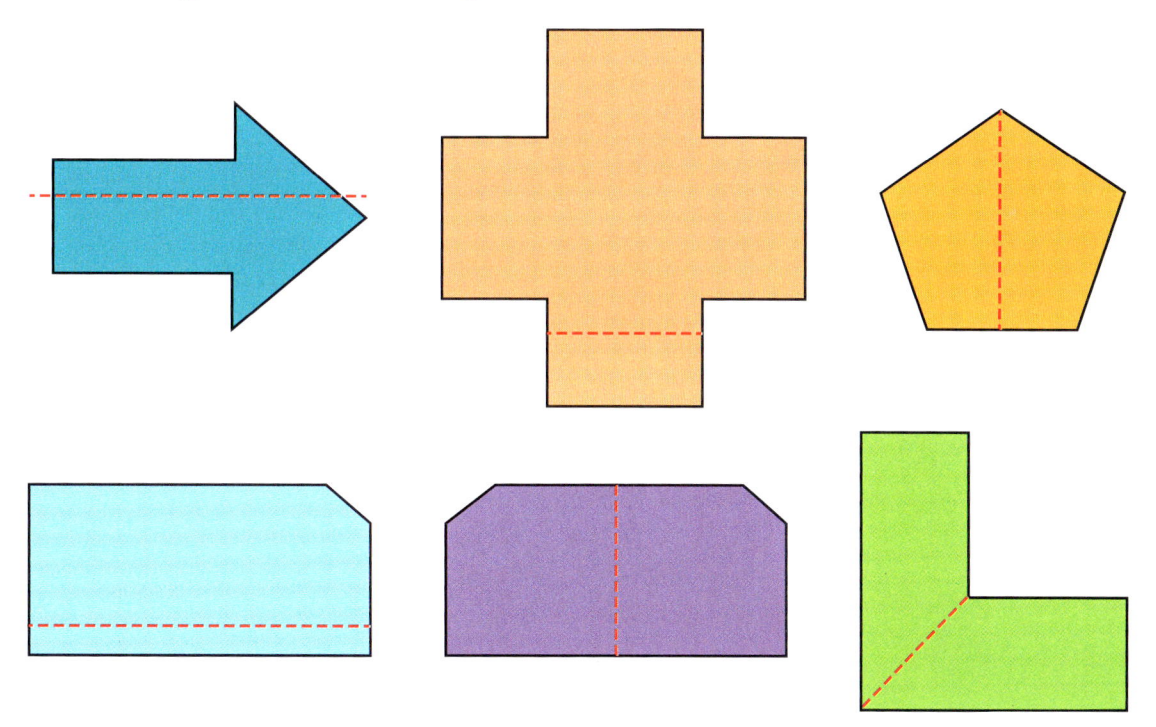

51

3 Fractions

4 This is one half of a house.

Draw the other half to make a whole house.

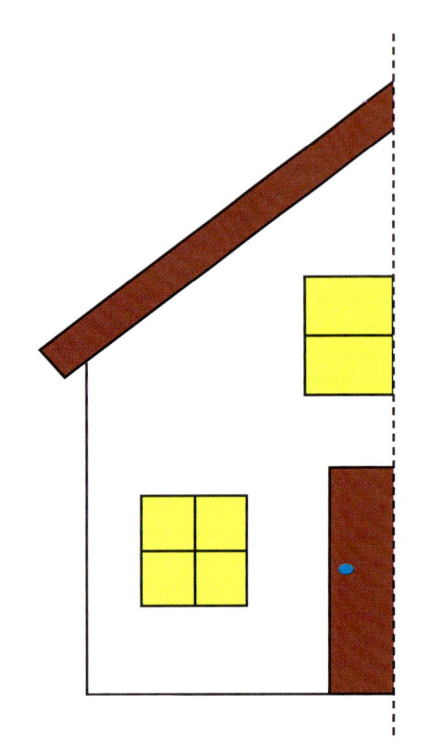

5 Draw half of each of these shapes.

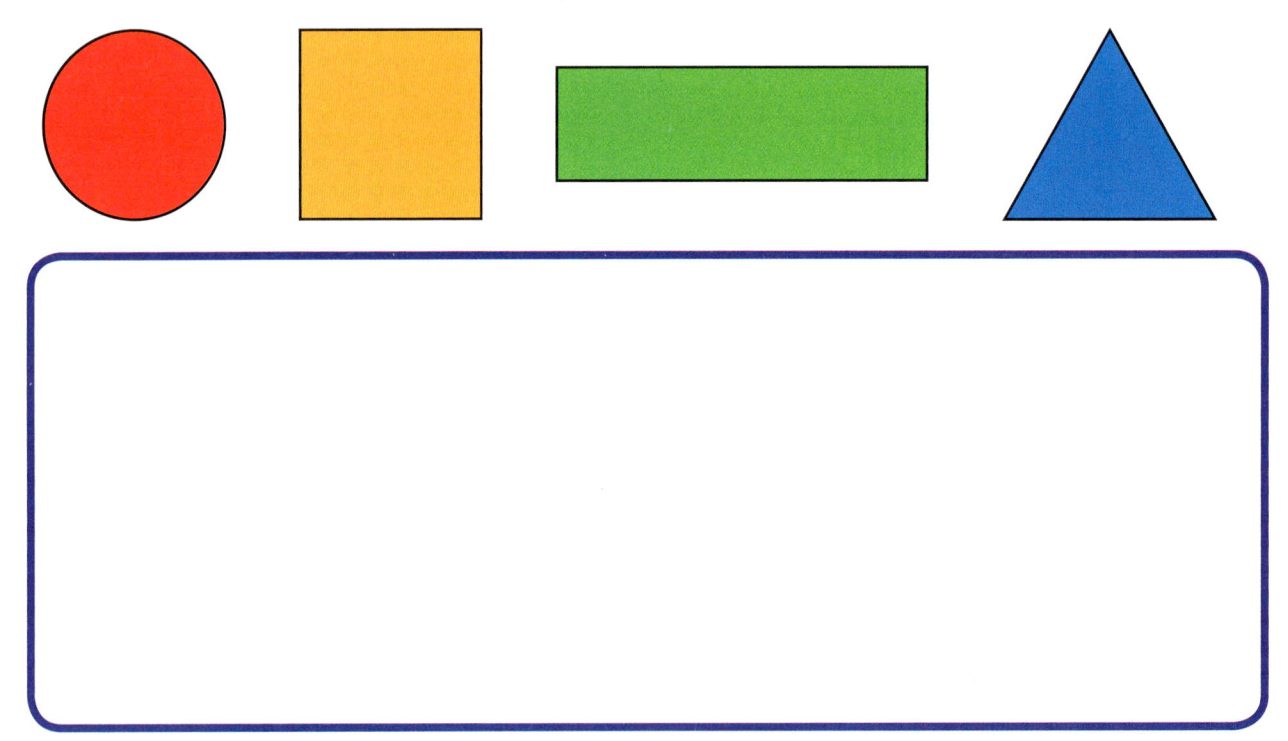

3.1 Fractions

Let's investigate

You will need: 2 paper squares the same size but different colours, scissors, glue, a piece of paper.

1. Fold one square in half, corner to corner.

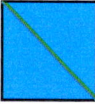

2. Cut along the fold line.
   You have 2 triangles.

3. Fold one of the triangles in half.

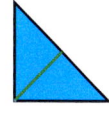

4. Cut along the fold.
   You now have 2 small triangles.

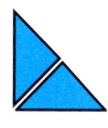

5. Fold the other square side to side.

6. Cut along the fold.
   You have 2 halves.

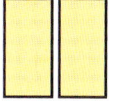

7. Fold them in half.

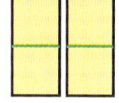

8. Cut along the fold.
   You have 4 small squares.

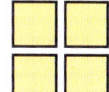

Make a pattern using all your shapes so that the edges fit together.

Compare your pattern with other patterns.

Is it the same or is it different?

What did you find easy when you were learning about fractions?
What did you find difficult?

3 Fractions

Look what I can do!

- I can find half of a shape.
- I can recognise when a shape is not split into halves.
- I understand that 2 halves of the same shape can fit together to make a whole.

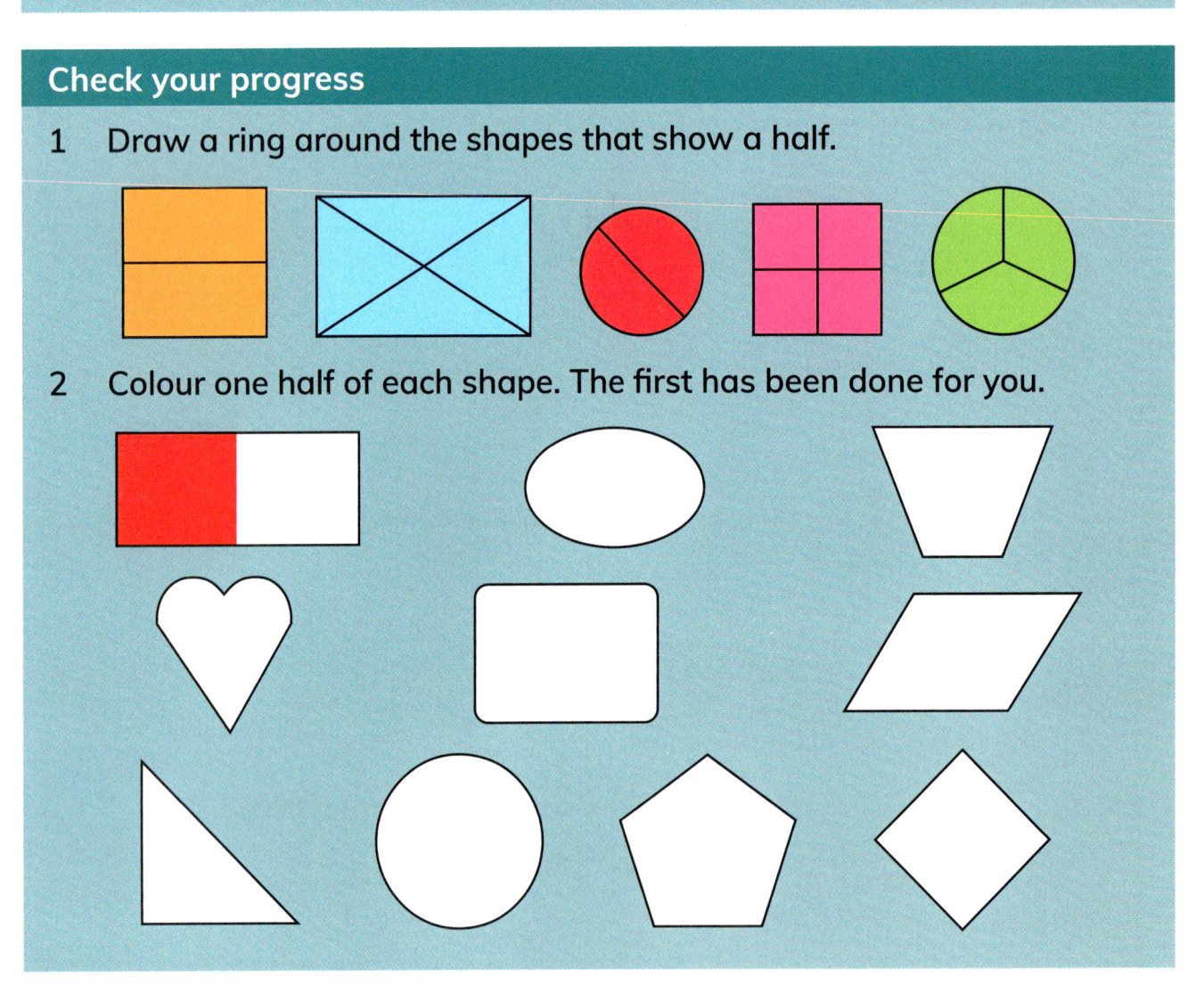

Check your progress

1 Draw a ring around the shapes that show a half.

2 Colour one half of each shape. The first has been done for you.

3.1 Fractions

Continued

3   Put a ✓ in the box if half of the shape is coloured.
    The first two have been done for you.

    Put a ✗ in the box if half is not coloured.

4   Colour the shapes that have equal parts.

    Cross out the shapes that do not have equal parts.

55

4 > Measures

Getting started

1. Draw a ring around the taller giraffe.

   Draw a taller tree next to the tall giraffe.

   Draw a shorter tree next to the short giraffe.

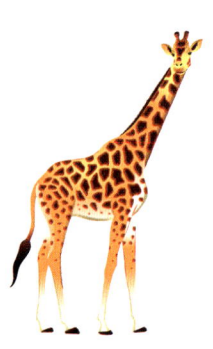

2. Draw a ring around the shorter house in each pair.

   a

   b

Knowing about length helps us to measure.

There are many different words for length.

> 4.1 Length

We are going to ...

- explore length and compare lengths
- use the correct words for different kinds of lengths.

We can measure how long things are   or how tall things are

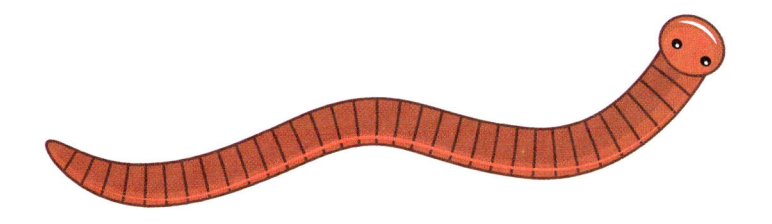

or how far apart they are.

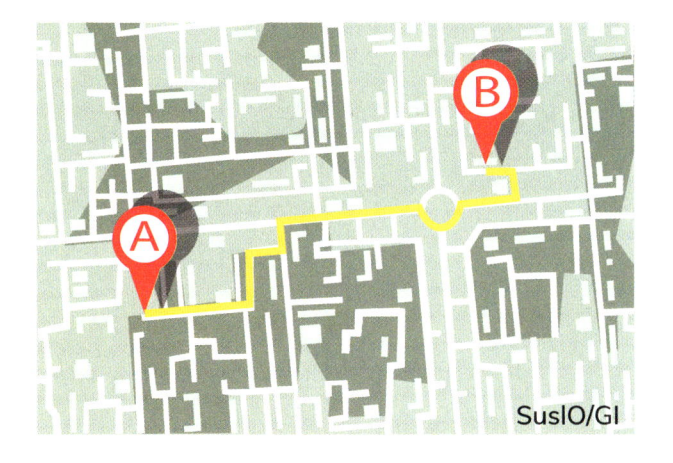

Length is the measurement of something from one end to the other.

length   long   short   tall   thin   wide

4 Measures

Exercise 4.1

Worked example 1

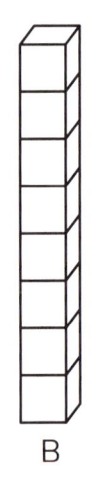

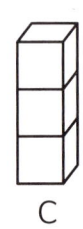

A   B   C

Colour the tallest tower of blocks red. Colour the shortest tower of blocks blue.

Answer:

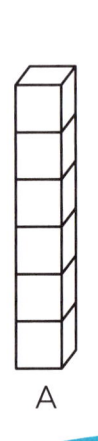

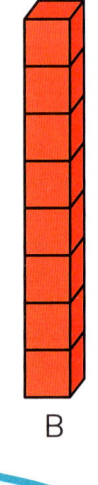

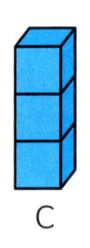

A   B   C

Tower B is higher than the others, so it is the tallest.

Tower C is lower than the others, so it is the shortest.

4.1 Length

1 Draw a ring around the taller animal in each pair.

2 How many cubes tall is each character?

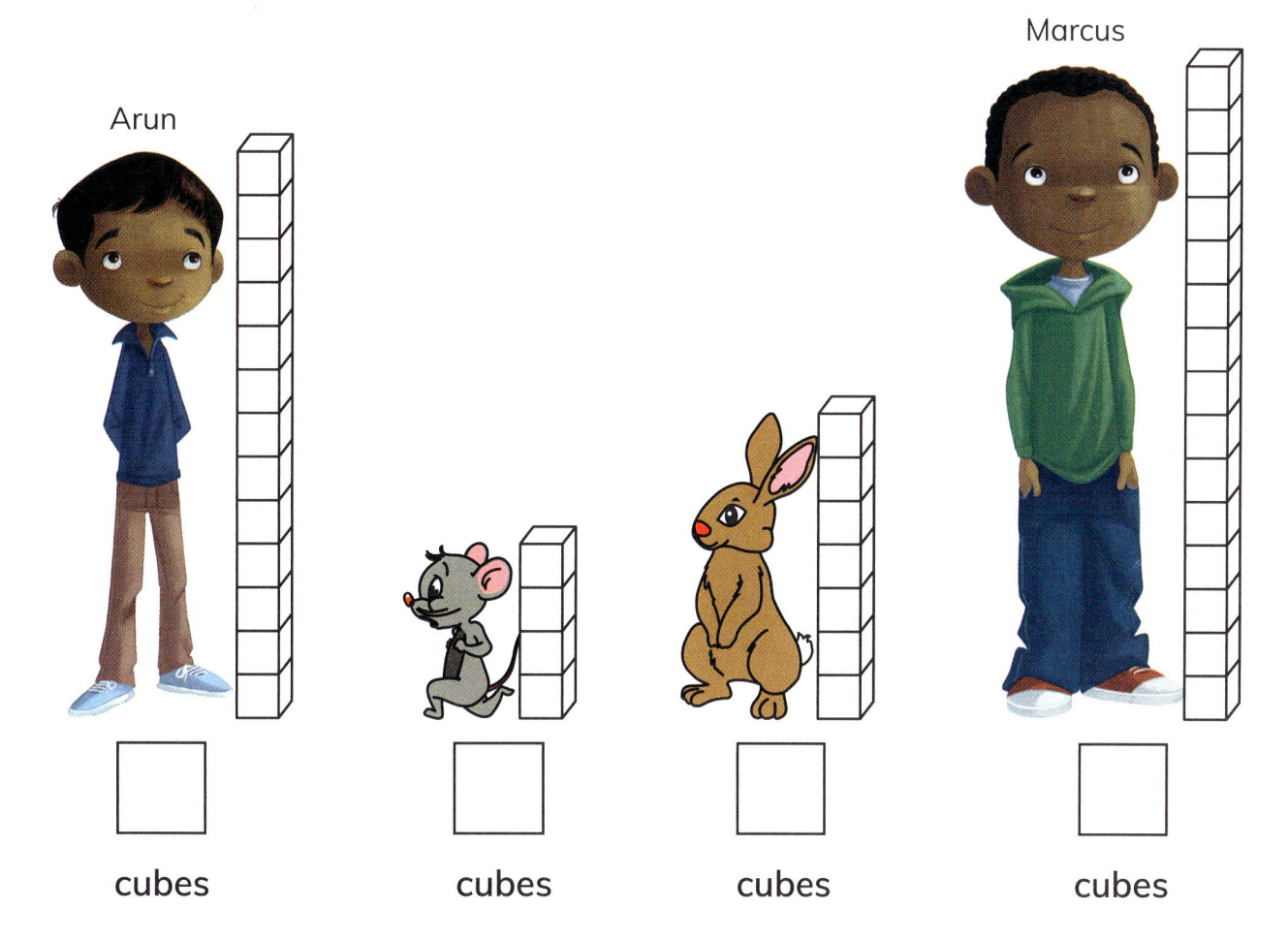

Arun

Marcus

☐ cubes   ☐ cubes   ☐ cubes   ☐ cubes

Who is taller than Arun? _____

Who is shorter than Marcus? _____

Put the characters in order from shortest to tallest.

Label them 1, 2, 3 or 4.

Now put the characters in order from tallest to shortest.

Label them a, b, c or d.

59

4 Measures

3 Talk to your partner.

Use the words taller and shorter to describe objects in your classroom.

Worked example 2

Look at these pencils.

Which is the longest? Which is the shortest?

Draw a ring around the longest and colour the shortest.

Answer:

---

4 Which is longer, your foot or your hand?

How can you find out?

My _____ is longer than my _____.

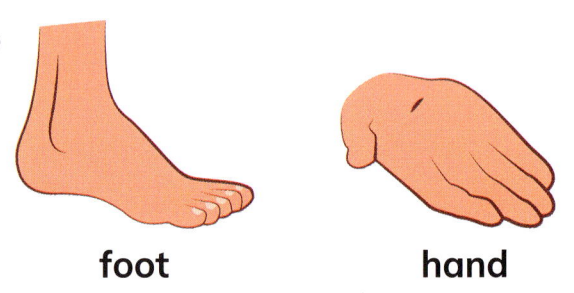

foot   hand

5 Which is shorter, your finger or your nose?

How can you find out?

My _____ is shorter than my _____.

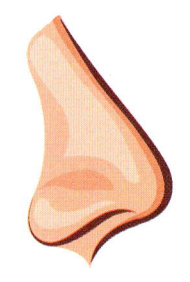

finger   nose

4.1 Length

6 Draw your family.

Draw them in order from the shortest to the tallest.

7 The height of something is how far it is from the bottom to the top.

The tree is taller than the flower.

Write the word taller or shorter below each object.

_____   _____

61

4 Measures

8 The length of something is how far it is from one end to the other.

The bus is longer than the car.

The car is shorter than the bus.

Write the word longer or shorter under each picture in the pairs below.

_____   _____

Draw 2 different objects.

Write longer or shorter under each picture.

9 Which river is wider? Tick ✓ the correct answer.

4.1 Length

Which lollipop is the thinnest? Tick ✓ the correct answer.

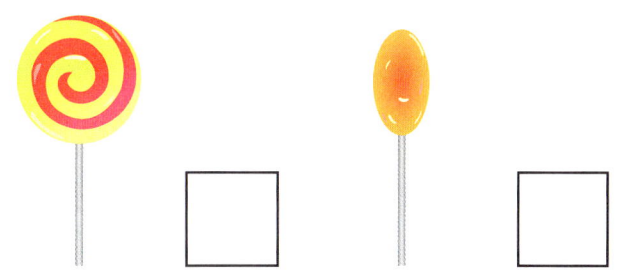

This is a wide door.

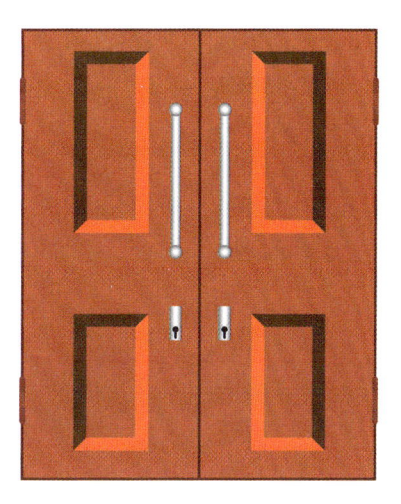

Draw a door that is thinner.

4 Measures

Let's investigate

Work with a partner to build a tower.

Use a spinner to choose the block colour.

Take turns to spin the spinner and collect a block.

If there is none of that colour left, miss your turn.

Keep playing until all of the blocks have been used.

Who has the taller tower?

Who has the shorter tower?

Put the blocks back on to the table and play the game again.

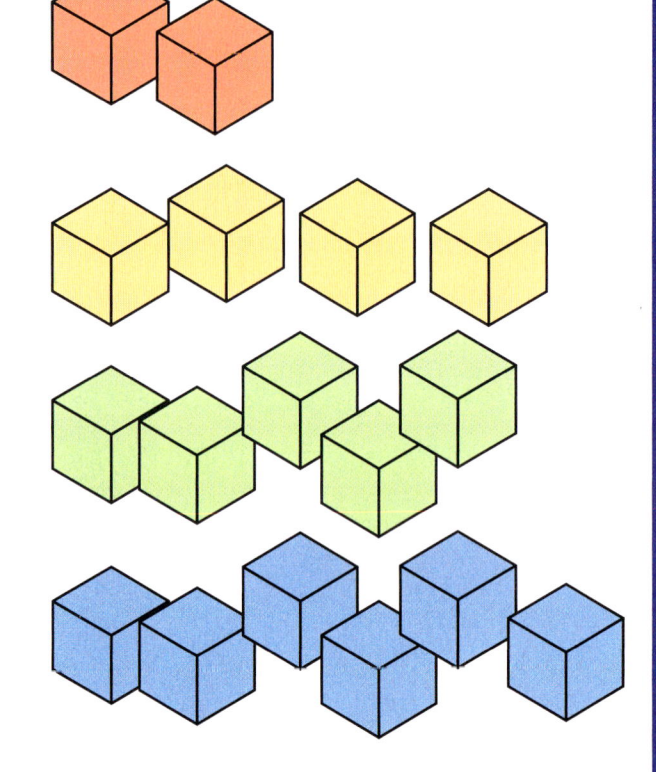

Did you learn anything new about length?
What was easy to do and what was difficult?

4.1 Length

Look what I can do!

- I can explore length.
- I can compare length.
- I can use the correct words for different kinds of lengths.

Check your progress

1 Draw a ring around the shortest frog.

2 Draw a ring around the tallest ostrich.

3 Draw a ring around the longest crocodile.

Project 1 Snakes

> # Project 1

Snakes

Your first challenge is to make a snake!

You could use card, paper, dough, pipe cleaners, ribbon, glue, tape, cubes, blocks… anything that you can find.

Put your snake near other people's snakes.

1 What is the same about your snakes?

   What is different?

2 Who has made the longest snake?

   Who has made the shortest snake?

   How do you know?

3 Whose snake is widest?

   Whose snake is thinnest?

   How do you know?

4 What else could you say about your snakes?

5 Working with numbers to 10

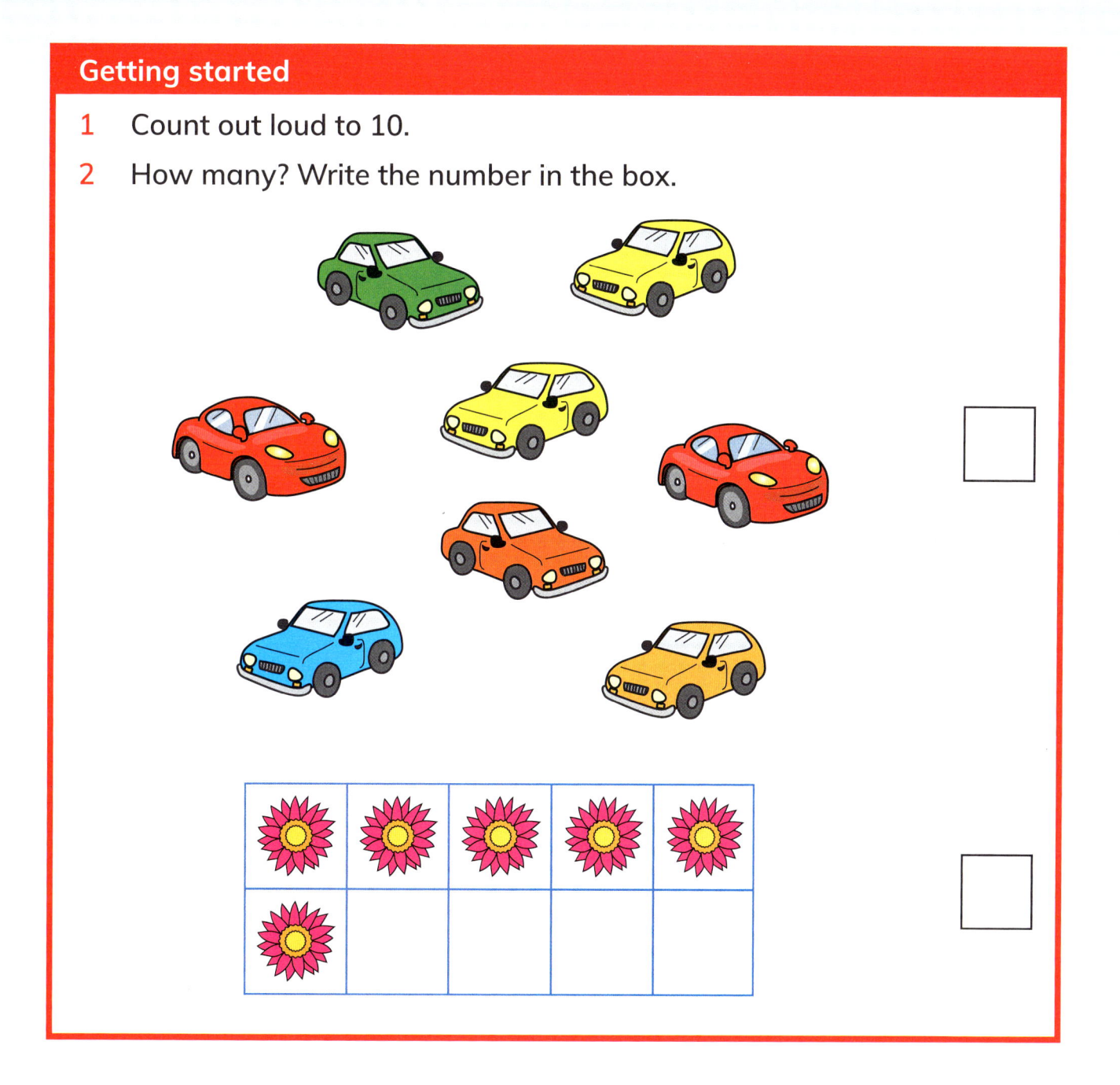

Getting started

1. Count out loud to 10.
2. How many? Write the number in the box.

67

5 Working with numbers to 10

Continued

3   Draw the domino pattern for 6.

Is 6 an odd or even number?

We often put two groups together to add them.

We want to know how many we have altogether.

Sometimes we know how many we have. If some are taken away, we want to know how many are left.

> 5.1 Addition as combining

We are going to …
- add quantities together by combining two sets
- begin to remember some number bonds.

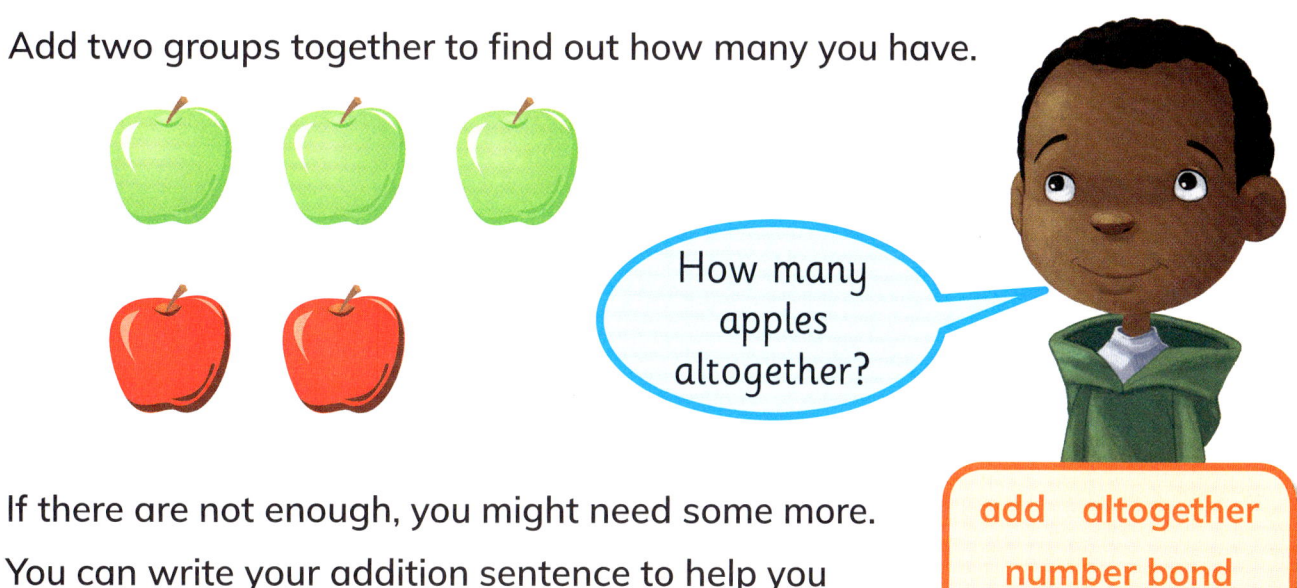

Add two groups together to find out how many you have.

How many apples altogether?

If there are not enough, you might need some more.

You can write your addition sentence to help you remember what you did.

**add   altogether
number bond
whole**

Exercise 5.1

1   Draw 1 more.

   Count how many objects there are now.

   Complete the number sentence.

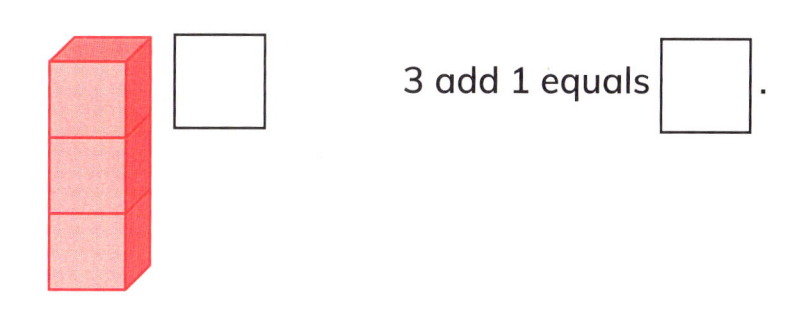

   3 add 1 equals ☐.

5 Working with numbers to 10

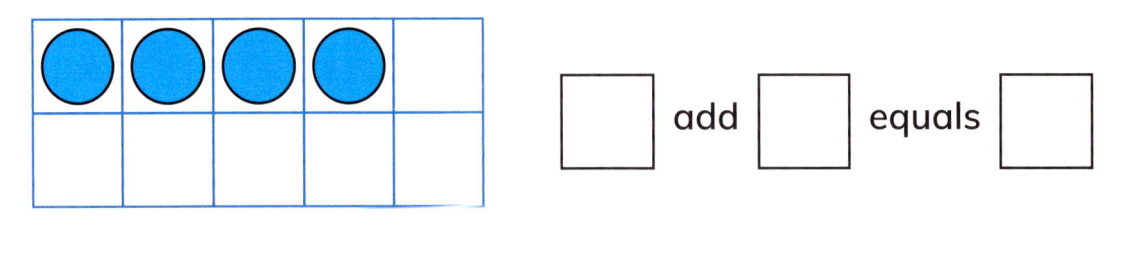

☐ add ☐ equals ☐

Worked example 1

5 add 1 equals ☐

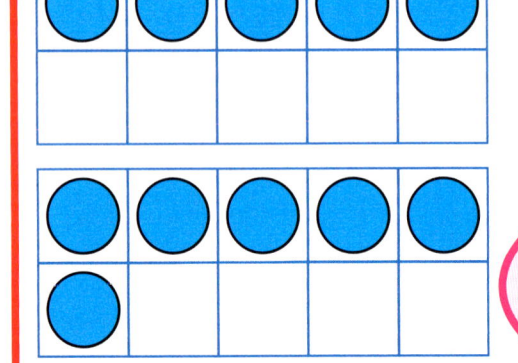

Put 5 counters on a ten frame.

Add 1 more. That's 6, I recognise it. 5 add 1 equals 6

Answer: 5 add 1 equals 6

2   Use counters and a ten frame to help you add 1 more.

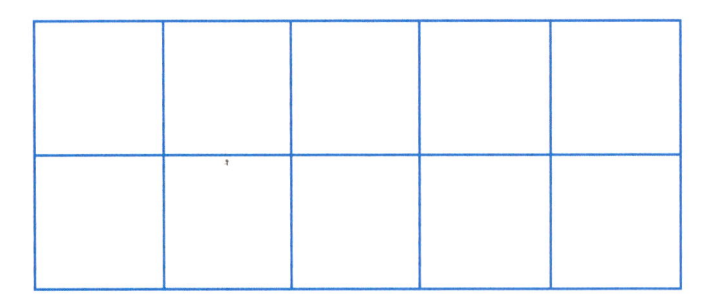

6 add 1 equals ☐   7 add 1 equals ☐

8 add 1 equals ☐   9 add 1 equals ☐

5.1 Addition as combining

> **Let's investigate**
>
> Sumi says when you add 1 more, you make the next counting number.
>
> Is Sumi correct?
>
> Discuss with your partner.

Worked example 2

Write a number sentence for the story.

First   Then   Now

Answer:

First

3

First, then

3 add 2

3 + 2

First, then, now

3 add 2 equals 5

3 + 2 = 5

There are 3 children playing football.

2 more children join them.

There are 5 children playing football. 3 add 2 equals 5.

The number sentence is 3 + 2 = 5.

71

5 Working with numbers to 10

3 Complete the number sentence for this story.

First   Then   Now

☐ add ☐ equals ☐

☐ + ☐ = ☐

4 Tell your partner what is happening in this story.
Write the number sentence.

First   Then   Now

5.1 Addition as combining

Worked example 3

3 add 2 equals ☐

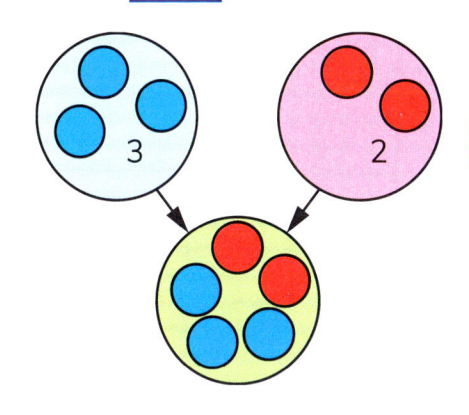

3 + 2 = ☐

How many altogether in this part-whole diagram?

Put the counters on a ten frame to find out.

Write the number sentence.

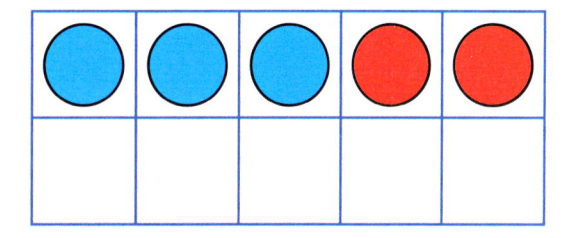

Answer: 3 add 2 makes 5.

3 + 2 = 5

*When the top row of the ten frame is full, there are 5 counters. 3 add 2 makes 5.
3 + 2 = 5*

*I combined all the counters. I counted 1, 2, 3, 4, 5.
3 + 2 = 5*

5 Working with numbers to 10

5 How many counters are there?

Combine the parts to find the whole.

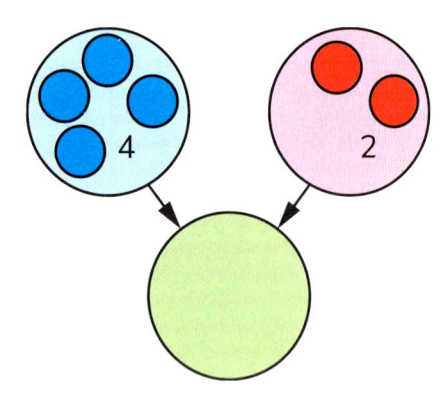

4 add 2 equals ☐.

4 + 2 = ☐

How many altogether?

6 Use the part-whole diagram to combine the parts.

Use the ten frame to help you find how many objects there are, which is called the total.

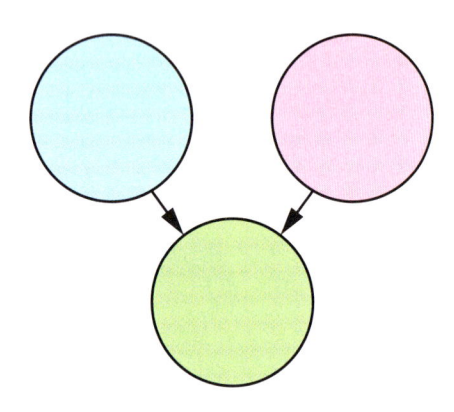

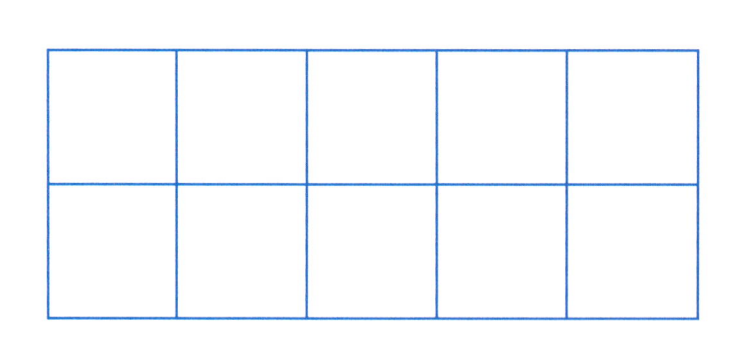

5 + 3 = ☐

3 + 5 = ☐

6 + 4 = ☐

4 + 6 = ☐

5.1 Addition as combining

7   Estimate the total number of spots on each domino.

Remember that an estimate is a good guess.

Write a number sentence for each domino.

Was your estimate close?

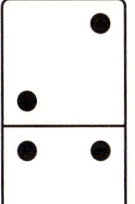

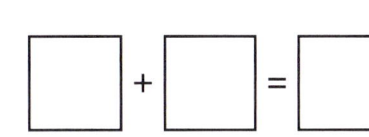

Estimate =

☐ + ☐ = ☐

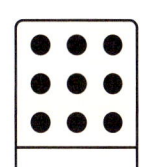

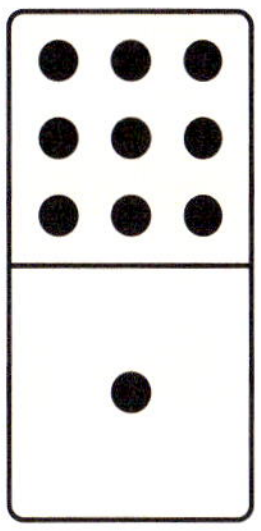

Estimate =

☐ + ☐ = ☐

8   Complete each part-whole diagram.

Write a number sentence for each diagram.

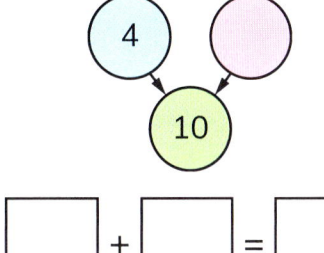

4 ◯ ◯
    10

☐ + ☐ = ☐

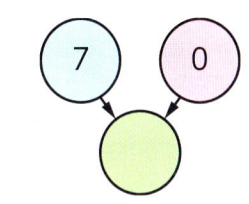

7 ◯ ◯ 0
    ◯

☐ + ☐ = ☐

How did you find the missing part?
Ask your partner what they did.

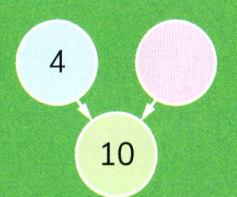

4 ◯ ◯
    10

9   Complete each addition wall.

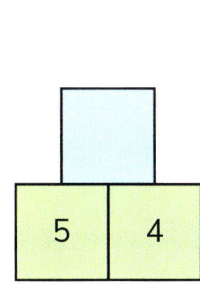

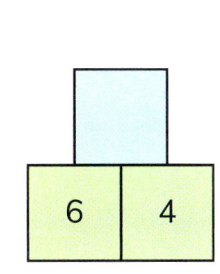

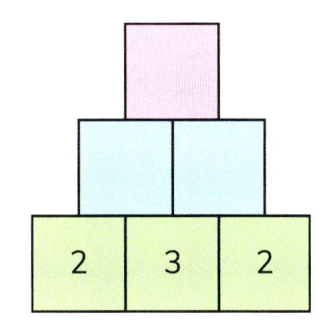

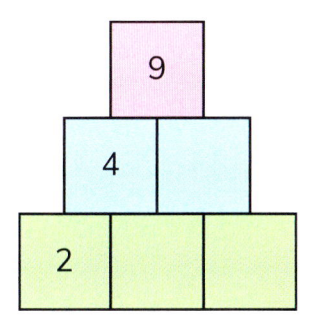

5 | 4

6 | 4

2 | 3 | 2

9
4
2 | ☐ | ☐

75

5 Working with numbers to 10

10 If 10 is the whole, what could the two parts be?

Use counters to help you find all the ways to make 10.

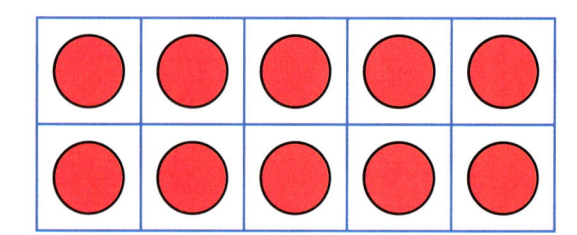

☐ + ☐ = 10   ☐ + ☐ = 10

☐ + ☐ = 10   ☐ + ☐ = 10

☐ + ☐ = 10   ☐ + ☐ = 10

☐ + ☐ = 10   ☐ + ☐ = 10

☐ + ☐ = 10   ☐ + ☐ = 10

☐ + ☐ = 10

Explain to your partner how you know you have found all the number sentences.

These calculations show the number bonds for 10.

5.1 Addition as combining

Let's investigate

Work with a partner. Choose a number from 5 to 9.

Make a poster showing all the number bonds for that number.

> A number bond is two numbers that add together to make a total. 5 + 1 = 6 is a number bond for 6.

How will you show each number bond?

How will you know that you have included all the number bonds for your number?

Look what I can do!

- I can add quantities together by combining two sets.
- I am beginning to remember some number bonds.

5 Working with numbers to 10

5.2 Subtraction as take away

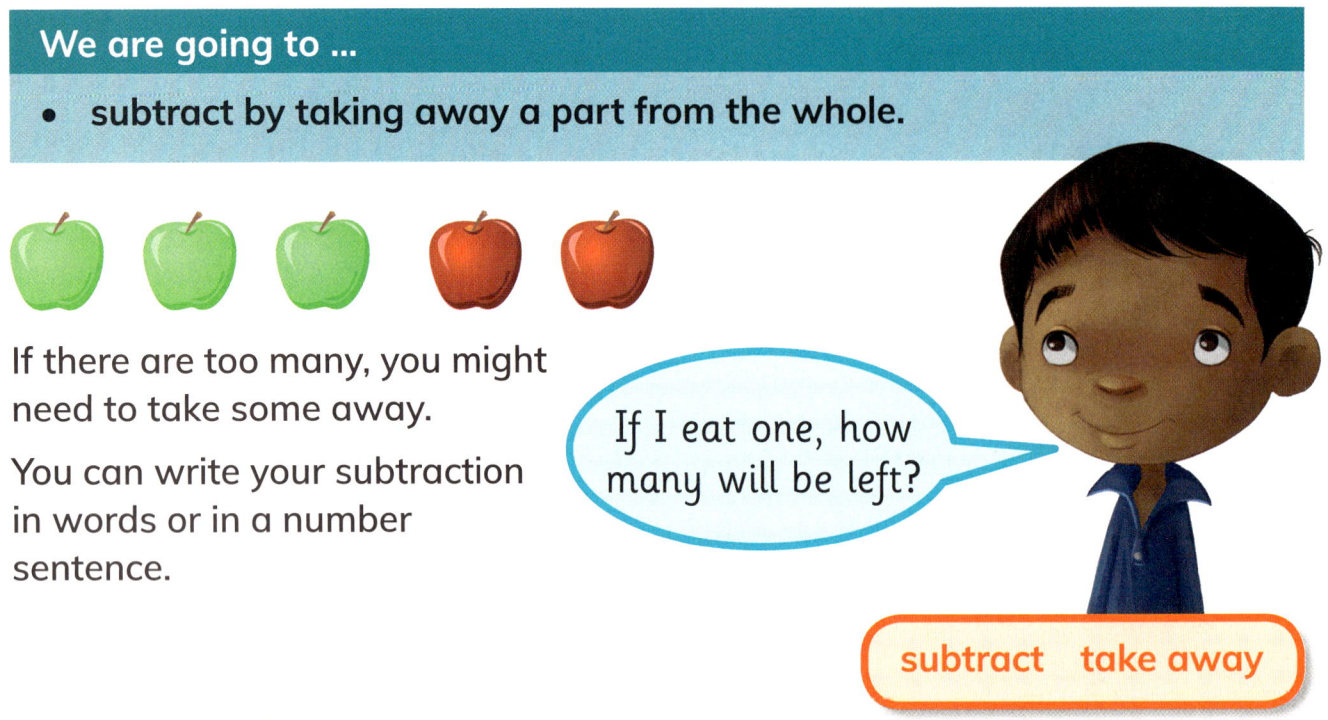

We are going to ...

- subtract by taking away a part from the whole.

If there are too many, you might need to take some away.

You can write your subtraction in words or in a number sentence.

If I eat one, how many will be left?

subtract   take away

Exercise 5.2

1   Cross out 1 bead and 1 counter. Count how many there are now.

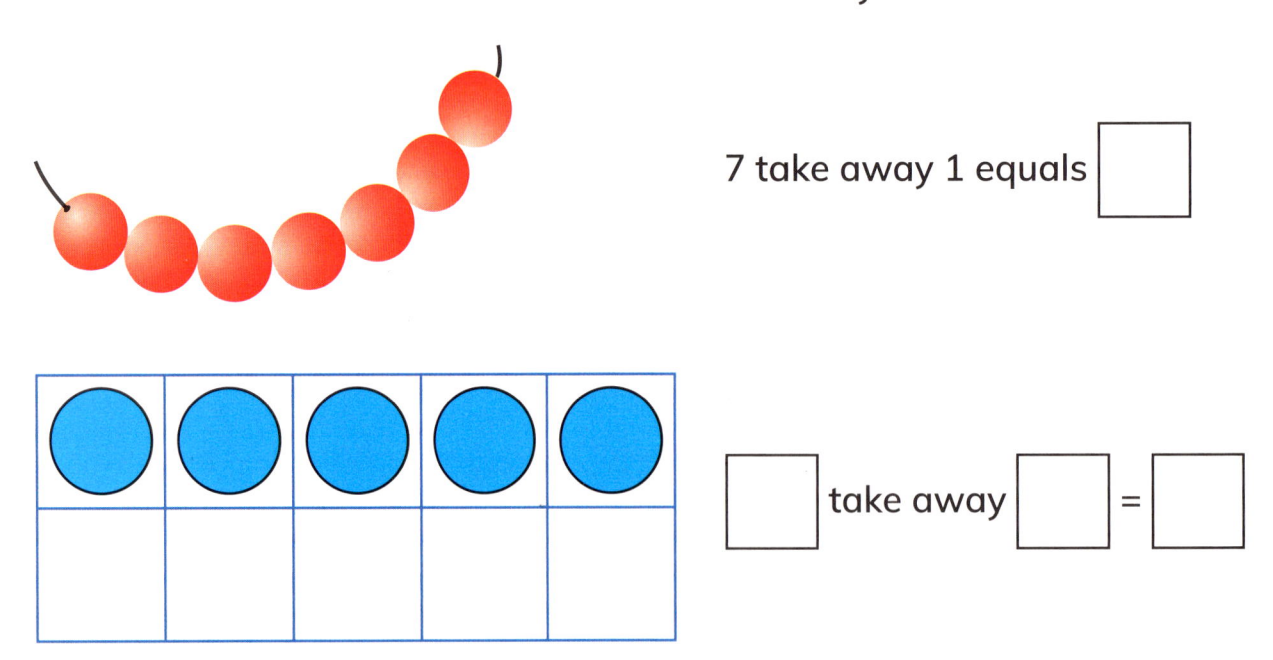

7 take away 1 equals ☐

☐ take away ☐ = ☐

5.2 Subtraction as take away

Let's investigate

Put 9 counters on the table in the domino pattern.

Take one counter away to make the domino pattern for 8.

Take one counter away to make the domino pattern for 7.

Repeat until there are no counters left.

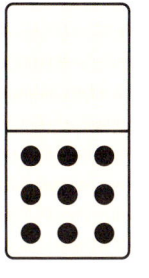

Tell your partner what you were thinking about as you took each counter away.

Worked example 4

Write a sentence for the story.

First   Then   Now

First
5

First, then
5 take away 2
5 − 2

First, then, now

Answer: 5 take away 2 equals 3
5 − 2 = 3

There were 5 ducks in the pond.

2 ducks left the pond.

There are 3 ducks left in the pond. 5 take away 2 equals. The number sentence is 5 − 2 = 3.

79

5 Working with numbers to 10

2 Tell your partner what is happening in this story.
Write the sentences.

First　　　　　　　Then　　　　　　　Now

☐ take away ☐ equals ☐ .

☐ – ☐ = ☐

3 Write the number sentence for this story.

First　　　　　　　Then　　　　　　　Now

5 take away 1 equals 4.

☐ – ☐ = ☐

5.2 Subtraction as take away

4   Write the number sentence for this story.

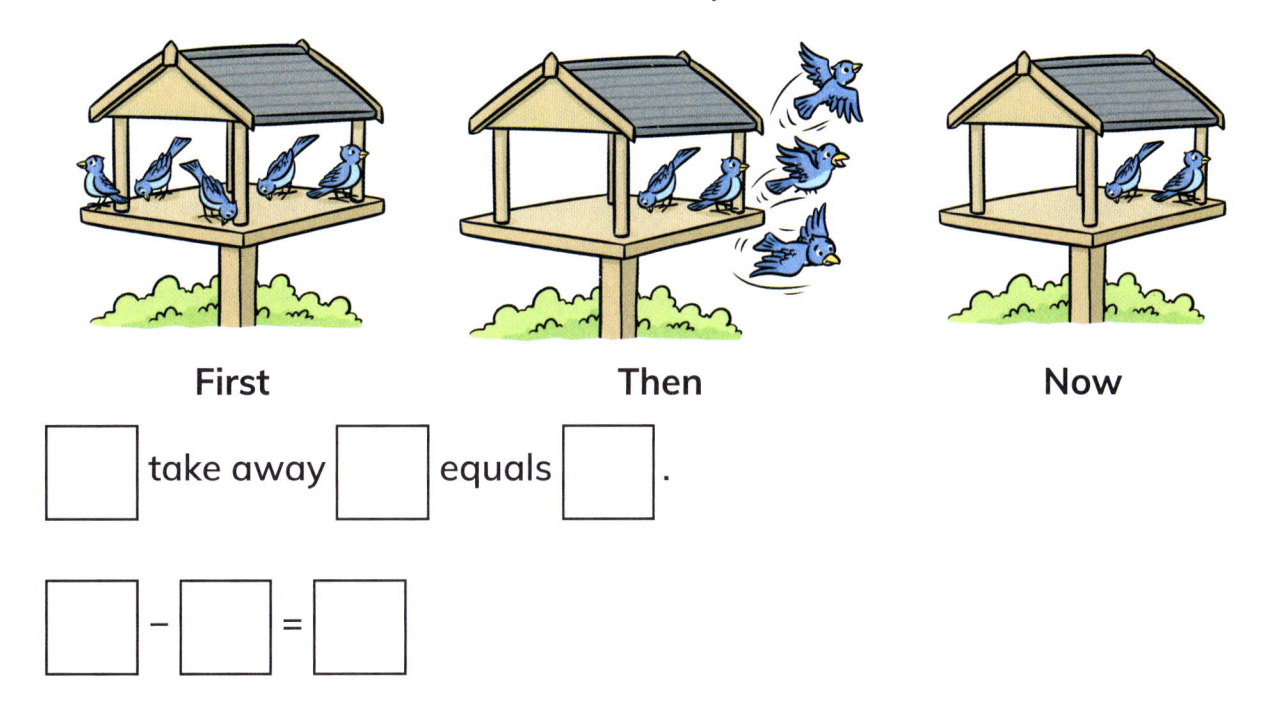

First   Then   Now

☐ take away ☐ equals ☐ .

☐ − ☐ = ☐

Worked example 5

4 take away 3 equals ☐

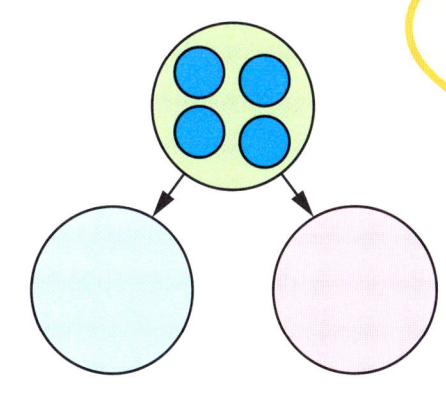

4 − 3 = ☐

4 is the whole, so I can put 4 counters in the whole circle.

5 Working with numbers to 10

Continued

Answer:

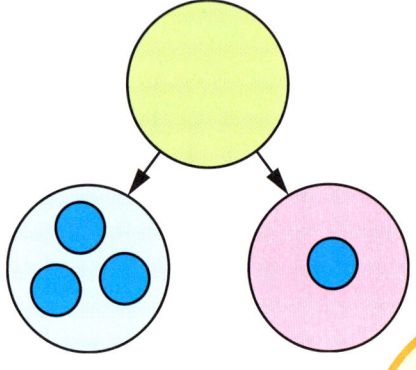

4 take away 3 equals 1.
4 − 3 = 1

3 is the part I need to take away, so I can put 3 of the counters in the first part circle.

I need to move what is left into the other part circle. Those counters are a part now, not the whole.

5   Find out how many are left over after taking a part away from the whole.

Use the diagram to help you.
Estimate your answer first.

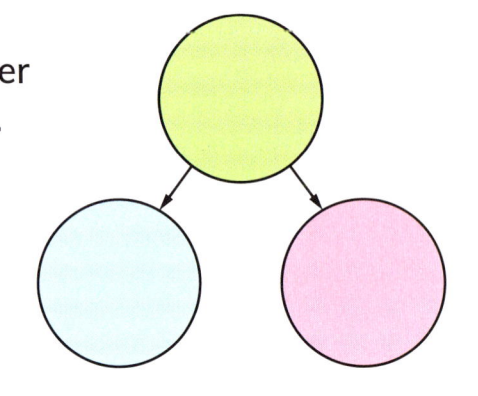

Estimate =

10 − 3 = ☐

Estimate =

9 − 4 = ☐

Estimate =

8 − 5 = ☐

Estimate =

7 − 6 = ☐

5.2 Subtraction as take away

> Can you take away a smaller number from a larger number?
> Is the part-whole diagram helpful?

6 Complete each part-whole diagram.

Estimate your answer first. Write a number sentence for each diagram.

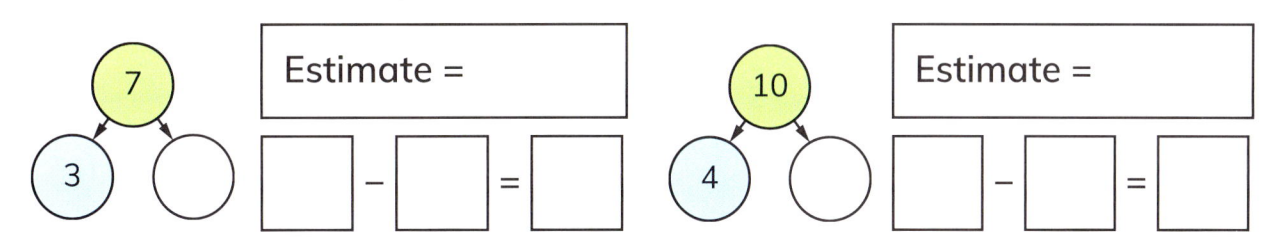

☐ − ☐ = ☐   (whole 7, part 3)   Estimate =

☐ − ☐ = ☐   (whole 10, part 4)   Estimate =

> How are these part-whole diagrams the same?
> How are they different?
> Do you use each diagram in the same way?

7 Complete each subtraction wall.

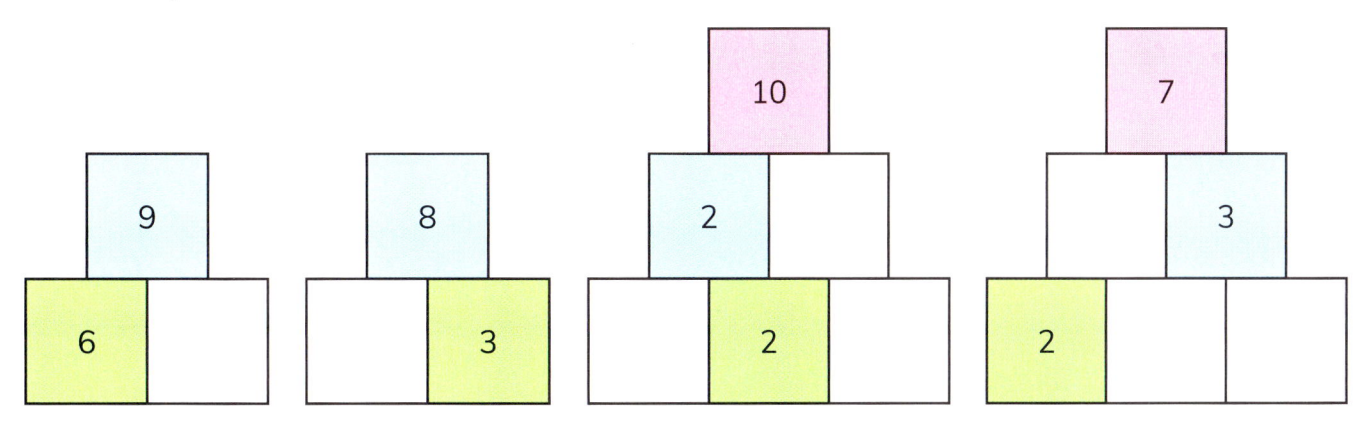

Wall 1: top 9, bottom-left 6
Wall 2: top 8, bottom-right 3
Wall 3: top (pink) 10, middle-left 2, bottom-left 2
Wall 4: top (pink) 7, middle-right 3, bottom-left 2

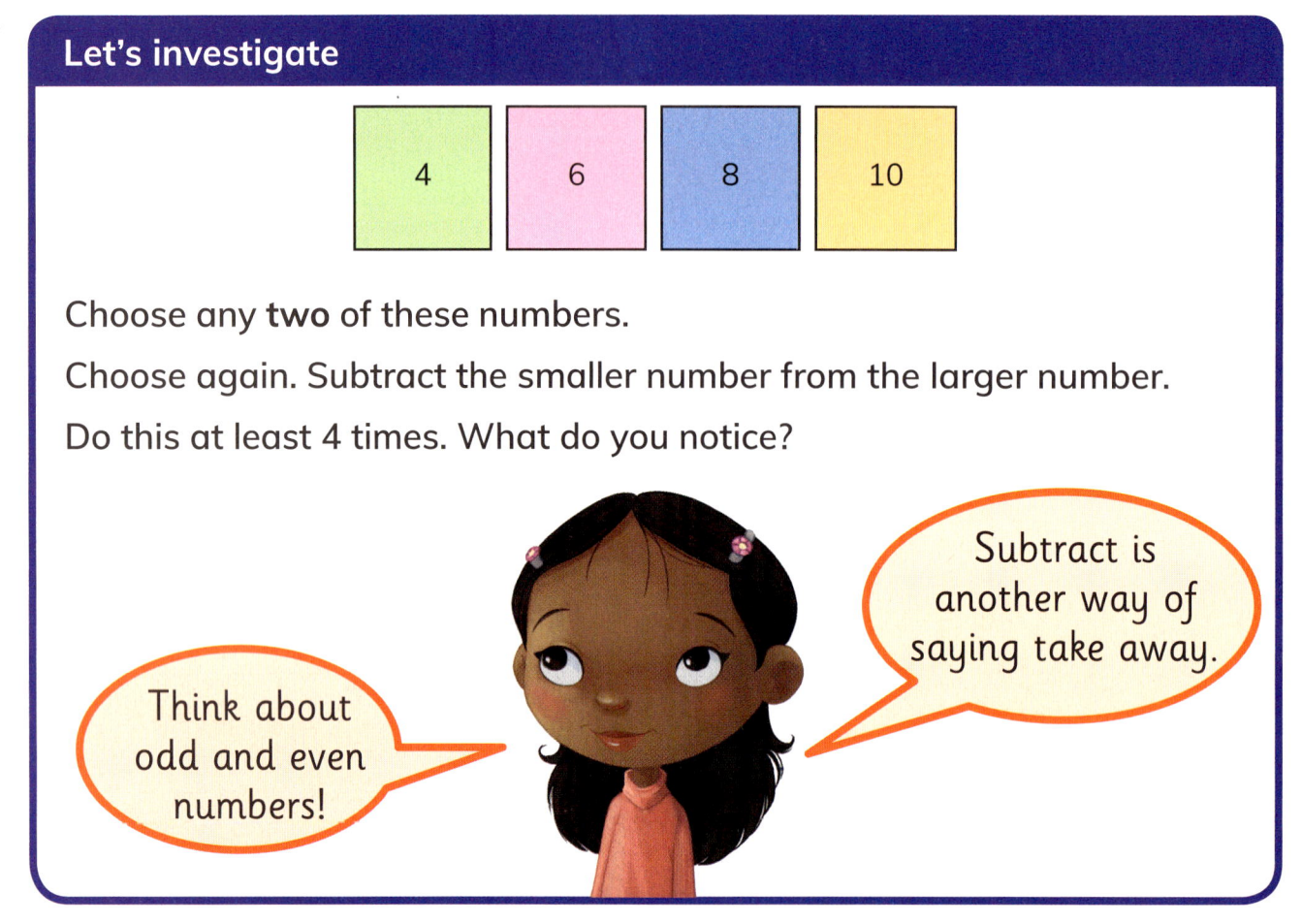

5 Working with numbers to 10

Let's investigate

| 4 | 6 | 8 | 10 |

Choose any **two** of these numbers.

Choose again. Subtract the smaller number from the larger number.

Do this at least 4 times. What do you notice?

Think about odd and even numbers!

Subtract is another way of saying take away.

Look what I can do!

- I can subtract by taking away a part from a whole.

5.2 Subtraction as take away

Check your progress

1. Complete each part-whole diagram. Write a number sentence for each diagram.

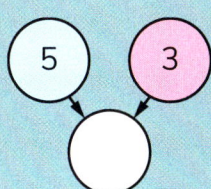

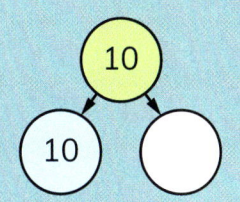

   ☐ add ☐ equals ☐   ☐ take away ☐ equals ☐

   ☐ + ☐ = ☐   ☐ − ☐ = ☐

2. Find all the number bonds for 7. What will you use to help you?

   ☐ + ☐ = 7   ☐ + ☐ = 7

   ☐ + ☐ = 7   ☐ + ☐ = 7

   ☐ + ☐ = 7   ☐ + ☐ = 7

   ☐ + ☐ = 7   ☐ + ☐ = 7

3. Complete each wall.

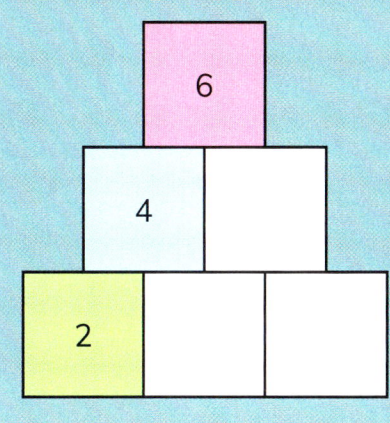

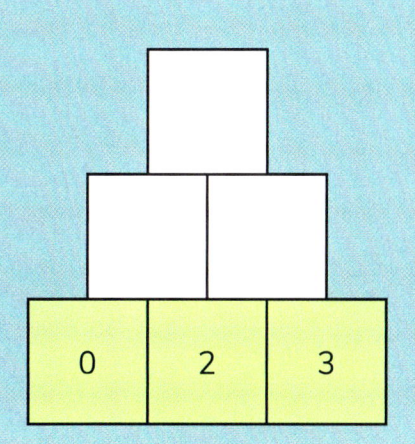

Project 2 Compare the rows

> # Project 2

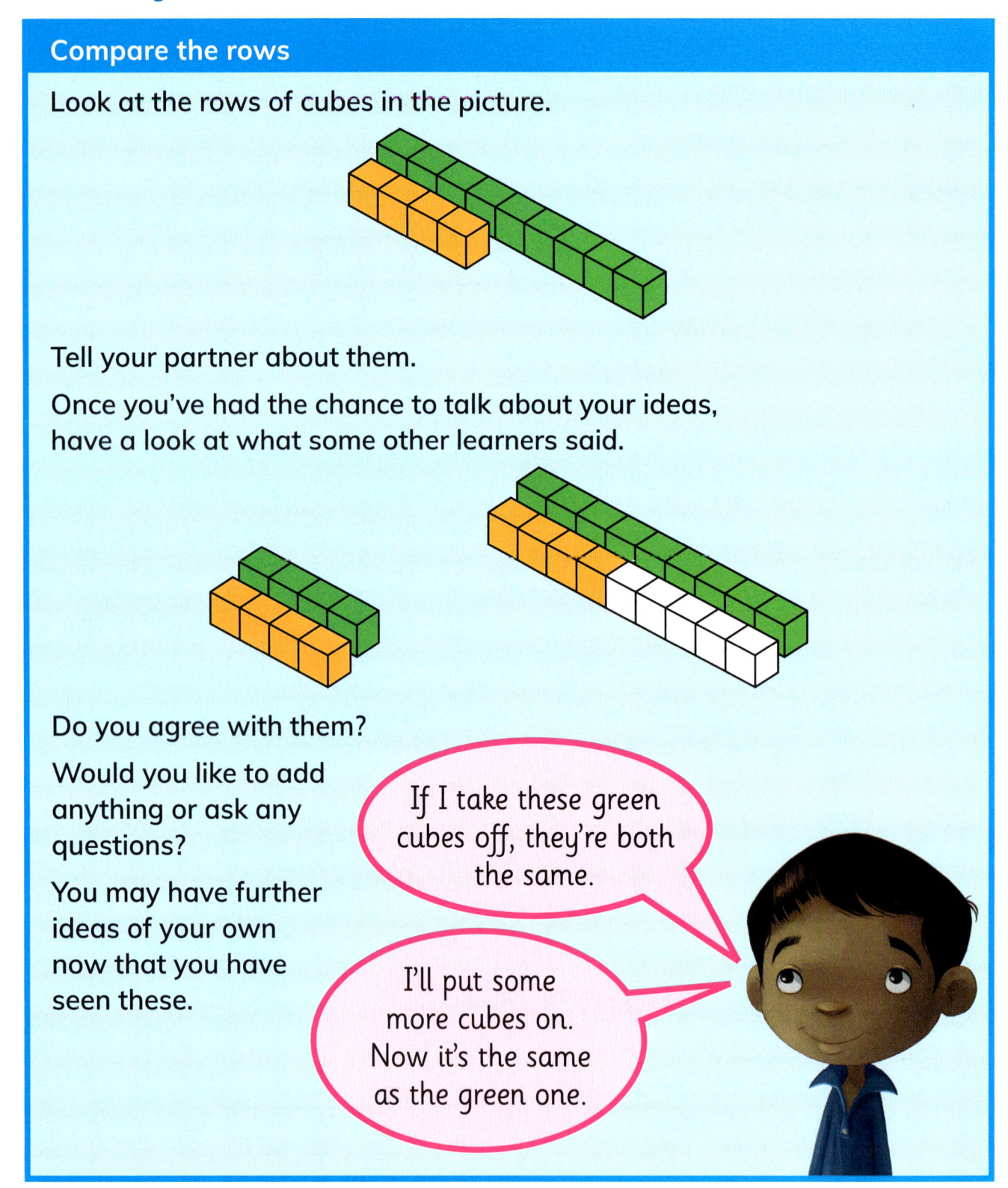

Compare the rows

Look at the rows of cubes in the picture.

Tell your partner about them.

Once you've had the chance to talk about your ideas, have a look at what some other learners said.

Do you agree with them?

Would you like to add anything or ask any questions?

You may have further ideas of your own now that you have seen these.

If I take these green cubes off, they're both the same.

I'll put some more cubes on. Now it's the same as the green one.

6 Position

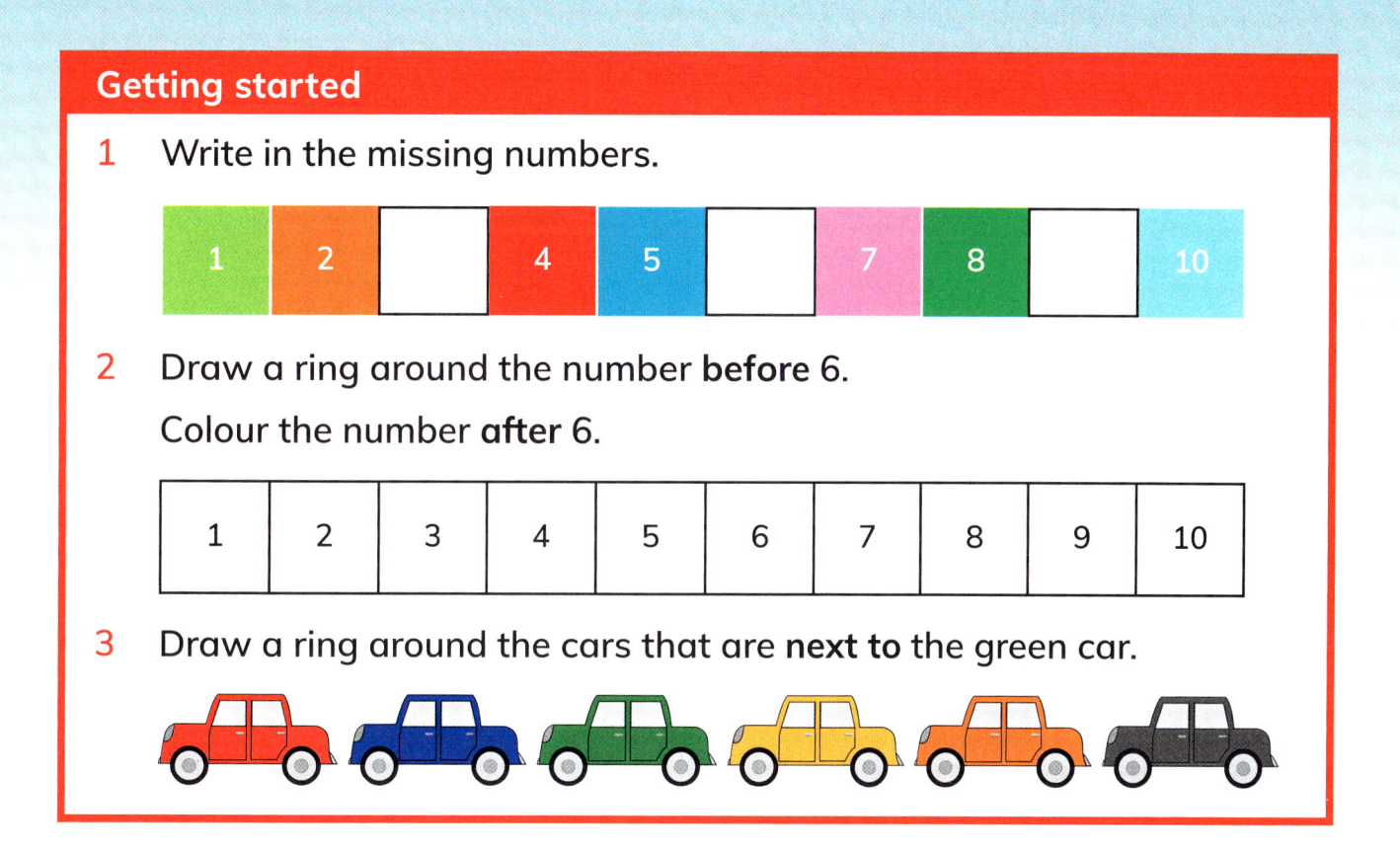

Getting started

1. Write in the missing numbers.

   | 1 | 2 | | 4 | 5 | | 7 | 8 | | 10 |

2. Draw a ring around the number **before** 6.
   Colour the number **after** 6.

   | 1 | 2 | 3 | 4 | 5 | 6 | 7 | 8 | 9 | 10 |

3. Draw a ring around the cars that are **next to** the green car.

You are learning about **position**.

Ordinal numbers help you to see the order that you do things in during your day.

For example, 1st you wake up, 2nd you get out of bed.

6 Position

Who is in front?

How many are on the podium?

Who is in front?

Who is behind?

> 6.1 Position

We are going to …

- recognise and use ordinal numbers
- use new words to describe position
- order ordinal numbers.

We need to know about position so that we can understand instructions.

We need to tell other people where we have put objects.

Ordinal numbers tell us the position of numbers or objects.

They don't tell us how much there is or how many things there are.

I put my ball under the chair.

above   behind
below   beside
in front of
next to   on
ordinal
position   under

Exercise 6.1

Worked example 1

There is a hot air balloon competition.

The balloon that flies the highest gets first prize.

Which balloon was 1st?

Which balloon was 7th?

6 Position

Continued

Answer:

"The green balloon flew the highest. It's above the others."

"The yellow balloon was 7th. It was lower than all the others."

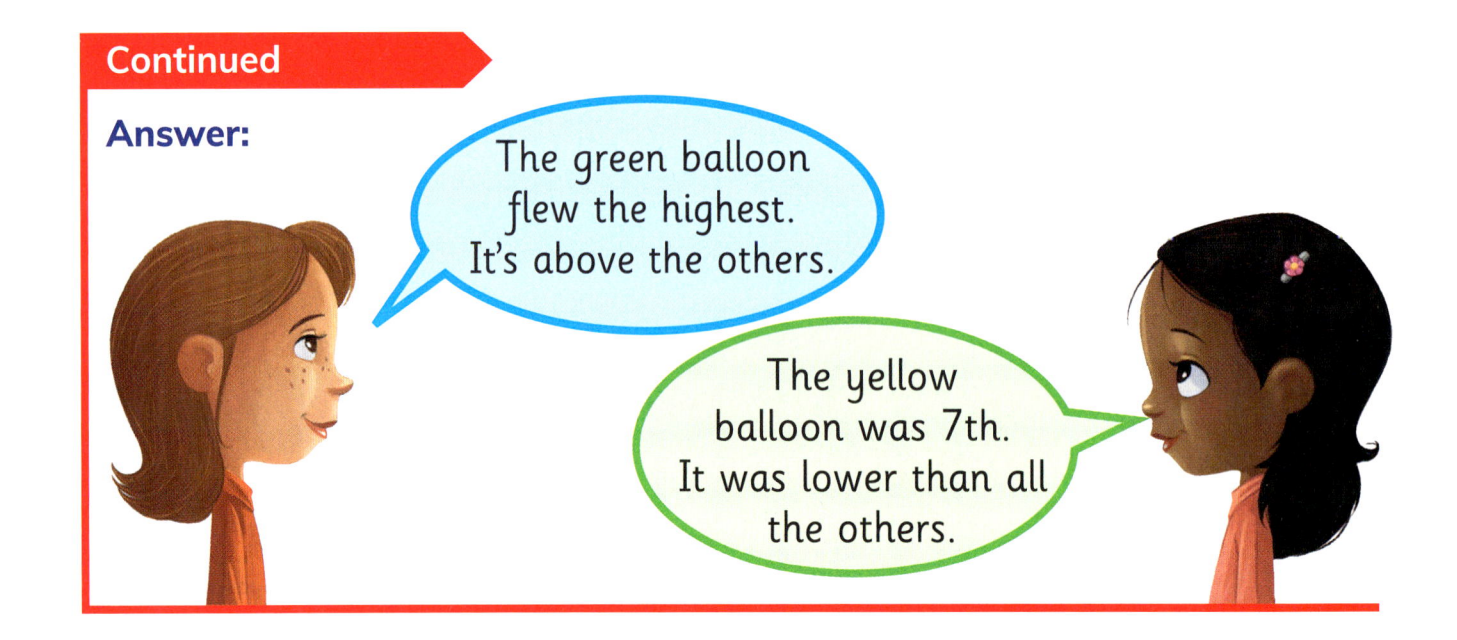

1   Look at the cars. For each question, write the position as a number and a word.

first   second   third   fourth   fifth   sixth   seventh   eighth

What colour is the car in front of the 5th car? _____

What position is the orange car? _____

What position is the white car? _____

What position is the pink car? _____

What colour and position is the car behind the blue car? _____

Which cars are beside the 3rd car? _____

6.1 Position

2 These colours have been lined up.

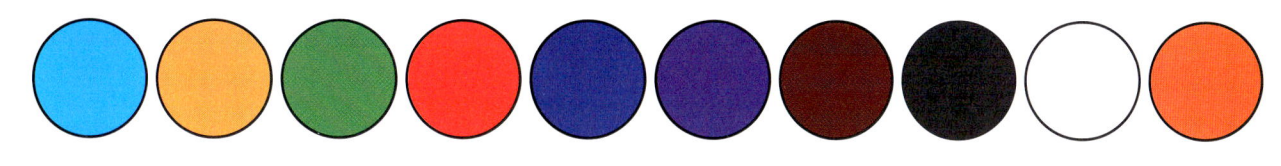

1st

Which colour is 4th? _____

Which colour is after the 5th colour? _____

Which colour is before the 3rd colour? _____

Which colour is beside the 1st colour? _____

3 Put a ring around the child who came 1st in the race.
   Colour the child who was 5th.

4 Join the words to match the position of the fox.

on   next to   in   behind   in front of

6 Position

5 Join the words to match the position of the ball.

above   below   between

6 Write the ordinal number of the coloured cake in each row of cakes. The first one is done for you.

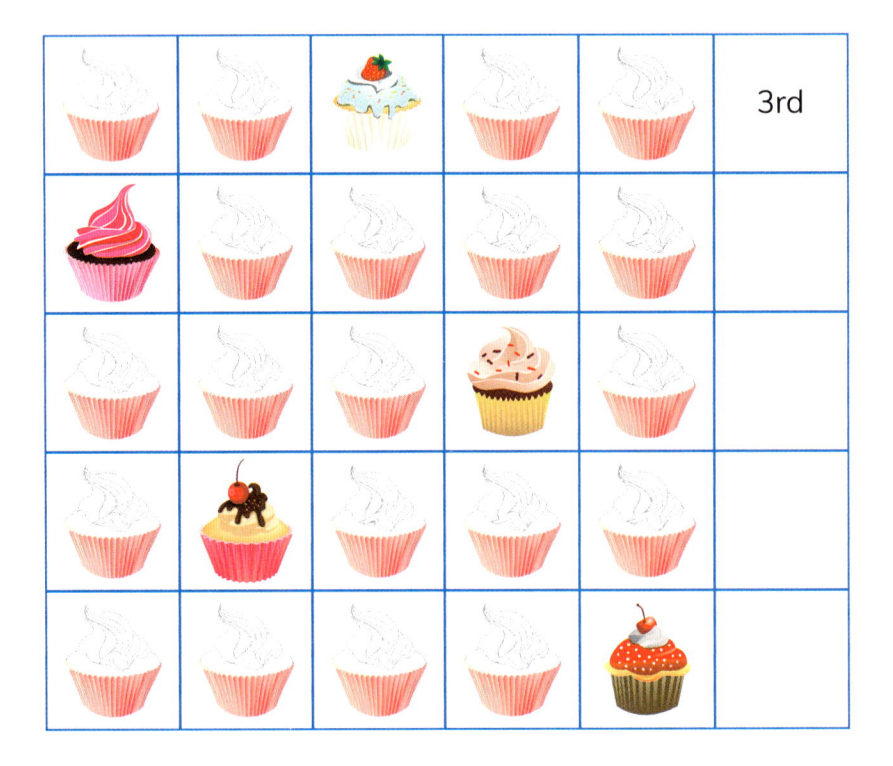

1st   2nd   3rd   4th   5th

		🧁			3rd
🧁					
			🧁		
	🧁				
				🧁	

6.1 Position

7 Draw a line from the word to the object.

on   under   in   next to

Fill in the missing words.

The cat is _____ the chair.

The chair is _____ the table.

The ball is _____ the table.

The flowers are _____ the vase.

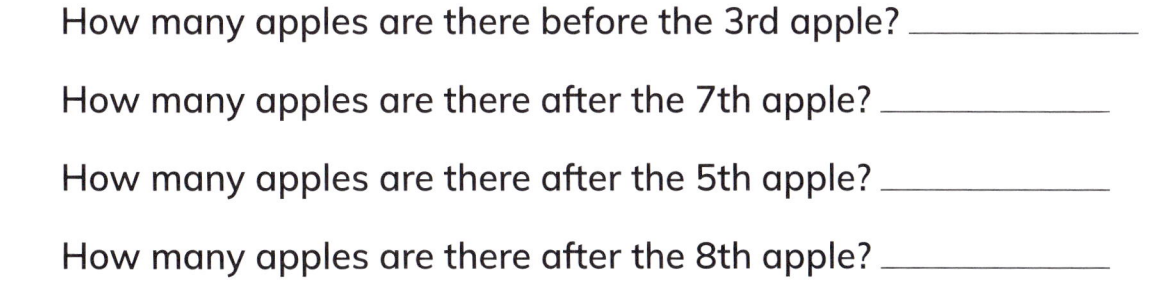

8

How many apples are there before the 3rd apple? _____

How many apples are there after the 7th apple? _____

How many apples are there after the 5th apple? _____

How many apples are there after the 8th apple? _____

93

6 Position

Let's investigate

You will need 3 cubes of different colours.

Put them in the order of red 1st, blue 2nd, yellow 3rd.

What different patterns can you make with red 1st?

You could have

Investigate the different patterns if you have yellow first.

Investigate the different patterns if you have blue first.

Colour the patterns you have made.

Label the cubes in each pattern 1st, 2nd, 3rd.

Now add a 4th cube colour.

How many patterns can you make?

6.1 Position

Look what I can do!

- I can recognise and use ordinal numbers.
- I can use new words to describe position.
- I can order ordinal numbers.

Check your progress

1 Write the number between.

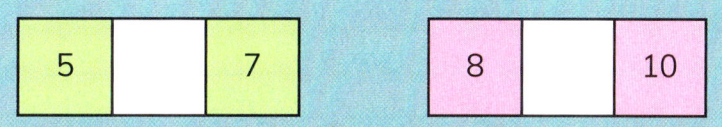

| 3 | | 5 | | 7 | | 9 |

| 5 | | 7 | | 8 | | 10 |

2 Join the hats and scarves to the correct people.
Use the ordinal numbers on the hats to help you.

95

6 Position

Continued

3   Draw or write what you see.

What is **on** the table?

What is **under** the table?

What is **between** the man and the table?

What is **behind** the chair?

What is **beside** the chair?

What is **in front of** the chair?

on	
under	
between	
behind	
beside	
in front	

4   Write in the missing ordinal numbers on the balloons.

1st   9th

96

7 Statistics

Getting started

1. Look at the bears.

   How many 🧸 bears are there? ☐

   How many other bears are there? ☐

   Draw a ring around the correct answer.

   There are **more** / **fewer** 🧸 bears than other bears.

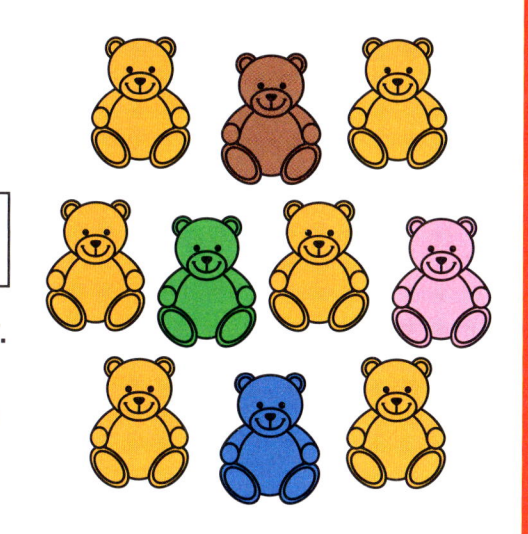

> How many different ways are there of sorting fruit and vegetables?

You are learning about sets and Venn diagrams so that you can:
- sort groups in different ways
- use and make sets and Venn diagrams of your own.

7 Statistics

> 7.1 Sets

We are going to …
- sort and count objects into sets
- use the words **group** and **set**
- understand **data**.

We need to know about organising into **sets** so that we can sort objects into which things belong together and which don't.

data   group   set   sort

When we sort we look for something that is the same.

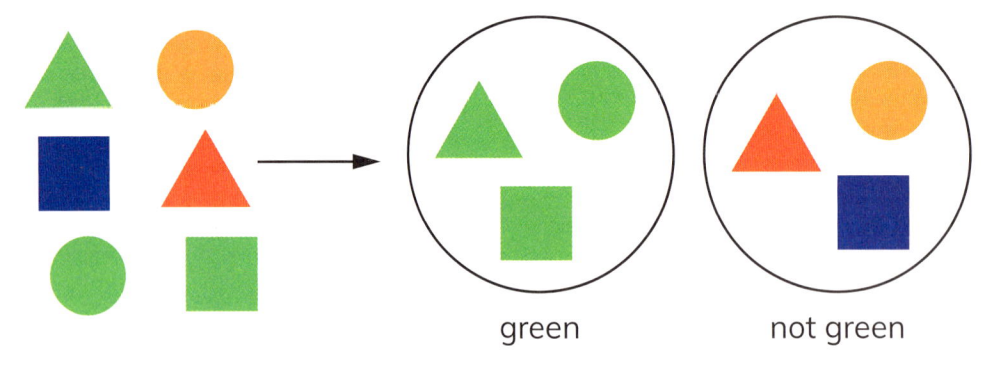

green   not green

> I've sorted this group of shapes into two sets. One set contains green shapes. The other set contains shapes that are not green.

Exercise 7.1

> **Worked example 1**
>
> Here is a group of children. Sort them into two sets. 
>
> Some of the children are girls.
>
> We label the circle **girls**.
>
> All the girls belong in this circle.
>
> Some of the children are boys.
>
> We label the circle **boys**.
>
> All the boys belong in this circle.

7 Statistics

1. Sort these animals into the 2 sets by writing the letters in the correct circle.

   not stripes   stripes

   How many animals have stripes? ☐

   How many animals do not have stripes? ☐

   Tick the set that has more animals.

2. Sort these vegetables into the 2 sets by writing the letters in the correct circle.

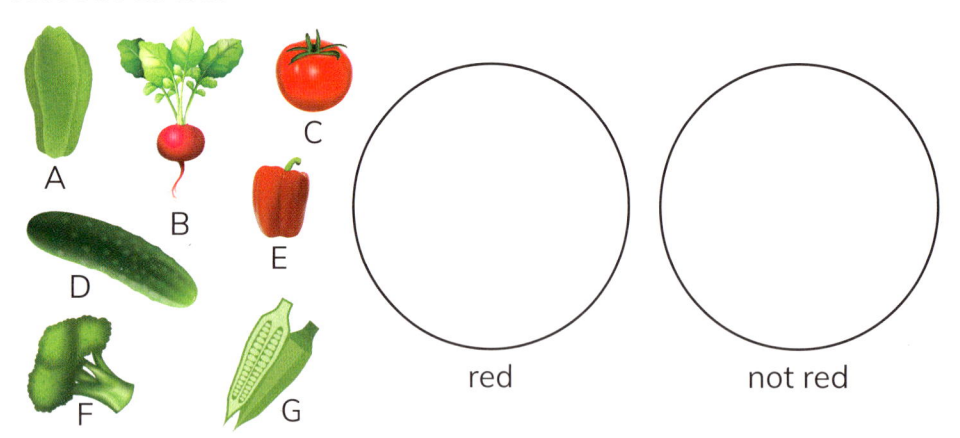

   red   not red

   How many are red? ☐   How many are not red? ☐

   Tick the set that has less.

7.1 Sets

Let's investigate

Work with a partner.

Find 2 different ways to sort the houses. Show 1 way in your book here. Your partner should show the other way in their book.

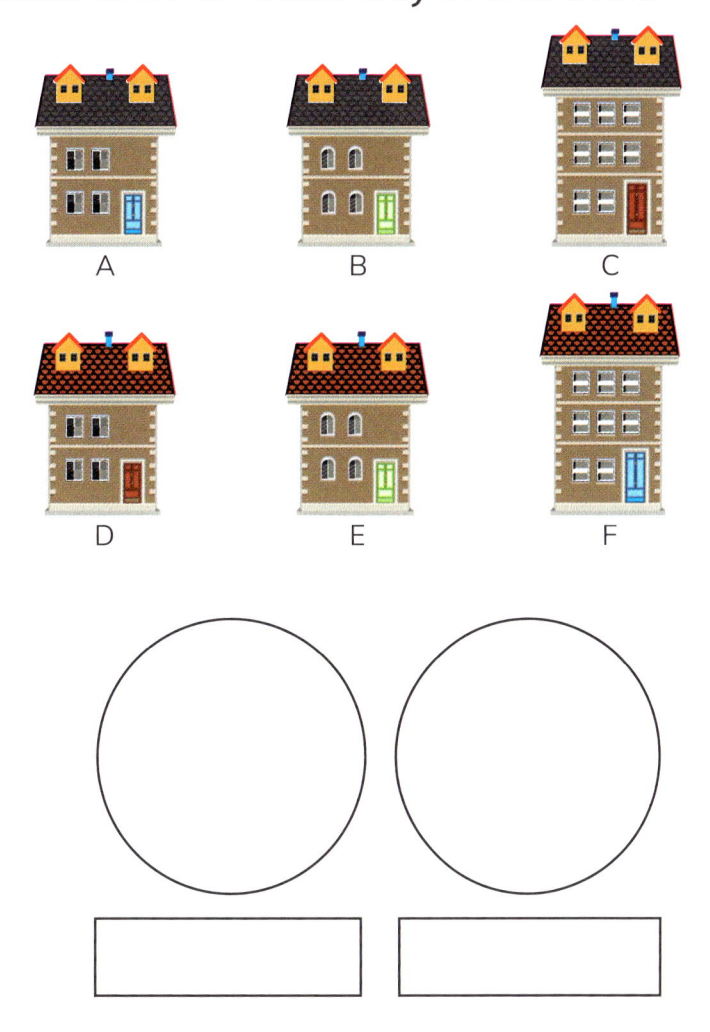

A   B   C

D   E   F

What have you learned about sets and sorting?

Write or draw one thing that you know now that you didn't know before.

101

7 Statistics

Look what I can do!

- I can sort objects into sets.
- I can count objects in sets.
- I can use the words **group** and **set**.

> 7.2 Venn diagrams

We are going to ...

- record, sort and show data using Venn diagrams
- describe data
- discuss what we have found out.

A Venn diagram helps you to organise data.

It can help you to compare different groups of things.

We need to know about sorting into sets so that we can organise objects that fit together.

When we sort, we look for things that are the same.

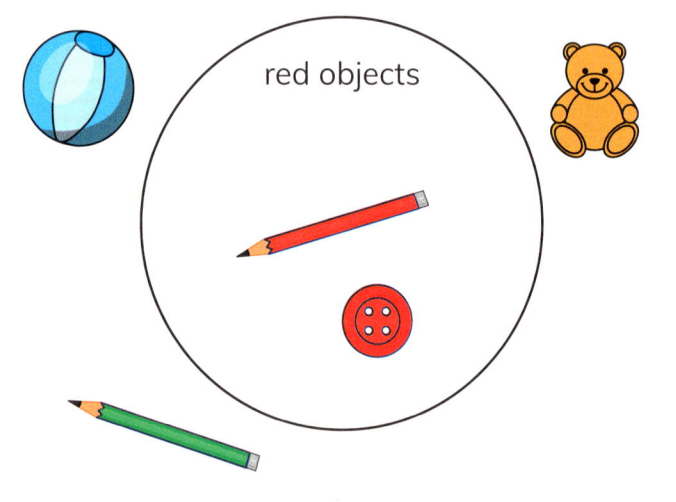

Venn diagram

7.2 Venn diagrams

Exercise 7.2

Worked example 1

Look at the stars.

Some have 5 points. Some do not.

Sort the stars by writing the letters in the correct part of the Venn diagram.

What do you notice?

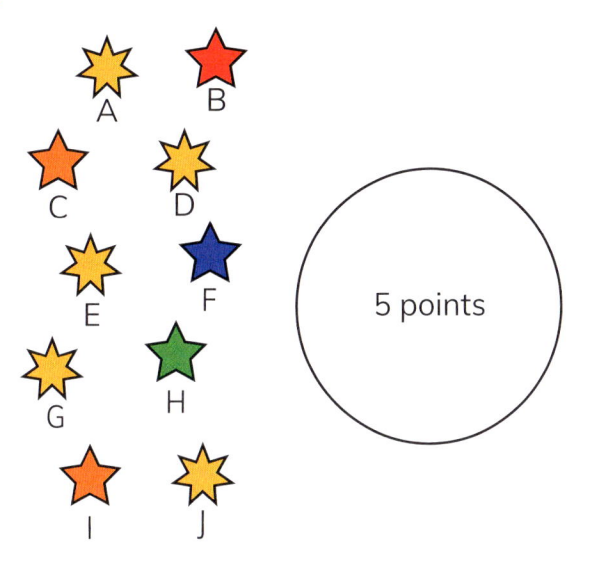

Answer:

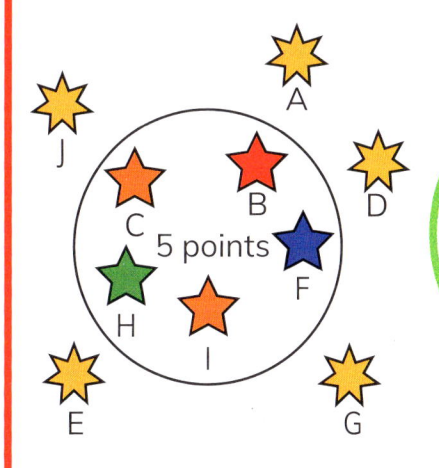

The stars that don't have 5 points go outside the circle. All the stars in the circle have 5 points.

103

7 Statistics

1. Work with your partner.

   Here is a group of shapes.

   Sort the shapes by writing the letters into the correct part of the Venn diagram.

   all faces flat

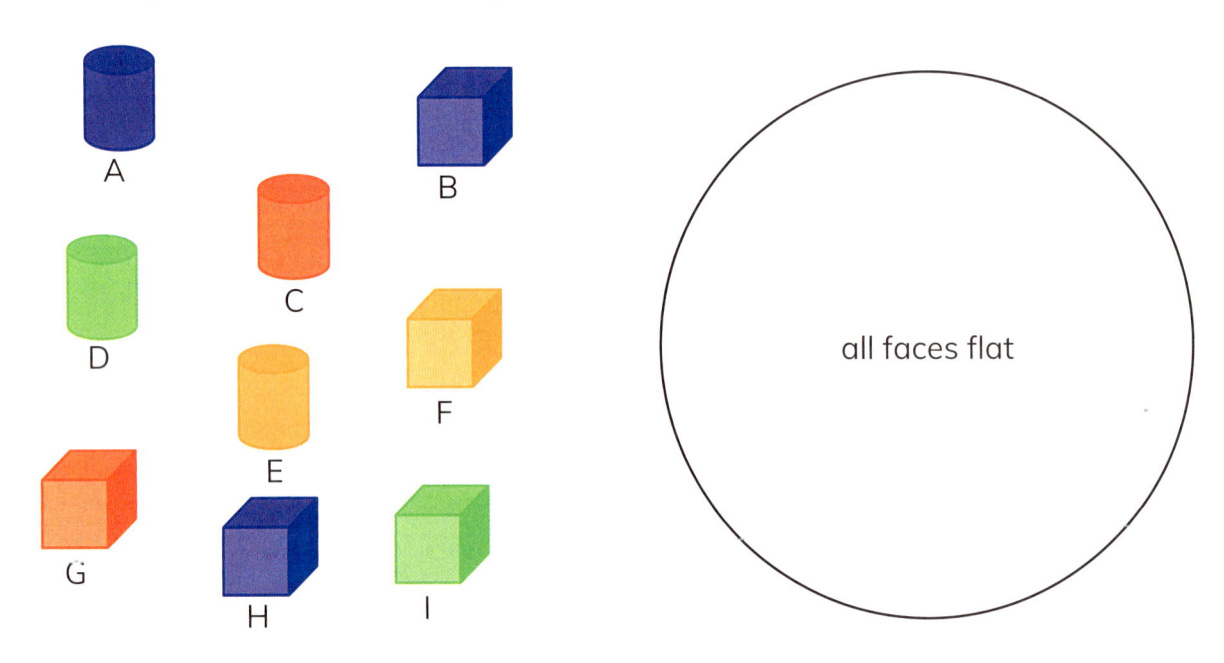

2. Sort the balloons by writing the letters into the correct part of the Venn diagram.

   not orange

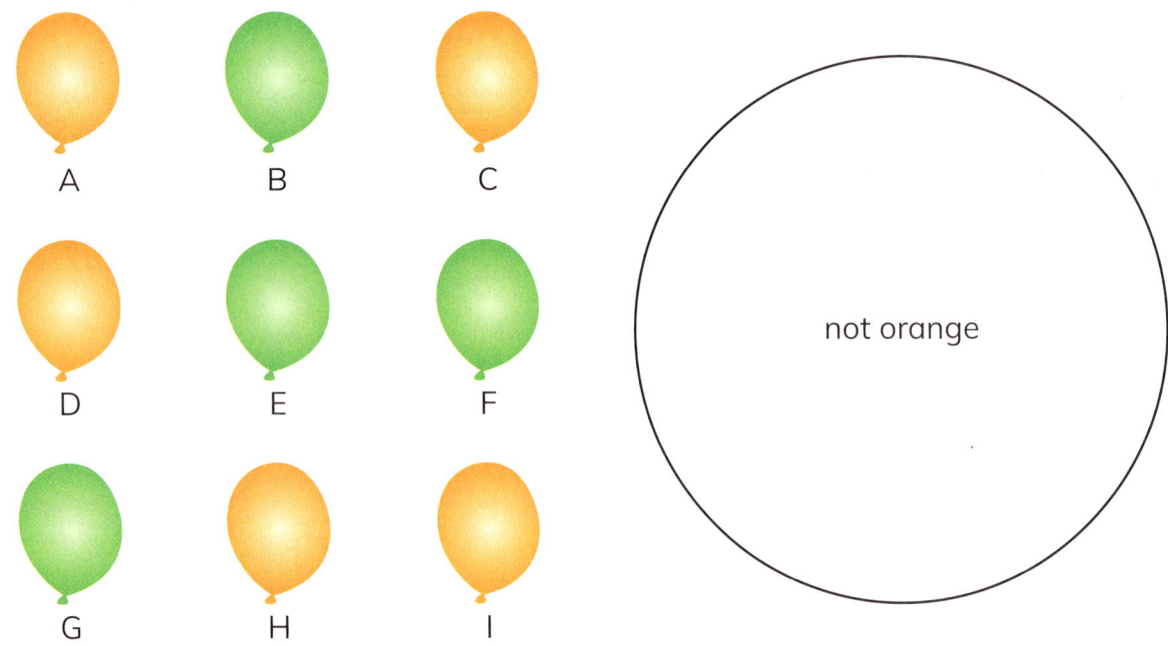

7.2 Venn diagrams

3 Sort the shapes by writing the letters into the correct part of the Venn diagram.

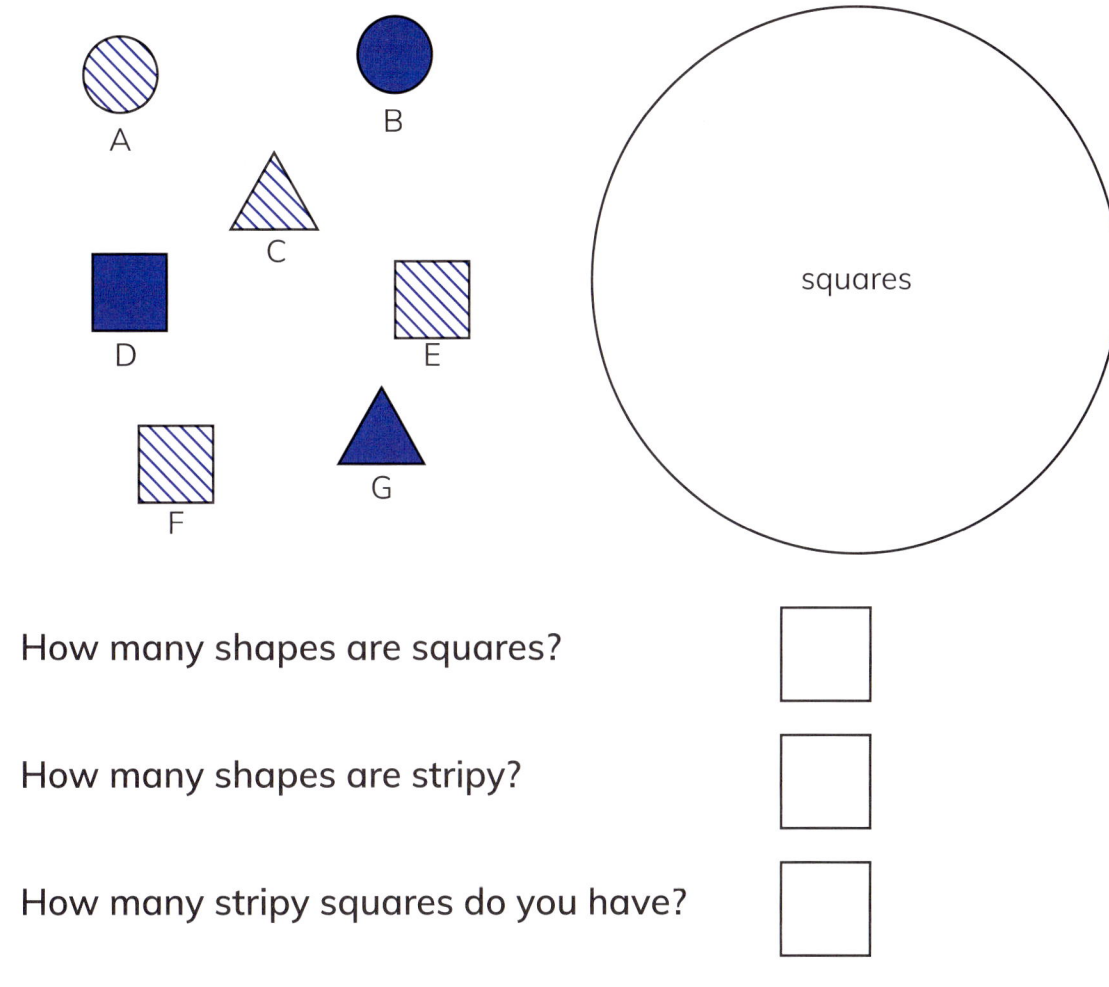

squares

How many shapes are squares? ☐

How many shapes are stripy? ☐

How many stripy squares do you have? ☐

Draw a ring around the correct word to complete each sentence.

There are **more stripy shapes / square shapes**.

There are **fewer stripy shapes / square shapes**.

7 Statistics

4   Sort the animals by writing the letters into the correct part of the Venn diagram.

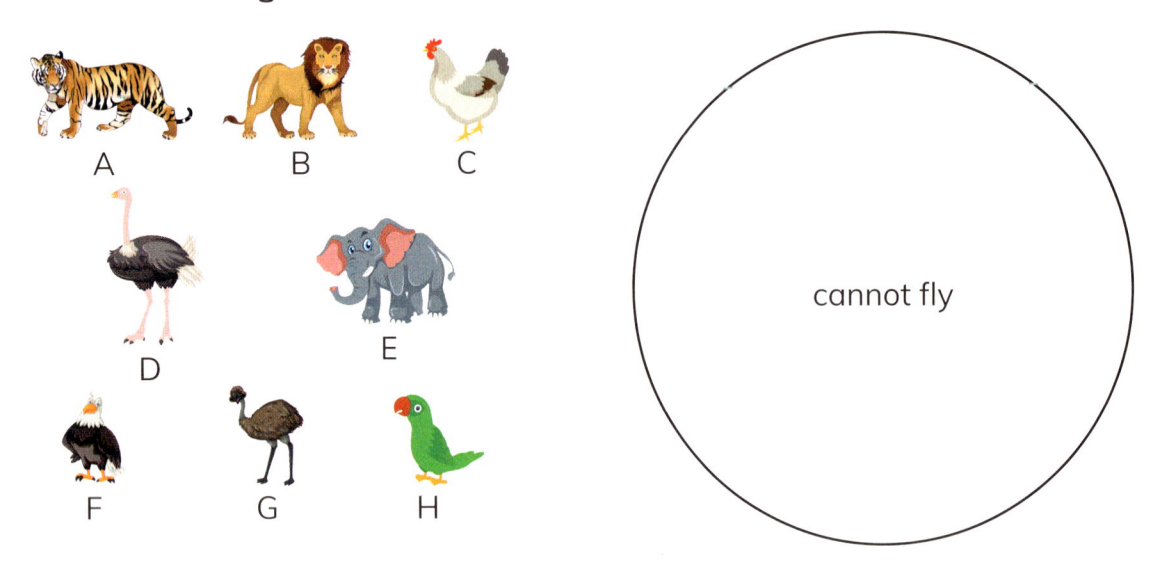

A   B   C
D   E
F   G   H

cannot fly

5   Work with a partner.

How can you find and record your favourite food?

Talk to your partner about what you like to eat.

Draw or write things you like in your circle.

Draw or write things you don't like outside your circle.
Your partner should do the same in their book.

I like

Now compare your answers with your partner's.

What did you both like most? Were they the same or different? What did you both like the least? Were they the same or different?

7.2 Venn diagrams

6   Draw a ring around each mistake in the Venn diagram.

I can see 4 mistakes.

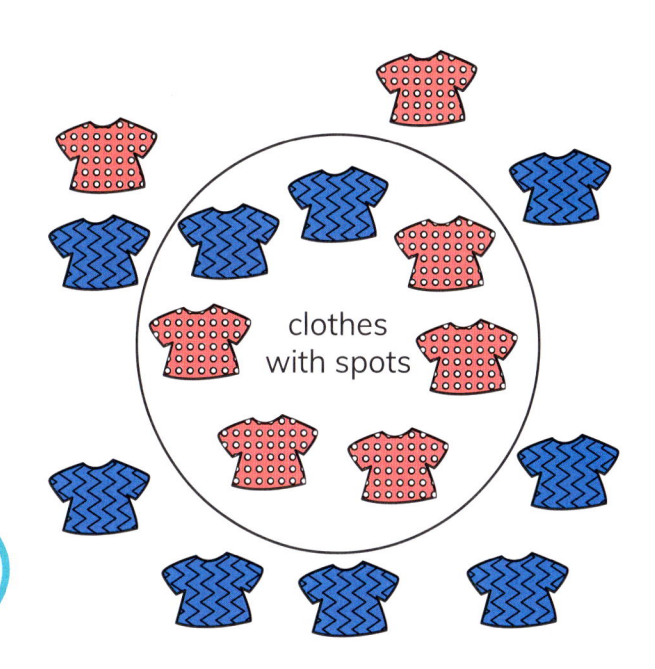

clothes with spots

Let's investigate

Look at this group of bugs.

A   B   C   D   E   F   G   H   I

Sort the bugs into a Venn diagram in 2 different ways.

Work with your partner.

Talk about the different ways you found.

Do you think there are more than 2 ways to sort the bugs?

Find 2 more different ways.

Use these labels.

Draw or write what you think.

Don't forget to label your diagram.

7 Statistics

How did your partner help you with Venn diagrams?
How did you help your partner?
What didn't you like doing? Why was that?

Look what I can do!

- I can record, sort and show data using Venn diagrams.
- I can describe data.
- I can discuss what I have found out.

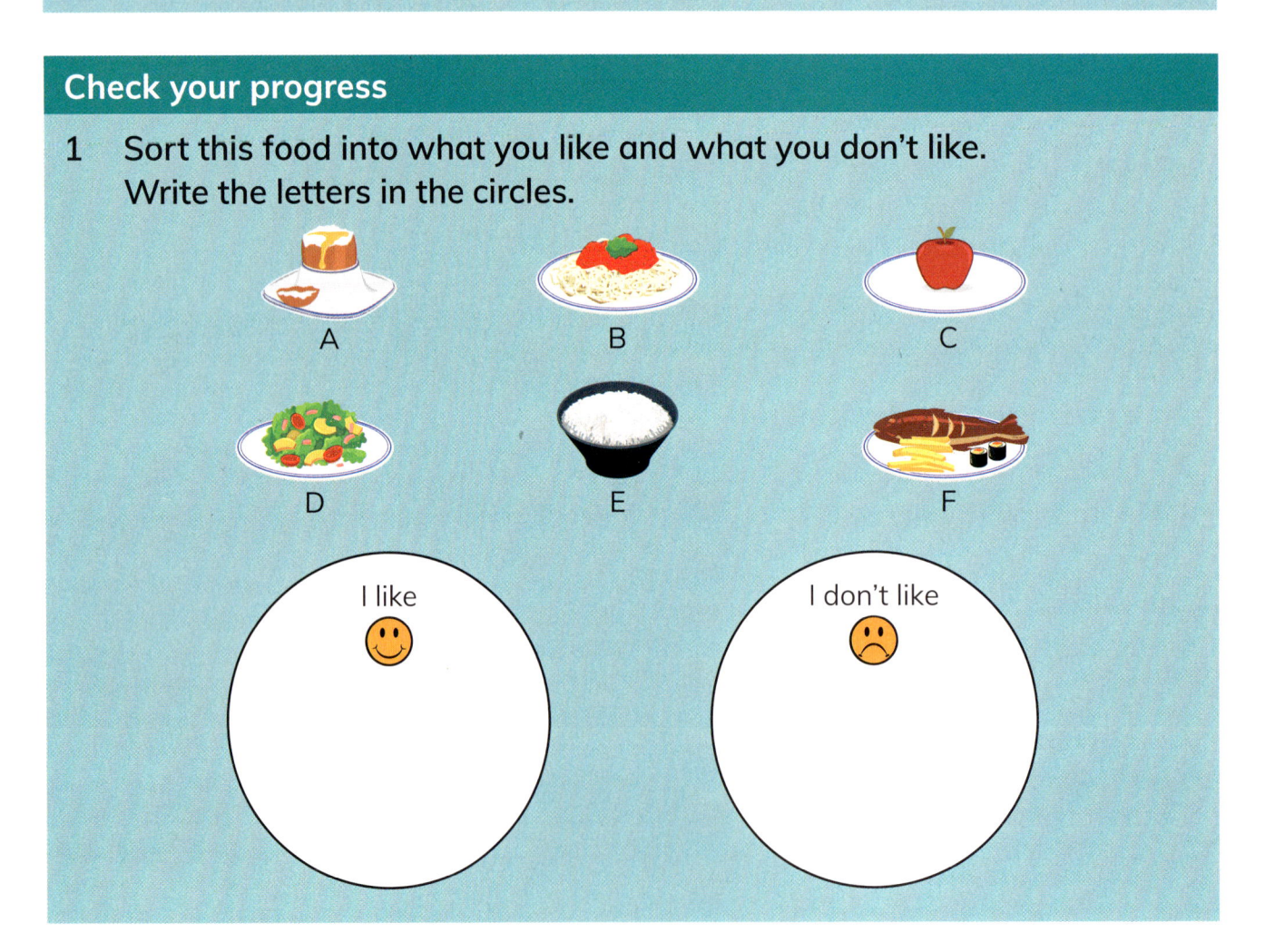

Check your progress

1. Sort this food into what you like and what you don't like. Write the letters in the circles.

A   B   C

D   E   F

I like

I don't like

7.2 Venn diagrams

Continued

2   Sort the bears by writing the letters into the correct part of the Venn diagram.

How many bears are red? ☐

How many bears are not red? ☐

3   Sort the ice creams and ice lollies by writing the letters into the correct part of the Venn diagram.

How many chocolate lollies are there? ☐

How many chocolate ice creams are there? ☐

How many items are not ice cream or lollies? ☐

8 Time

Getting started

1 When do you get up?

2 When do you go to bed?

Being able to tell the time and work with time is very important.

You will be learning about the days of the week and the facts about clocks.

A clock has numbers and hands.

The long hand is the minute hand.

The short hand is the hour hand.

On a clock we measure time in minutes and hours.

On a calendar we measure time in days.

There are 7 days in a week.

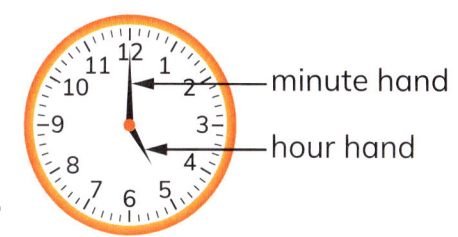

> 8.1 Time

We are going to ...

- **learn about the days of the week**
- **learn about clocks**
- **learn how to tell the o'clock and half past times.**

Telling the time is an important thing to know how to do and can be very useful. Clocks can help you:

- wake up in time for school
- tell you when it is time for lunch
- tell you when your favourite TV show is about to start.

Once you have learned how to read a clock, you can use it every day of your life.

afternoon   clock   evening   half past   hands   hour   minute
morning   o'clock   today   tomorrow   week   yesterday

8 Time

Exercise 8.1

1   Complete each sentence by drawing a line from the word to the space.

   In the _____ I get out of bed.

   In the _____ I get into bed.

   Today is _____.

   Tomorrow will be _____.

   Yesterday was _____.

morning	afternoon
evening	Monday
Tuesday	Wednesday
Thursday	Friday
Saturday	Sunday

Worked example 1

What is the same about all of these clocks?

Answer:

All of the clocks have the long **hand** pointing to the top.

8.1 Time

2 There are 7 days in a week.
   Write the missing days.
   Use the list to help you.

   Monday   Tuesday
   Wednesday   Thursday
   Friday   Saturday
   Sunday

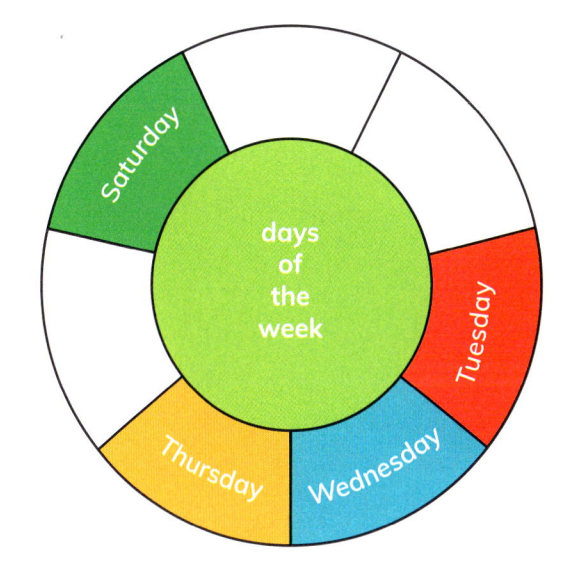

3 Write the times under these clocks.

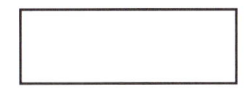

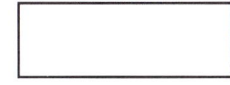

4 Write the o'clock time under each clock.

113

8 Time

5 What o'clock time does the clock show?

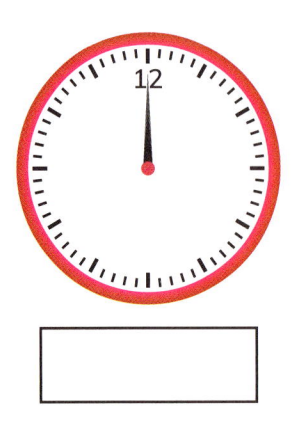

[ ]

6 Draw a ring around the correct time.

4 o'clock   5 o'clock   6 o'clock

7 o'clock   8 o'clock   9 o'clock   1 o'clock   2 o'clock   3 o'clock

7 The long hand is pointing to 6.

What **half past** time does the clock show?

_____

10.1 3D shapes

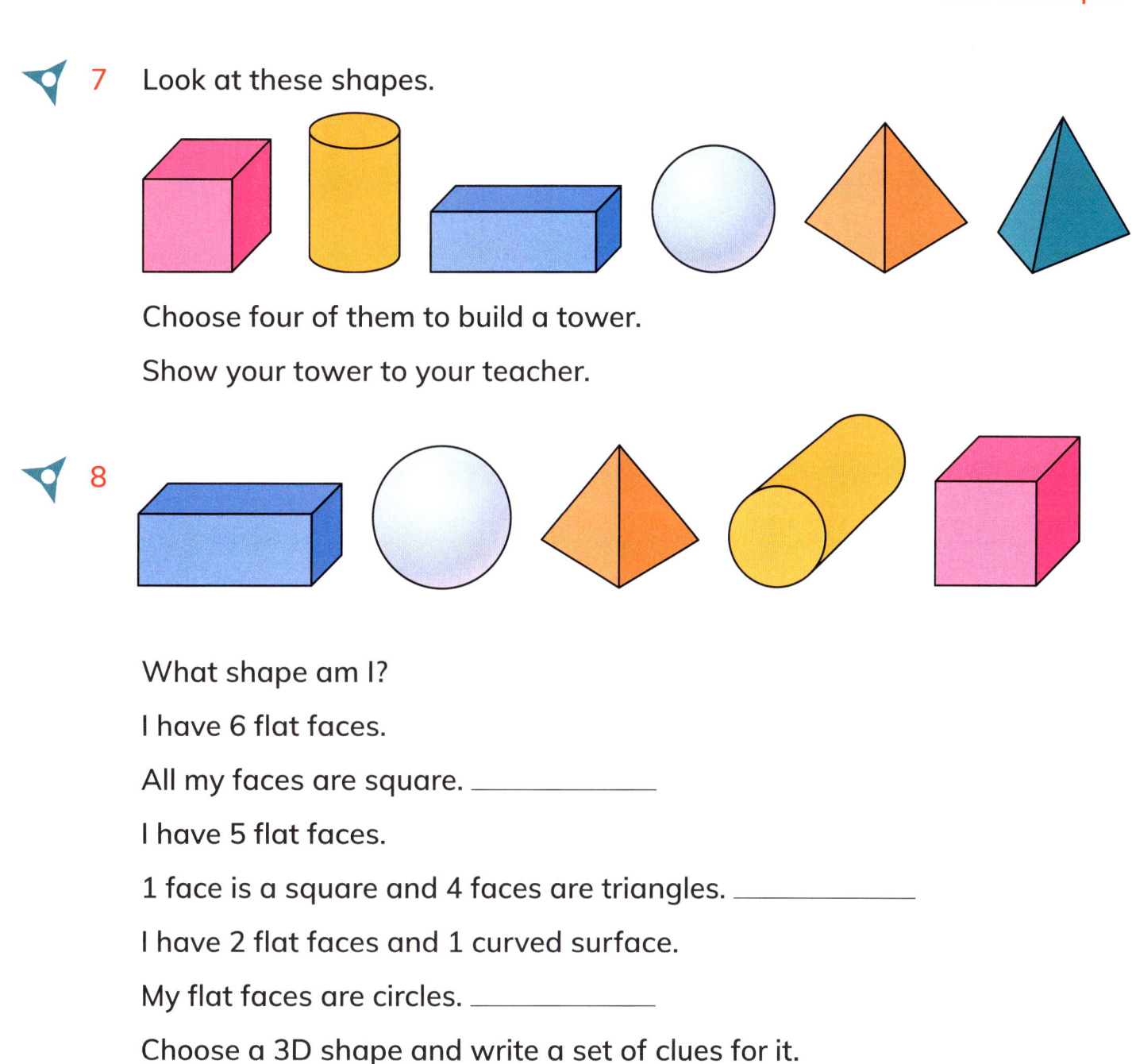

7   Look at these shapes.

Choose four of them to build a tower.

Show your tower to your teacher.

8

What shape am I?

I have 6 flat faces.

All my faces are square. _____

I have 5 flat faces.

1 face is a square and 4 faces are triangles. _____

I have 2 flat faces and 1 curved surface.

My flat faces are circles. _____

Choose a 3D shape and write a set of clues for it.

_____

_____

_____

145

10 Geometry (2)

Let's investigate

Work with a partner.

You need 5 cubes of the same size.

Pick up one cube. Count how many faces it has. Write your answer in the table.

Number of cubes in the shape	Number of faces
1	
2	
3	
4	
5	

Now put two cubes together. Count how many faces the new shape has. Is there a different number of faces?

Keep adding cubes and counting the number of faces. Write your findings in the table.

What happens to the number of faces when you add more cubes?

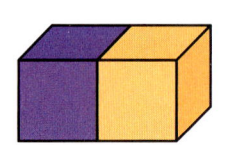

What have you found out about faces of 3D shapes?

Look what I can do!

- I can identify, describe and sort 3D shapes.
- I can explore faces and edges.

> 10.2 2D shapes

> **We are going to …**
> - identify, describe and sort 2D shapes
> - identify when a 2D shape looks the same when it is turned around
> - find what is the same and what is different between 2D and 3D shapes.

Playing with and making patterns using 2D shapes will help you to learn much more about them.

Make a pattern using the same shape but turning it around.

We can rotate the shape.

Some 2D shapes fit together with no spaces.

Some 2D shapes will always have spaces between them.

This is important when you want to make patterns for buildings, floors or sewing.

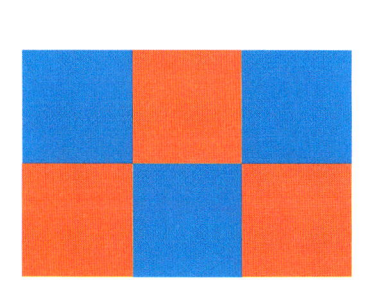

hexagon   pentagon
rectangle   rotate

Some shapes look different when they are turned around, but they are still the same shape.

147

10 Geometry (2)

Exercise 10.2

Worked example 2

Draw lines from the shapes to the correct circles.

Count how many 2D and 3D shapes there are.

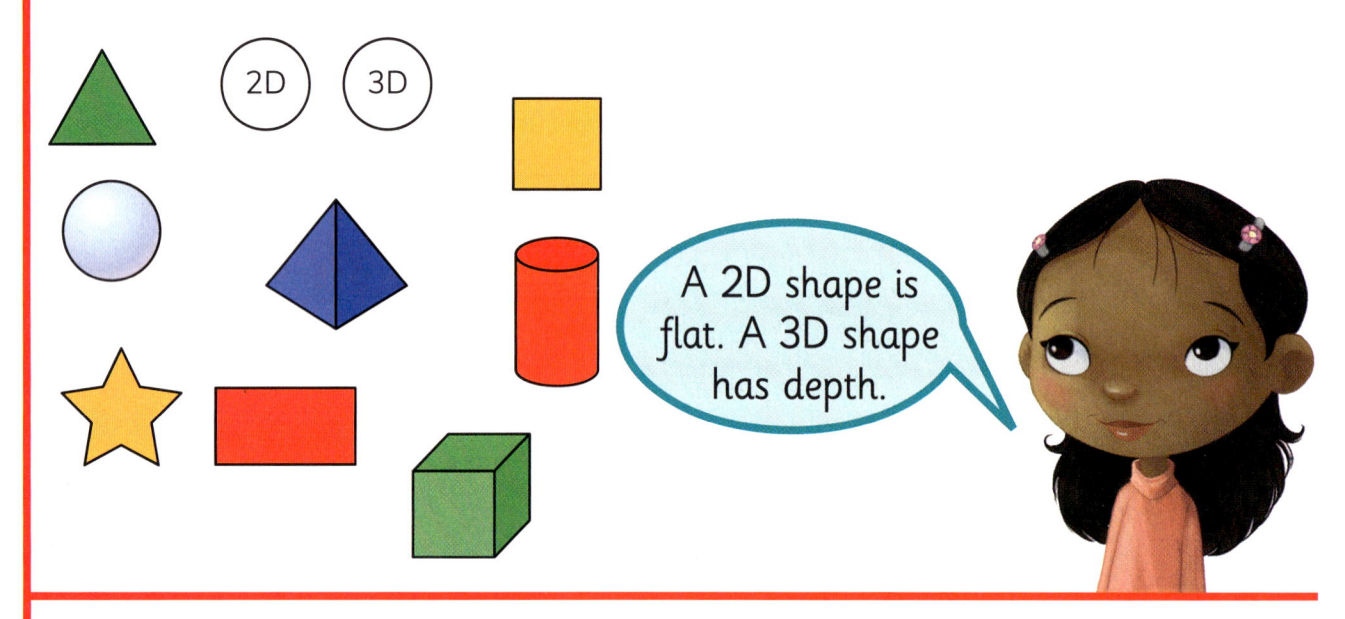

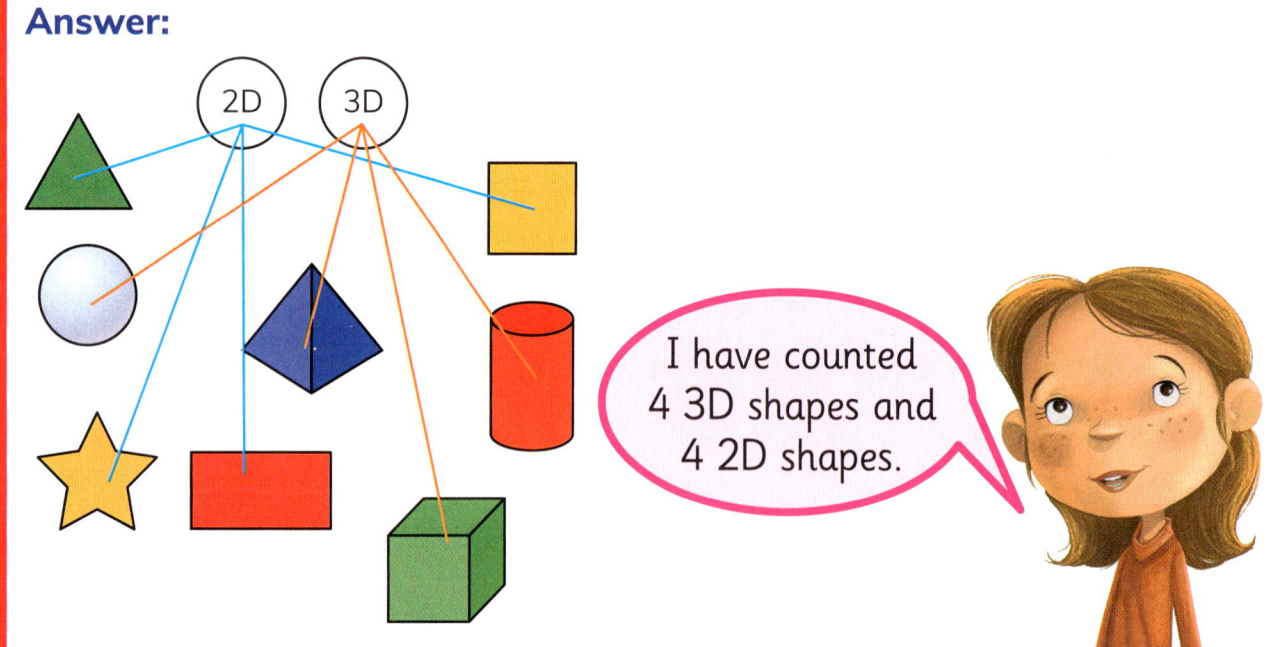

A 2D shape is flat. A 3D shape has depth.

Answer:

I have counted 4 3D shapes and 4 2D shapes.

10.2 2D shapes

1   Draw a ring around the triangles.

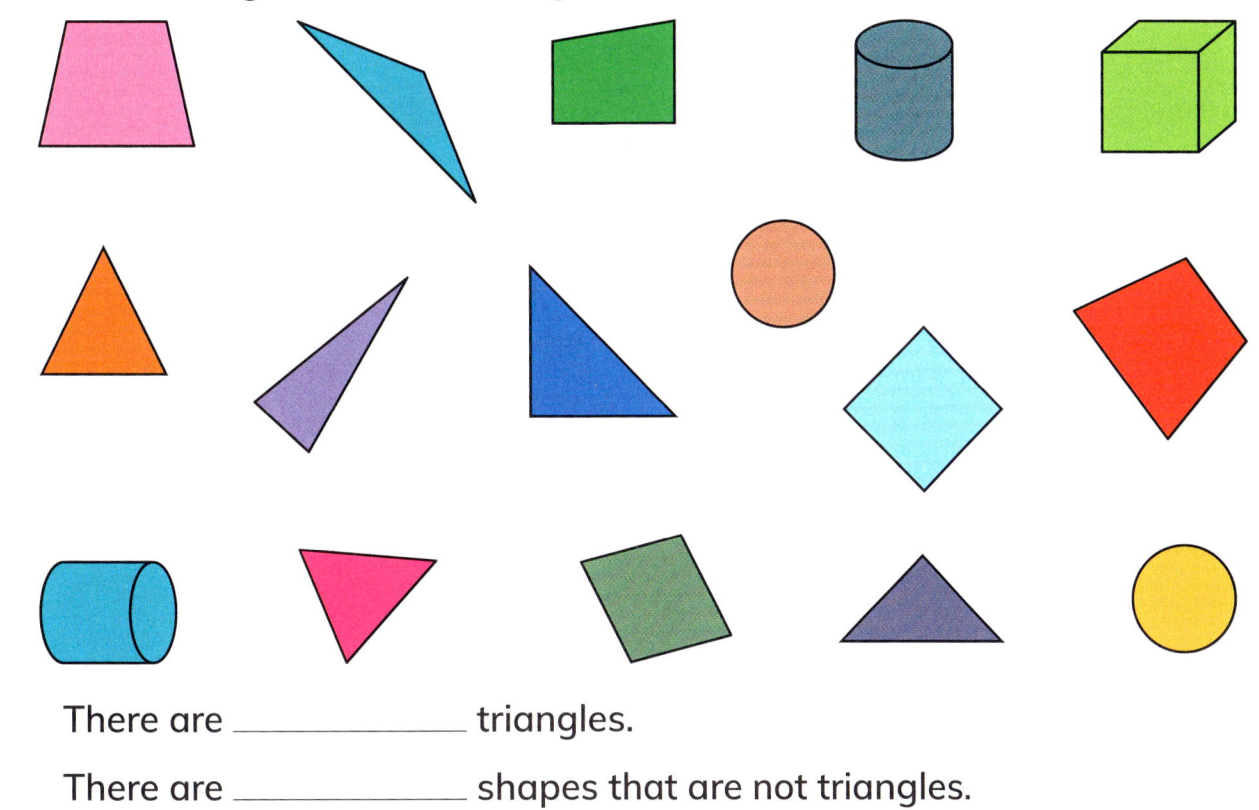

   There are _____ triangles.

   There are _____ shapes that are not triangles.

2   Big triangles can be made by using lots of small triangles.

   Use just 2 colours to make your own triangle pattern.

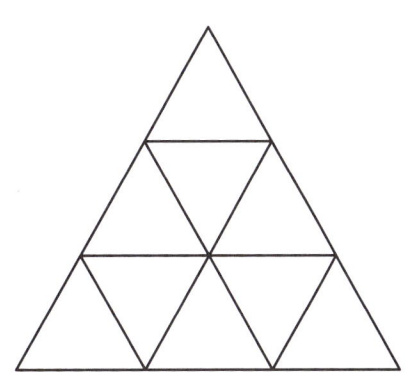

149

10 Geometry (2)

3. Play this game with a partner.

   You are trying to make squares.

   Take turns to spin a spinner.

   Take that number of sticks to make a square.

   You may not have enough or you may have too many.

   The first person to make 4 squares is the winner.

   You can make other shapes.

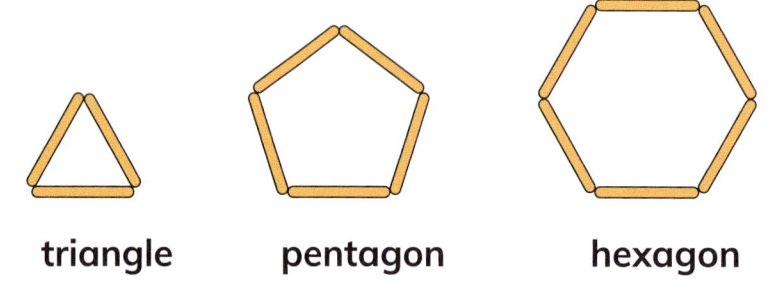

   triangle   pentagon   hexagon

4. Put together two squares to make a new shape.

   How many different shapes or patterns can you make with two squares?

   Draw 2 different ones that you can make.

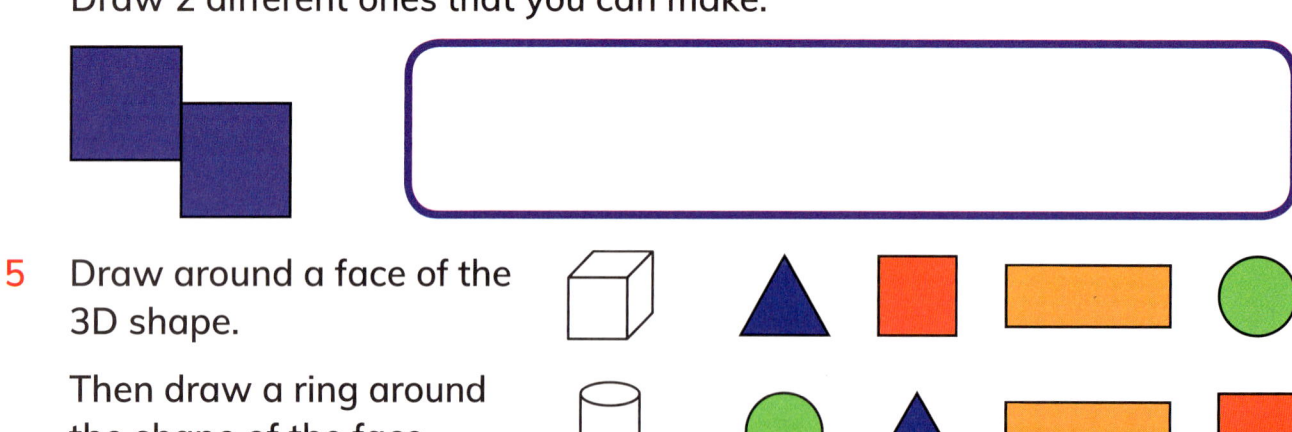

5. Draw around a face of the 3D shape.

   Then draw a ring around the shape of the face.

10.2 2D shapes

Let's investigate

You will need lots of triangles.

Make a star shape with some triangles.

How many different star shapes can you make?

How about this one?

Or this one?

What other shapes can you make?

What if you used different types of triangles together to make a star?

Where have you seen these 2D shapes before?
When you made patterns with squares and triangles, did they look like anything you had seen before?

10 Geometry (2)

6. For each shape, tick if it is a 2D shape or a 3D shape.

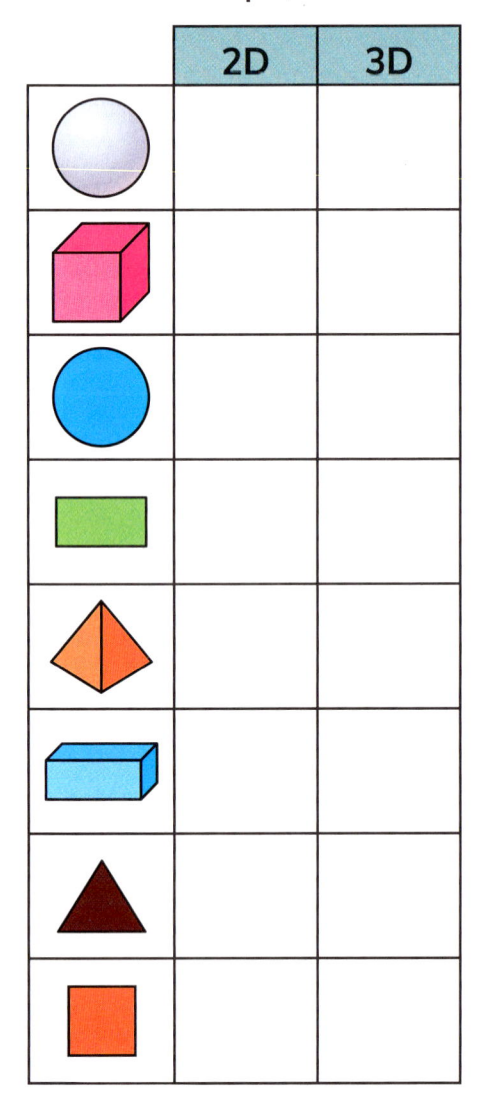

	2D	3D
sphere		
cube		
circle		
rectangle		
pyramid		
cuboid		
triangle		
square		

How did you know whether a shape was 2D or 3D?

Look what I can do!

- I can identify and name 2D shapes.
- I can identify when a 2D shape looks the same when it is turned around.
- I can find what is the same and what is different between 2D and 3D shapes.

10.2 2D shapes

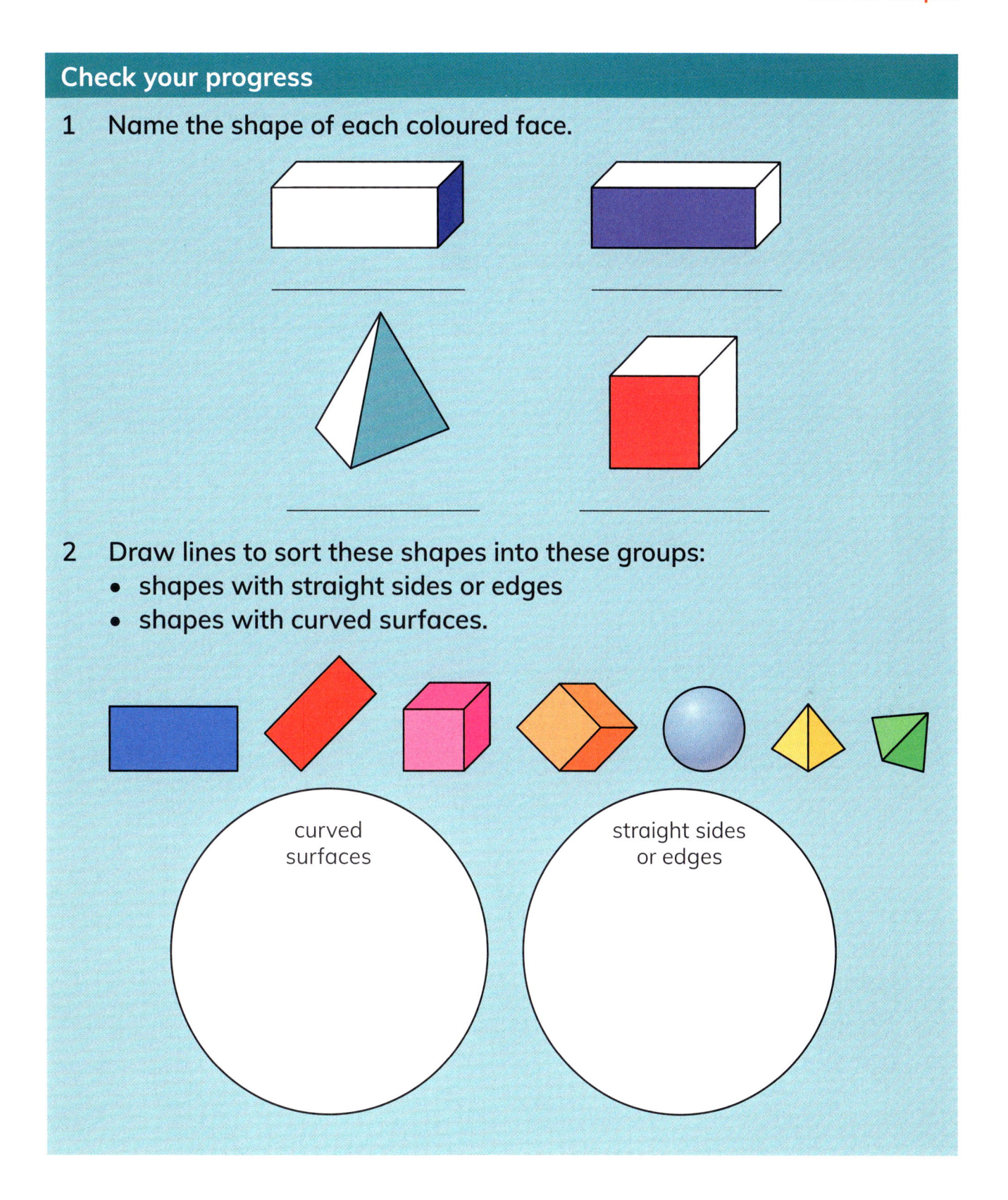

Check your progress

1   Name the shape of each coloured face.

    _____   _____

    _____   _____

2   Draw lines to sort these shapes into these groups:
    - shapes with straight sides or edges
    - shapes with curved surfaces.

    curved surfaces   straight sides or edges

10 Geometry (2)

Continued

3   Put together 4 triangles to make a picture or a pattern.

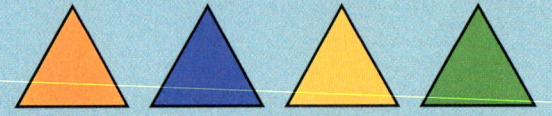

Draw 2 different patterns you can make.
Use the colours to make different patterns.

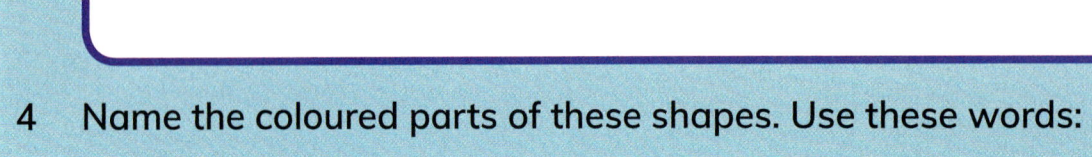

4   Name the coloured parts of these shapes. Use these words:
- face
- edge

> Project 4

Which one doesn't belong?

Look at this group of shapes.

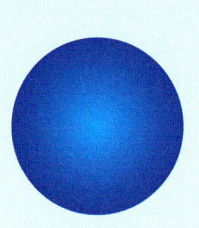

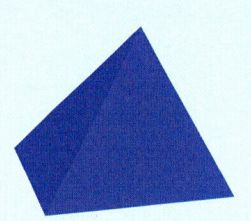

Which one doesn't belong?

Why?

Talk to your partner about these shapes.

Which one do they think doesn't belong?

Can you find a way for another shape to be the one that doesn't belong?

Could it be any of the shapes?

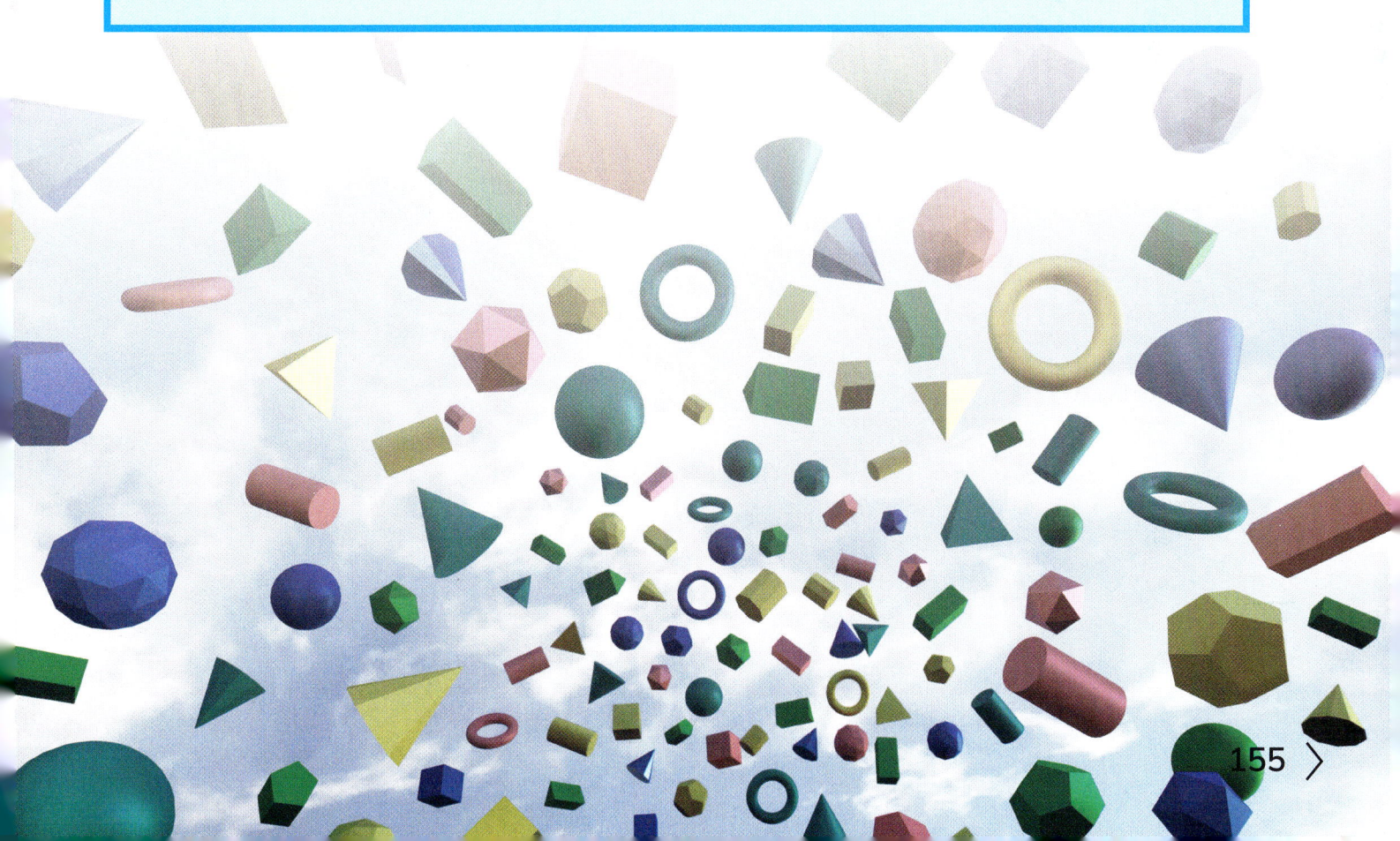

11   Fractions (2)

Getting started

1   Colour one half of each shape.

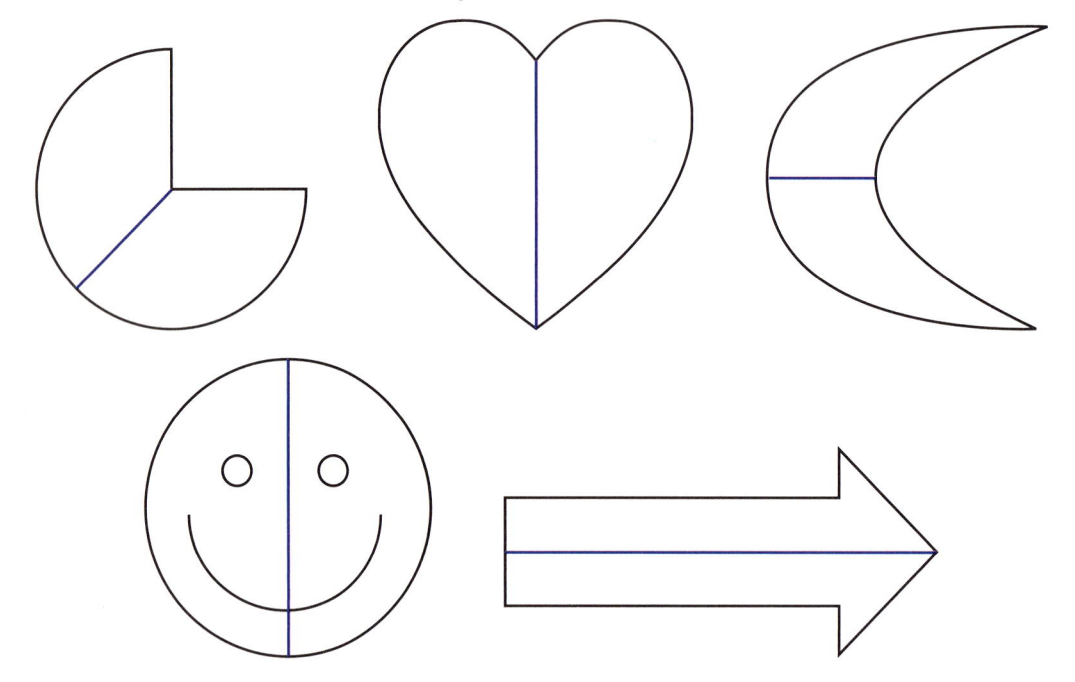

2   Draw lines to show a half.

11 Fractions (2)

What do I know about halves?

How do I know if it is a half?

A fraction is a part of a whole.

This can be numbers or objects or sets of objects.

You need to know about halves when sharing your sweets, your toys and even your pizza.

A full jug can be halved into 2 equal glasses of juice and then poured back into the jug to make the whole again.

You need to know about a half when telling the time.

11 Fractions (2)

> 11.1 Halves

> **We are going to ...**
> - find halves of objects, sets and quantities
> - put halves together to make a whole
> - record halves using half, $\frac{1}{2}$, equal and the same as.

We need to know about wholes and halves for all sorts of different reasons.

Half of a sandwich.

Half a jug of water.

At half past 4 I go swimming.

$\frac{1}{2}$ halve

You can also halve numbers. Half of 10 is 5.

$$10 \longrightarrow 55$$

11.1 Halves

Worked example 1

Colour one half of each shape.

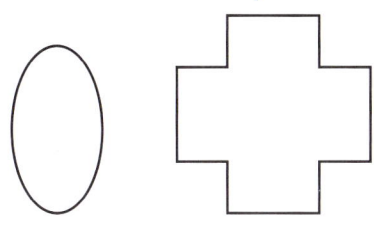

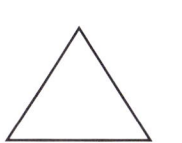

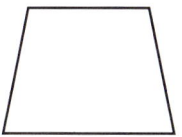

Answer:

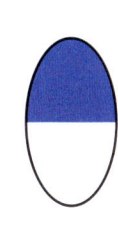

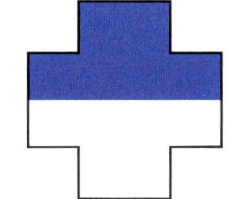

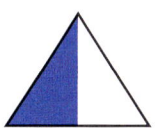

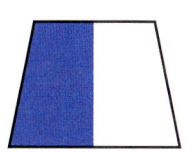

Exercise 11.1

1   When you cut something into two parts and both are the same size, each one is a half.

We can write it as $\frac{1}{2}$.

Here is $\frac{1}{2}$ of a cake.

Here is $\frac{1}{2}$ of another cake.

Do the two halves make a whole cake?

11 Fractions (2)

2 Draw the other half of this face.

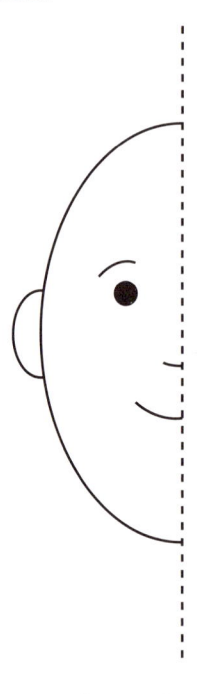

3 Join the word **half** to the shapes that show a half.

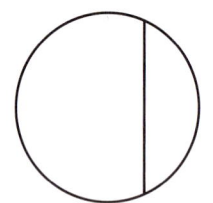

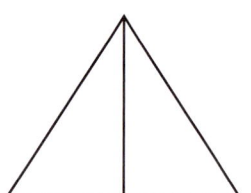

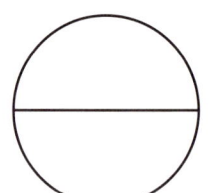

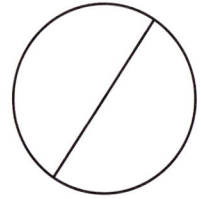

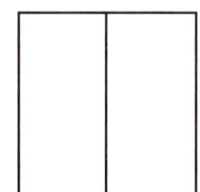

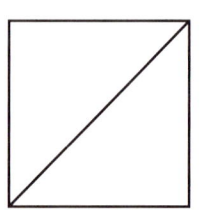

11.1 Halves

4 A half is part of a whole.

A half is part of a set.

Draw a line through each set to show $\frac{1}{2}$.

How many snails in the whole set? ☐

How many snails in half the set? ☐

5 Remember when you share **equally** between two, both sets have **the same** amount.

Jamil needs $\frac{1}{2}$ of these eggs for his cakes.

Sairah needs $\frac{1}{2}$ of these eggs for her cookies.

Draw a line to show half.

How many eggs are needed for the cakes? ☐

How many eggs are needed for the cookies? ☐

161

11 Fractions (2)

6 How many?

= _____ apples

= _____ apples

= _____ cakes

Let's investigate

How can you **halve** each cookie?

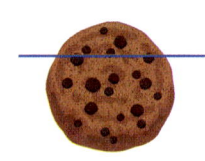

Work with a partner.

Draw lines to show the two halves of each cookie.

7 Use counters to find half of these numbers:

4 ☐   8 ☐   18 ☐

11.1 Halves

Working in pairs, tell your partner how you would halve a cookie.

How would you make both parts the same size?

What would you do if they were not the same size?

Look what I can do!

- I can find halves of objects, sets, quantities and numbers.
- I can put halves together to make a whole.
- I can record halves using half, $\frac{1}{2}$, equal and the same as.

Check your progress

1. A farmer has 10 sheep.

    He has 2 fields.

    He puts $\frac{1}{2}$ of the sheep in each field.

    How many sheep are in each field?

163

11 Fractions (2)

Continued

2. Lomi goes for a picnic. Her friend goes with her.
   This is what she takes:

   2 bottles of water

   4 apples

   6 sandwiches

   4 cookies.

   They share everything equally.
   Draw what Lomi has on this picnic cloth.

   Draw what her friend has on this picnic cloth.

> Project 5

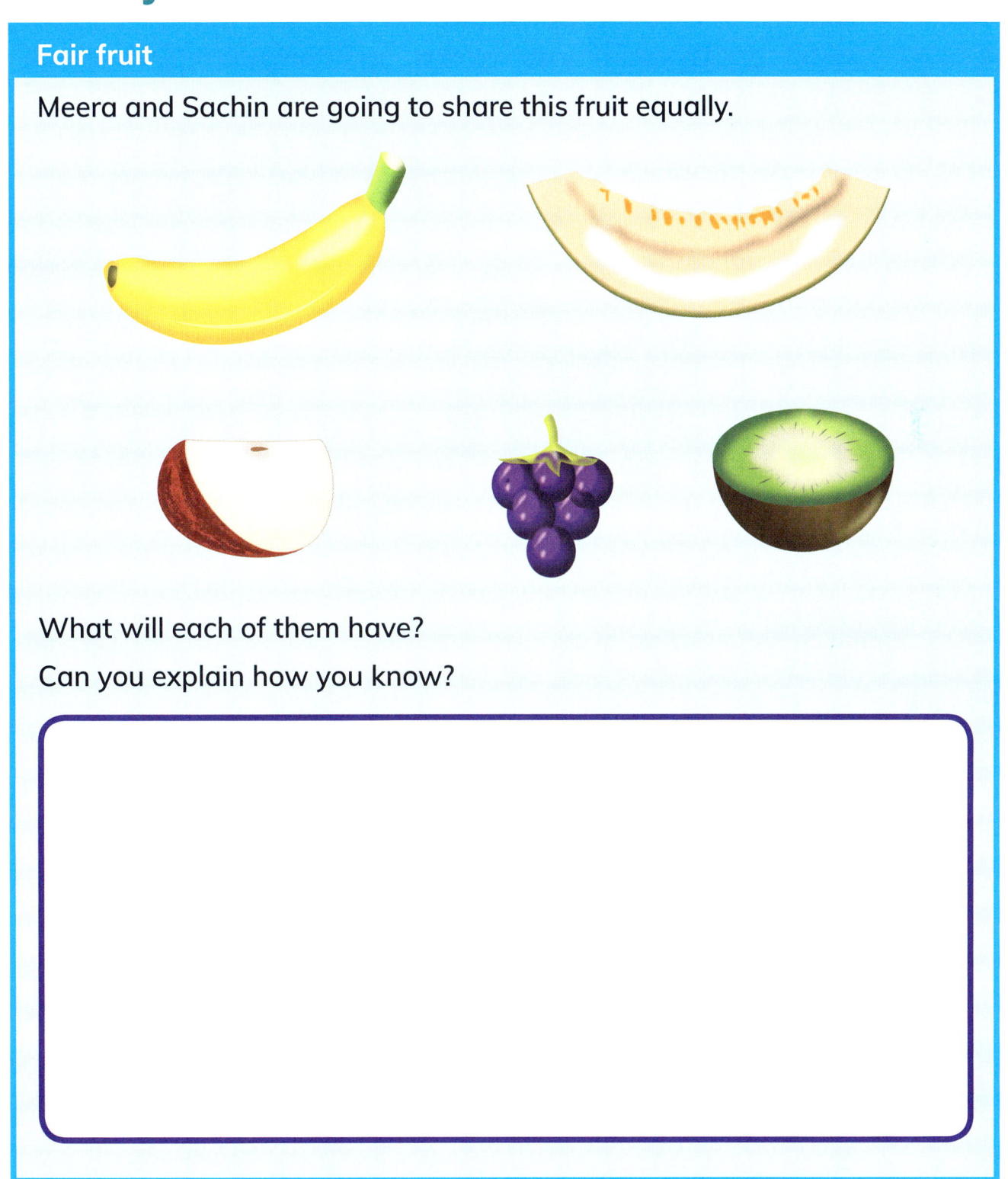

Fair fruit

Meera and Sachin are going to share this fruit equally.

What will each of them have?

Can you explain how you know?

12 Measures (2)

Getting started

1. Draw a ring around the heaviest animal.

2. Draw a ring around the shortest pencil.

3. Draw a ring around the tallest tree.

12 Measures (2)

This unit is about measuring length, mass, capacity and temperature.

We measure different things in different ways.

Length looks at how long, short or high something is.

It can also be used to measure distance.

Mass looks at how heavy something is.

Capacity looks at how much something can hold.

It looks at the space inside a container.

Temperature looks at how hot or cold something is.

12 Measures (2)

> 12.1 Mass and capacity

We are going to ...
- explore and compare mass
- explore and compare capacity.

The more mass an object has, the heavier it is.

Capacity is how much an object can hold.

This jug can hold more water than the cup. It has a bigger capacity.

balance scales   capacity   empty   full   heavy   light   mass

Worked example 1

Which is heavier?

Answer:
The shoe is heavier than the cube.
The cube is lighter than the shoe.

12.1 Mass and capacity

Exercise 12.1

1   Talk to your partner.

Which is heavier? Which is lighter?

How do you know?

2   Talk to your partner.

Which is heavier? Which is lighter?

How do you know?

Draw a ring around the correct answer.

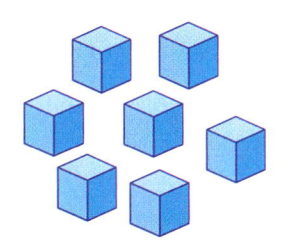

are heavier / lighter than

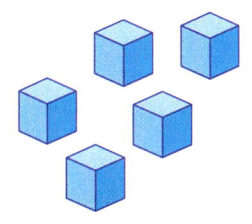

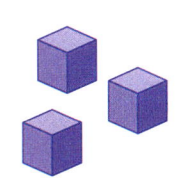

are heavier / lighter than

169

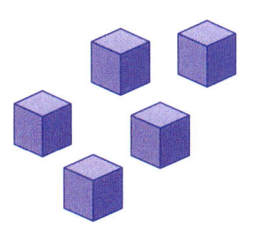

12 Measures (2)

3 Draw a ring around the correct word.

The [cow] is **heavier than / lighter than / the same as** the [horse].

The [horse] is **heavier than / lighter than / the same as** the [mouse].

4 To **balance** the scales you need the same mass on both sides.

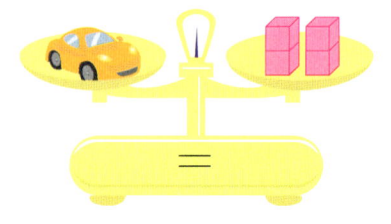

These scales balance.
The car has the same mass as 4 cubes.

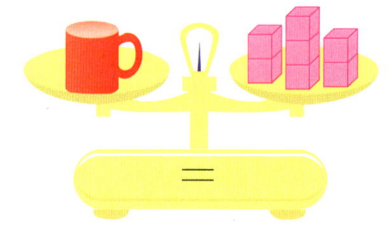

These scales balance.
The mug has the same mass as 7 cubes.

How many cubes will balance the car and the mug?

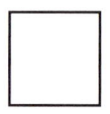

5 Draw a ring around the objects that hold the most in each box.

12.1 Mass and capacity

Let's investigate

Work with your group.

You will need:
- 5 cups of the same size and shape.
- 6 cups in different sizes and shapes.
- a jug, a funnel and some rice.

Challenge 1

Use cups that are the same shape and size.

Share out all the rice equally between the cups.

Draw a line on the side of the cups to show where the rice comes to.

As a group, talk about how you can share out the rice equally.

Challenge 2

Repeat the challenge using cups of different sizes.

What do you notice?

Did you change your mind about the way you shared the rice?

If you did this again, would you do it the same or differently? Explain why.

What did you find difficult about these challenges?

What did you learn in Challenge 1 that helped you in Challenge 2?

12 Measures (2)

6 Solve the puzzle to help the king find his drink.

empty   nearly empty   nearly full   full

A nearly empty jug and a nearly full jug will make a full jug.

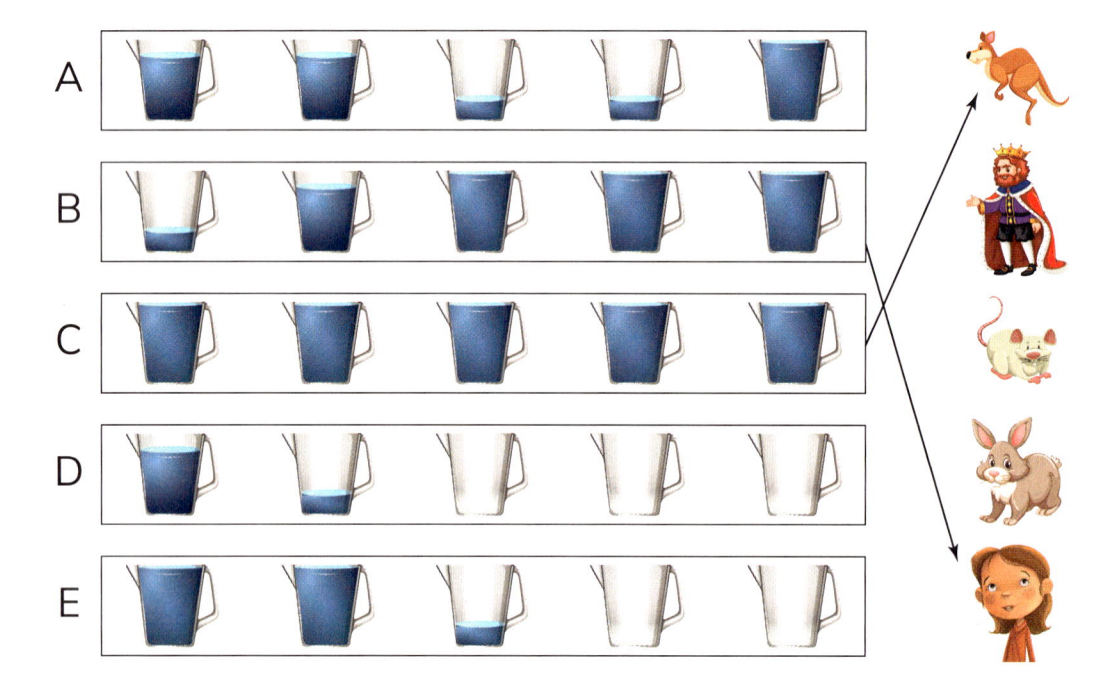

Match the jugs to the characters.

The kangaroo drinks the jugs that are full.

The mouse has 3 empty jugs.

The rabbit has 2 empty jugs.

The king drinks more than the mouse but less than the girl.

The girl drinks less than the kangaroo.

Does the king drink A B C D E?

Draw a ring around the correct answer.

12.2 How do we measure?

> **Look what I can do!**
>
> - I can explore and compare mass.
> - I can explore and compare capacity.

› 12.2 How do we measure?

> **We are going to …**
>
> - explore instruments with numbered scales
> - choose the correct instrument to measure different things.

You use mass and capacity when cooking, and temperature when baking.

You use height and length when you buy new clothes or shoes.

When you keep yourself warm or cool, you are using what you know about temperature.

You need to know about weight when lifting heavy or light objects.

This section explores how you measure each of these things.

temperature   thermometer

173

12 Measures (2)

Exercise 12.2

1. Which ruler would be most helpful for measuring the length of a pencil? Why?

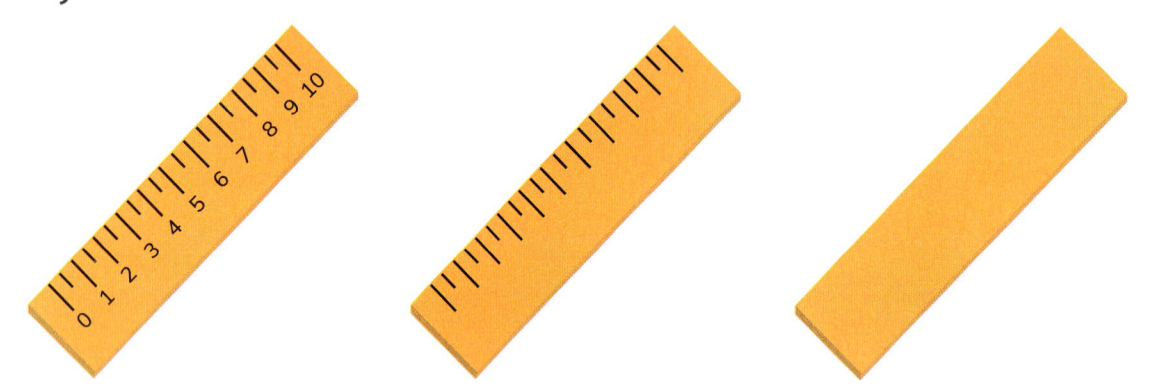

2. Look at each thermometer and draw a ring round the word that matches the temperature.

   Is it hot, cold or warm? Talk to your partner.

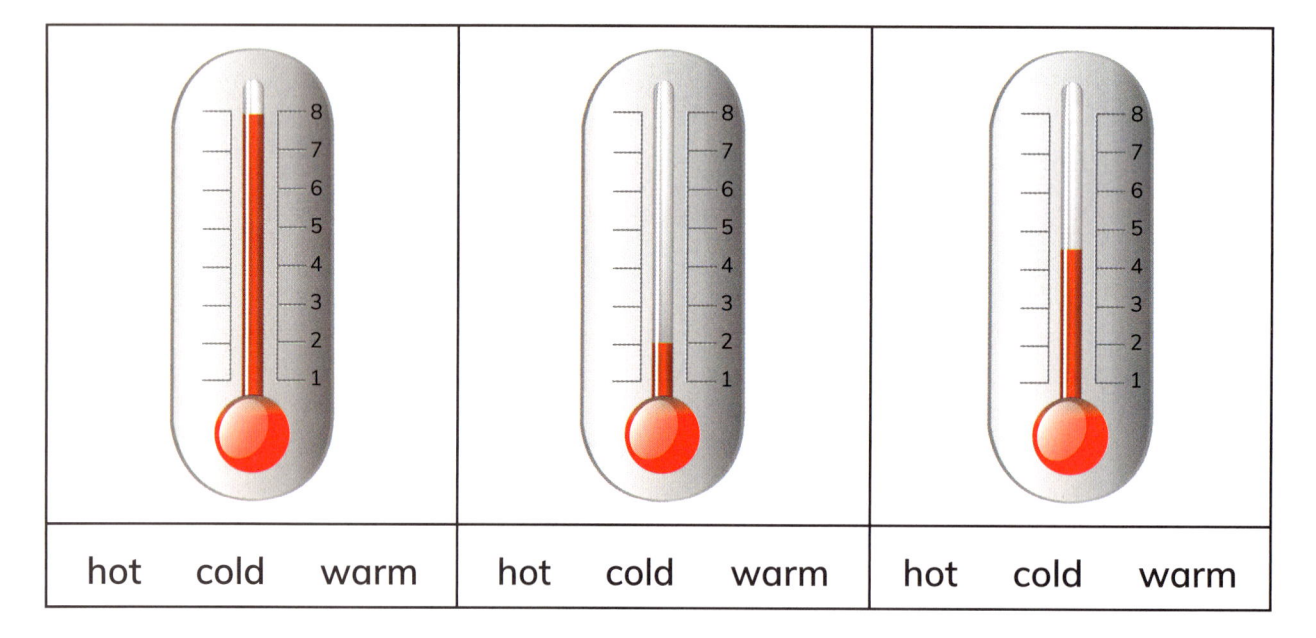

   | hot   cold   warm | hot   cold   warm | hot   cold   warm |

12.2 How do we measure?

3 Colour in the instrument you would use to measure the capacity of a bottle.

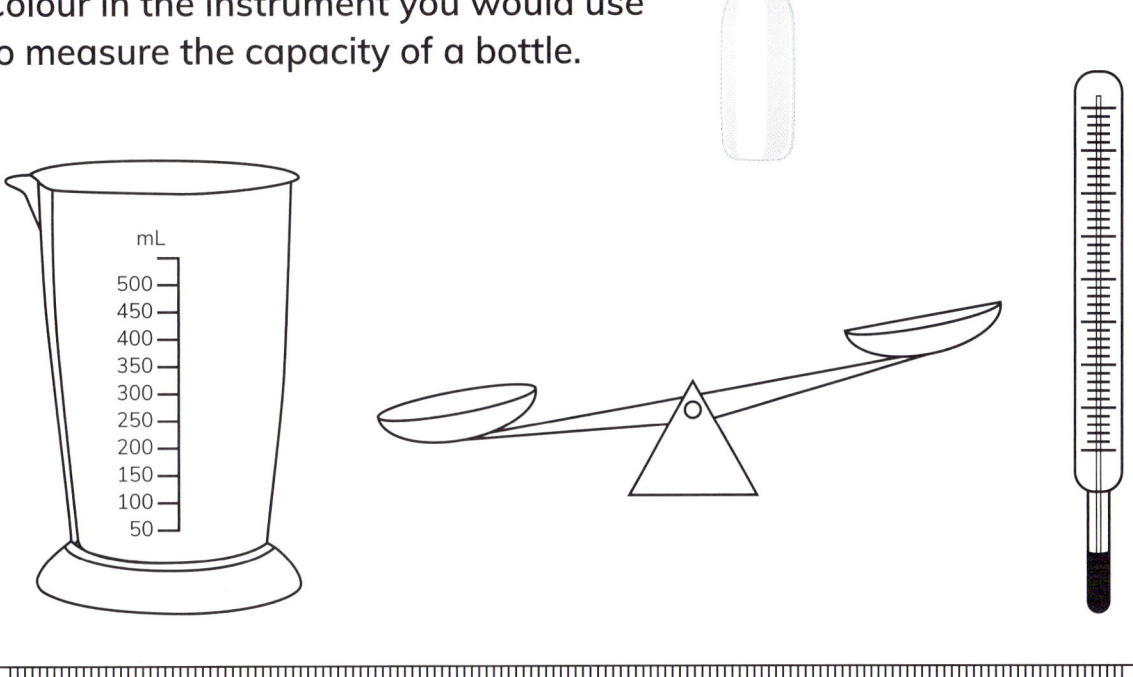

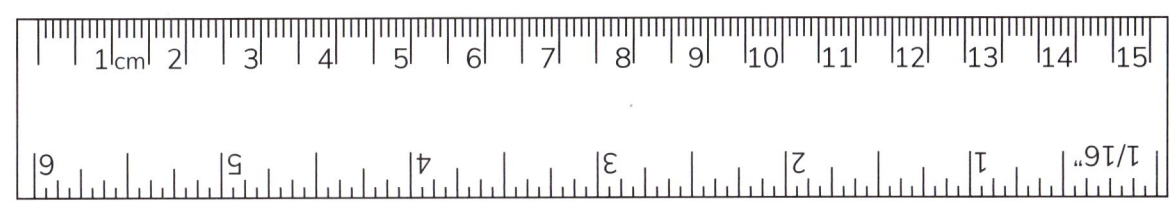

4 Draw a ring around the jug containing the most juice.

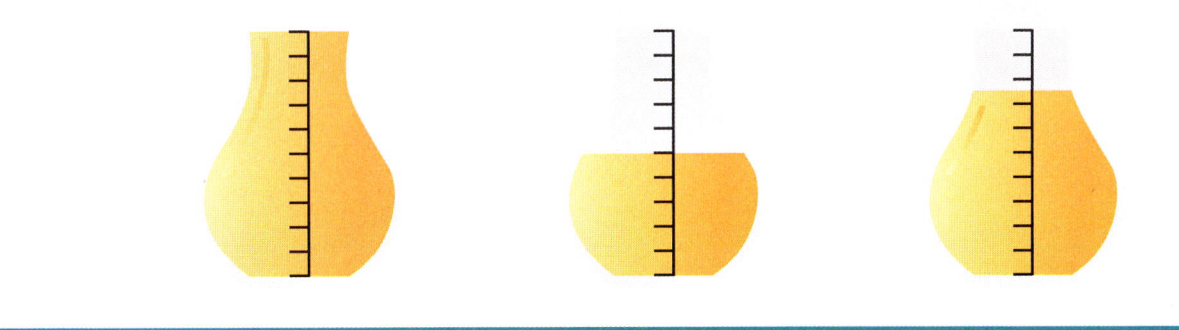

Look what I can do!

- I can choose the correct instrument to measure length, mass, capacity and temperature.

12 Measures (2)

Check your progress

1. Draw the objects on the balance scales.

   Which is heavier? Which is lighter?

   The elephant is _____ than the snake.

   The flower is _____ than the tree.

   The car is _____ than the plane.

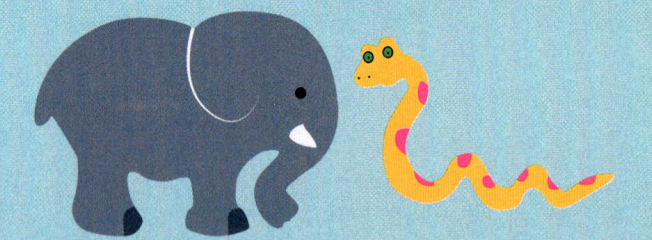

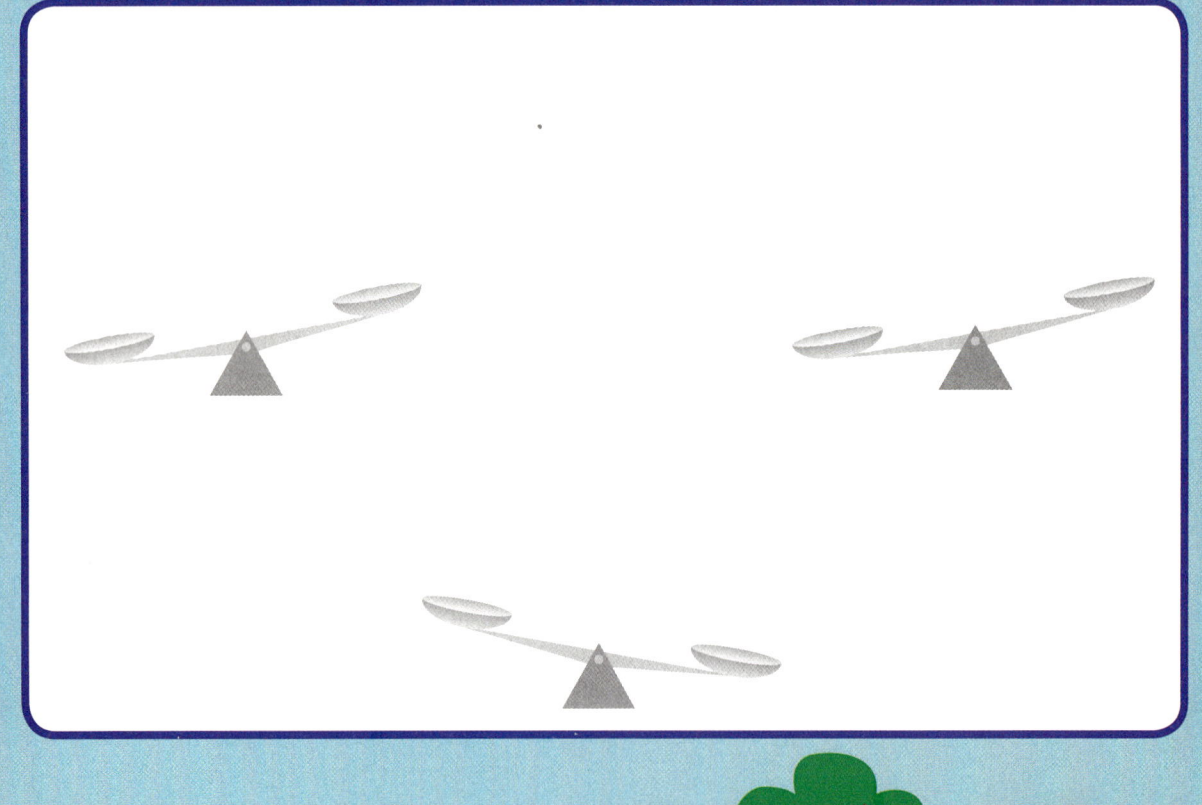

12.2 How do we measure?

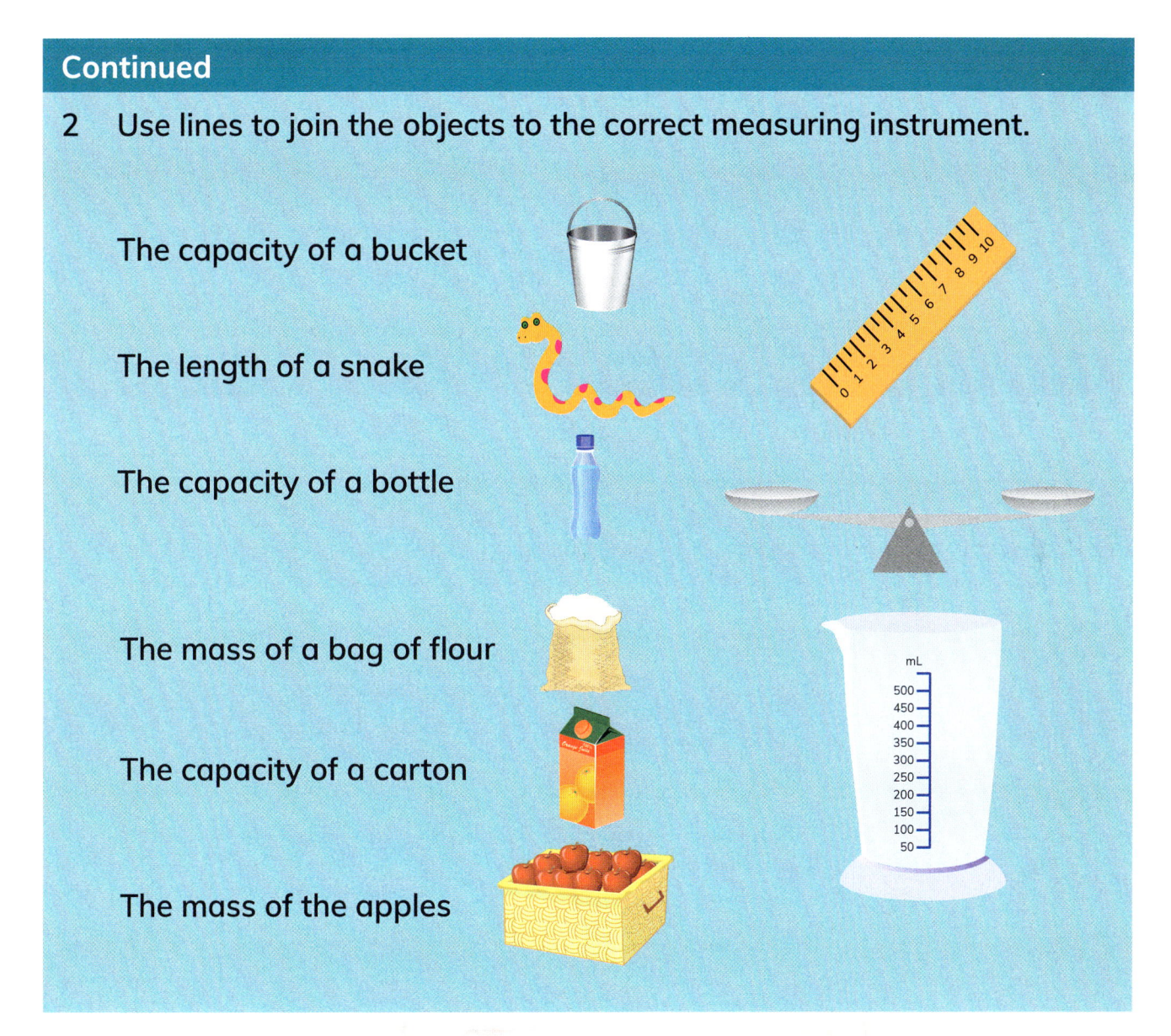

Continued

2   Use lines to join the objects to the correct measuring instrument.

The capacity of a bucket

The length of a snake

The capacity of a bottle

The mass of a bag of flour

The capacity of a carton

The mass of the apples

13 > Working with numbers to 20

Getting started

1 Complete each part-whole diagram.

   Write a matching number sentence for each diagram.

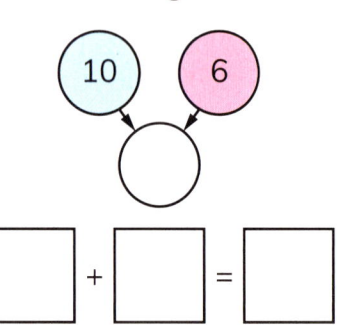

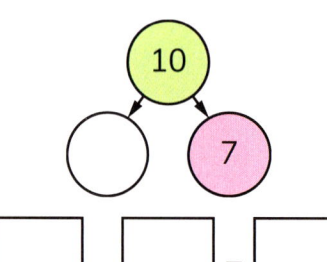

   (10) (6)   (10)
      ↘ ↙   ↙ ↘
       ○   ○   (7)

   ☐ + ☐ = ☐   ☐ − ☐ = ☐

2 Add and subtract to complete the wall.

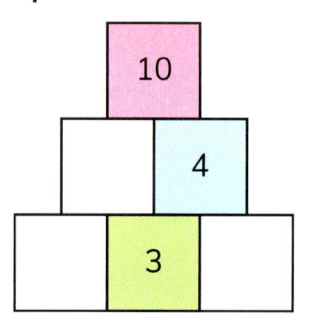

   ```
         [10]
      [  ][ 4]
      [  ][ 3][  ]
   ```

3 Use the number line to help you compare these numbers.

   Write **fewer** or **greater** to complete the sentences.

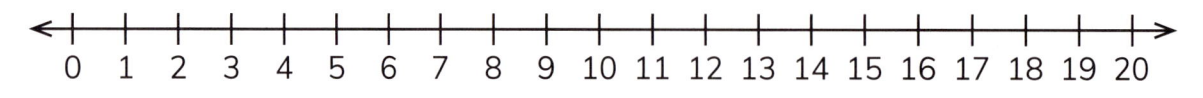

   ←|—|—|—|—|—|—|—|—|—|—|—|—|—|—|—|—|—|—|—|—|→
     0 1 2 3 4 5 6 7 8 9 10 11 12 13 14 15 16 17 18 19 20

   9 is _____ than 12.   12 is _____ than 9.

   16 is _____ than 11.   11 is _____ than 16.

13 Working with numbers to 20

There are different methods to add and subtract.

You will use a number line to help you count on or back from any number.

You will begin to explore money.

You need to recognise what you have so that you can spend it on the things you want to buy.

I must remember to buy more eggs.

13 Working with numbers to 20

> 13.1 Addition by counting on

We are going to …

- add by counting on, using a number line to help
- separate numbers into smaller numbers to help with addition
- use complements to 10 to help with addition.

We often add some more to what we have.
If you have 9 marbles and win 4 in a game,
it is better to count on 4 from 9 to see that you
have 13 rather than have to count them all.

Using a number line to help, you will be able to count on
from a number instead of having to count everything.

calculation   complement   method   regroup   solve

Exercise 13.1

Worked example 1

11 + 6 = ☐

Answer: 11 + 6 = 17

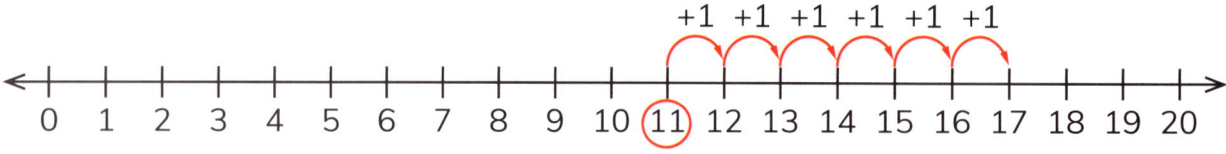

Draw a ring around 11.
Count on 6.

12, 13, 14, 15, 16, 17.
11 + 6 = 17

13.1 Addition by counting on

1 Count on in ones. Draw your jumps.

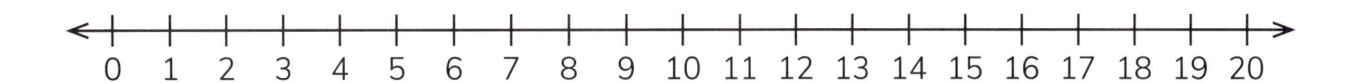

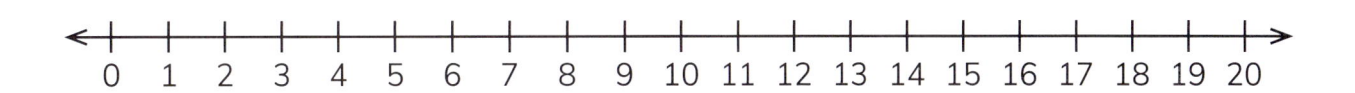

13 + 4 = ☐

（number line 0–20）

9 + 7 = ☐

（number line 0–20）

2 Here is Erin's number line.

What calculation is she solving?

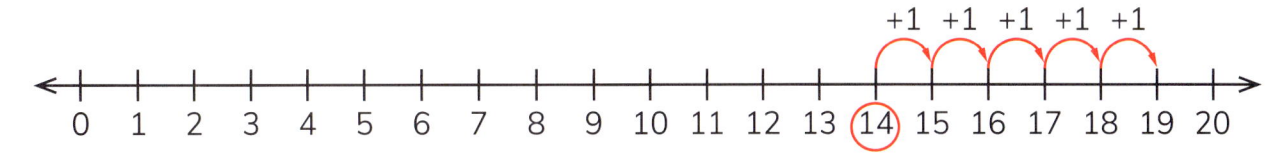

（number line 0–20 with 14 circled and five +1 jumps from 14 to 19）

181

13 Working with numbers to 20

Worked example 2

12 + 7 = ☐

Answer: 12 + 7 = 19

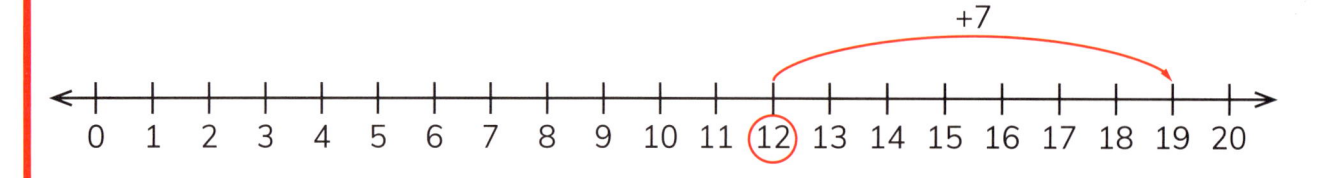

+7
0 1 2 3 4 5 6 7 8 9 10 11 (12) 13 14 15 16 17 18 19 20

Draw a ring around 12.
Count on 1, 2, 3, 4, 5, 6, 7.
Draw 1 jump.
Drawing one jump is quicker than drawing 7 jumps!
12 + 7 = 19.

3   Count on in ones.

Draw and label **one** jump to find each total.

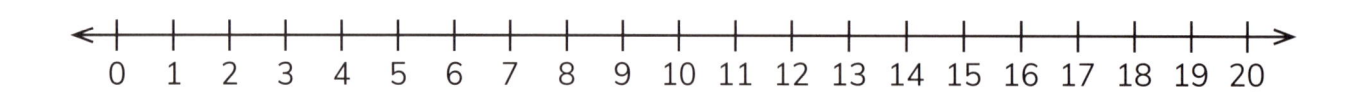

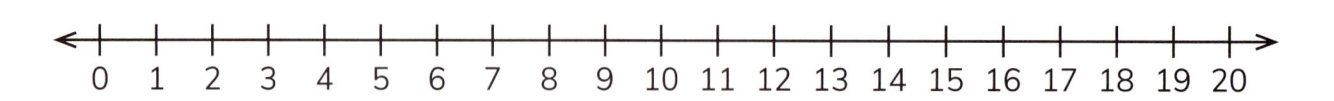

6 + 9 = ☐

0 1 2 3 4 5 6 7 8 9 10 11 12 13 14 15 16 17 18 19 20

11 + 8 = ☐

0 1 2 3 4 5 6 7 8 9 10 11 12 13 14 15 16 17 18 19 20

13.1 Addition by counting on

4   Here is Tomas' number line.

　　What calculation is he solving?

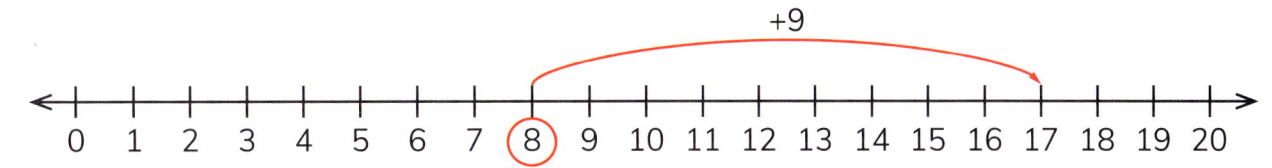

$$+9$$

0 1 2 3 4 5 6 7 ⑧ 9 10 11 12 13 14 15 16 17 18 19 20

> **Let's investigate**
>
> What happens when you add 0 to a number?
>
> How could you show adding to 0 on a number line? For example, 0 + 4.
>
> 0 1 2 3 4 5 6 7 8 9 10 11 12 13 14 15 16 17 18 19 20

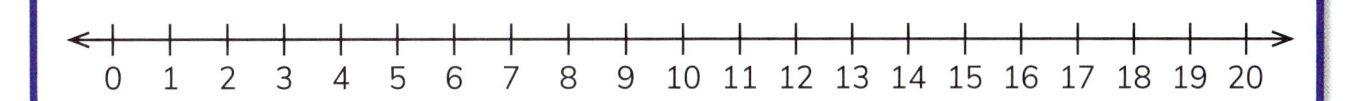

5   Regroup 9 in two different ways.

　　Regroup 15 in two different ways.

183

13 Working with numbers to 20

Worked example 3

7 + 6 = ☐

Answer: 7 + 6 = 13

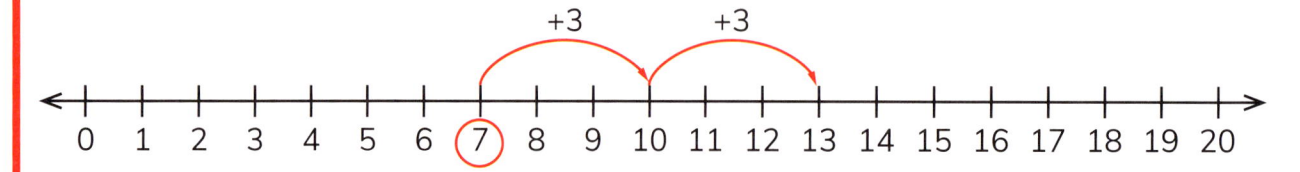

```
        +3    +3
0 1 2 3 4 5 6 (7) 8 9 10 11 12 13 14 15 16 17 18 19 20
```

I have added 3.
I need to add 3 more.
That's another jump
of 3. 7 + 6 = 13.

Draw a ring around 7.
7 and 3 are complements to 10.
Regroup 6 into 3 and 3.

13.1 Addition by counting on

6 Use **complements** to 10 to help you add.

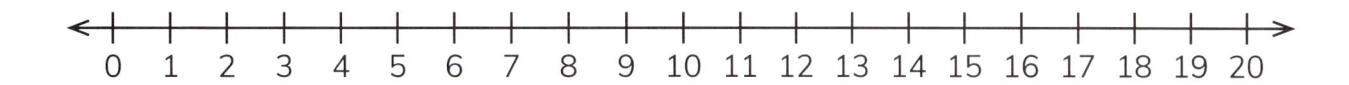

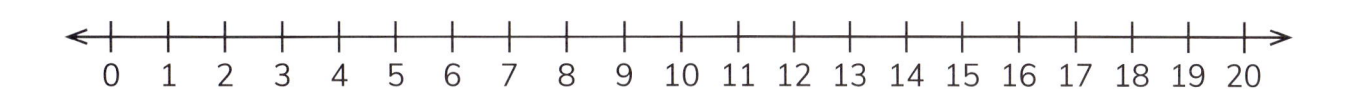

8 + 7 = ☐

← 0 1 2 3 4 5 6 7 8 9 10 11 12 13 14 15 16 17 18 19 20 →

9 + 5 = ☐

← 0 1 2 3 4 5 6 7 8 9 10 11 12 13 14 15 16 17 18 19 20 →

What makes the number line useful when adding by counting on?

Share your ideas with a partner.

Let's investigate

Work in a small group to make a poster to show the three methods you have used to add using a number line.

How will you make each **method** easy to understand?

7 Aliya drew a jump of 3 and a jump of 2. She started from number 7.

What was her calculation?

13 Working with numbers to 20

8 Choose a number from each circle to add together on a number line.

Do this twice. Choose which method to use each time.

Write your number sentence.

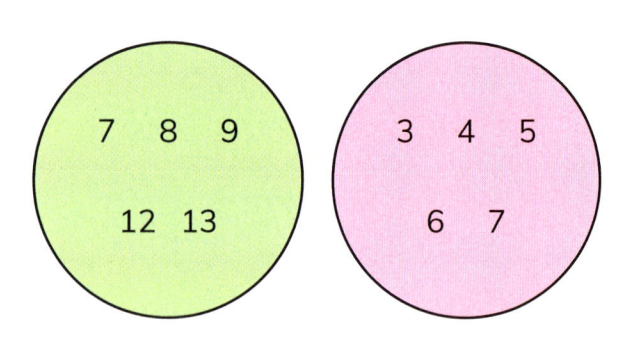

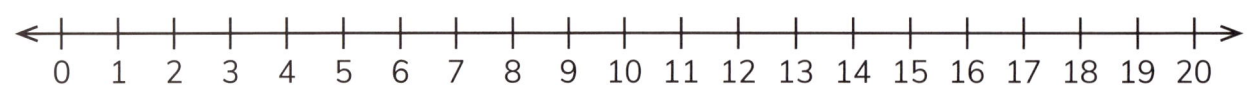

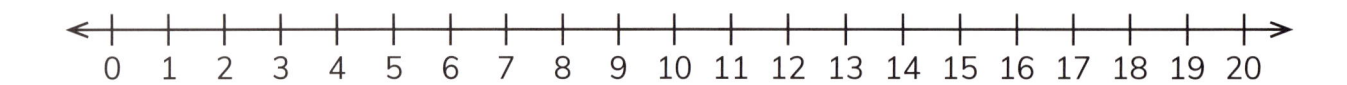

Green circle: 7 8 9 12 13

Pink circle: 3 4 5 6 7

0 1 2 3 4 5 6 7 8 9 10 11 12 13 14 15 16 17 18 19 20

☐ + ☐ = ☐

0 1 2 3 4 5 6 7 8 9 10 11 12 13 14 15 16 17 18 19 20

☐ + ☐ = ☐

Worked example 4

6 + 9 = 15   7 + 8 = 15

6 + 9 = ☐ + ☐

Answer:

6 + 9 = 7 + 8

> Number facts on each side of the equals sign have the same value.

186

13.1 Addition by counting on

9   Work in a group of 4.

Use the calculations from question 8 to help you find equivalent facts.

☐ + ☐ = ☐ + ☐   ☐ + ☐ = ☐ + ☐

☐ + ☐ = ☐ + ☐   ☐ + ☐ = ☐ + ☐

Let's investigate

Sumi says you can always use any of the three methods to add on a number line. It does not matter what the numbers are.

Do you agree? Explain your thinking to your partner.

Look what I can do!

- I can add by counting on, using a number line to help.
- I can split numbers into smaller numbers to help with addition.
- I can use complements to 10 to help with addition.

13 Working with numbers to 20

> 13.2 Subtraction by counting back

We are going to ...
- subtract by counting back, using a number line to help
- split numbers into smaller numbers to help with subtraction
- use complements to 10 to help with subtraction.

Sometimes we need to find how many objects are left.

If there are 14 biscuits and 9 are eaten, are there enough left for 6 people to have 1 each?

You can work out if you need to buy more biscuits when you are shopping.

compose   decompose

13.2 Subtraction by counting back

Exercise 13.2

Worked example 5

11 − 6 = ☐

Answer: 11 − 6 = 5

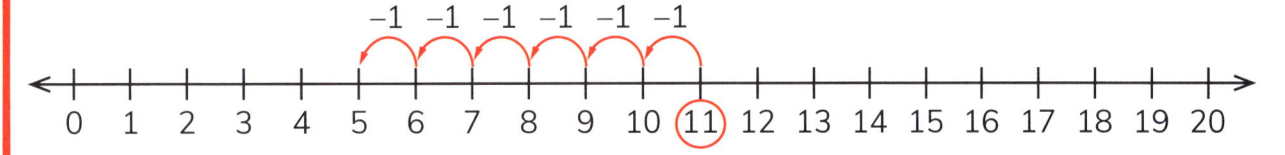

Count back 1, 2, 3, 4, 5, 6. I drew a jump each time I counted. 11 − 6 = 5

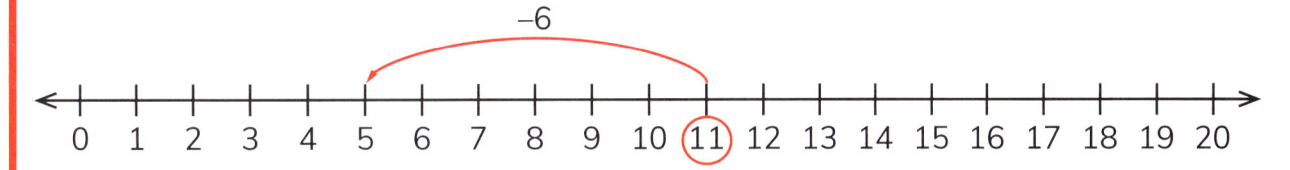

Count back 1, 2, 3, 4, 5, 6. I drew one jump of 6. 11 − 6 = 5

Both methods work.

13 Working with numbers to 20

1 Count back. Draw your jumps.

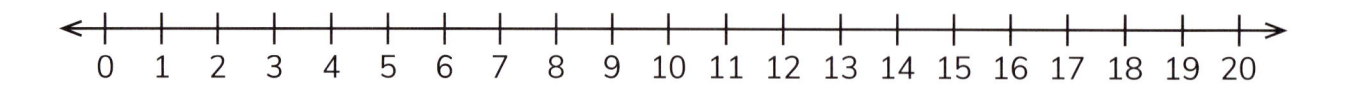

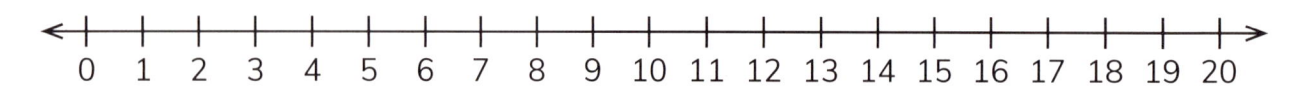

13 − 4 = ☐

←—+—→
 0 1 2 3 4 5 6 7 8 9 10 11 12 13 14 15 16 17 18 19 20

9 − 6 = ☐

←—+—→
 0 1 2 3 4 5 6 7 8 9 10 11 12 13 14 15 16 17 18 19 20

2 This is Sammy's number line. What calculation is he solving?

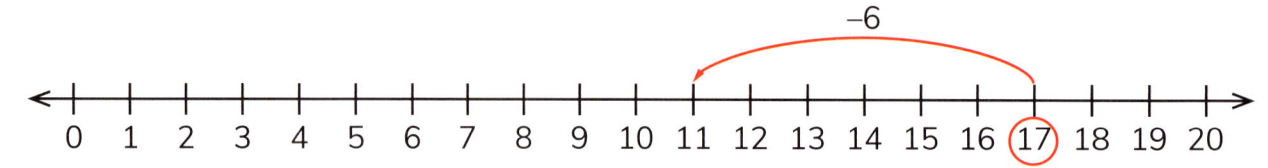

←—+—→
 0 1 2 3 4 5 6 7 8 9 10 11 12 13 14 15 16 (17) 18 19 20

(jump of −6 from 17 back to 11)

3 This is Erin's number line. What calculation is she solving?

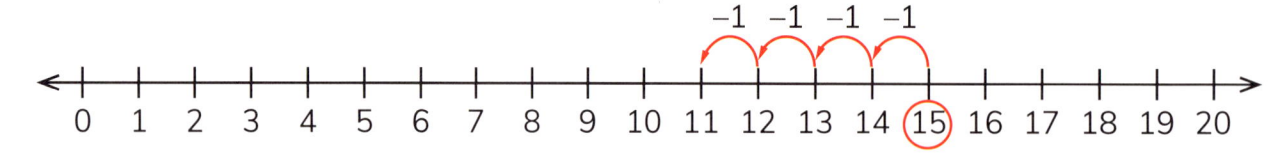

←—+—→
 0 1 2 3 4 5 6 7 8 9 10 11 12 13 14 (15) 16 17 18 19 20

(four jumps of −1 from 15 back to 11)

13.2 Subtraction by counting back

Worked example 6

18 − 13 = ☐

Answer: 18 − 13 = 5

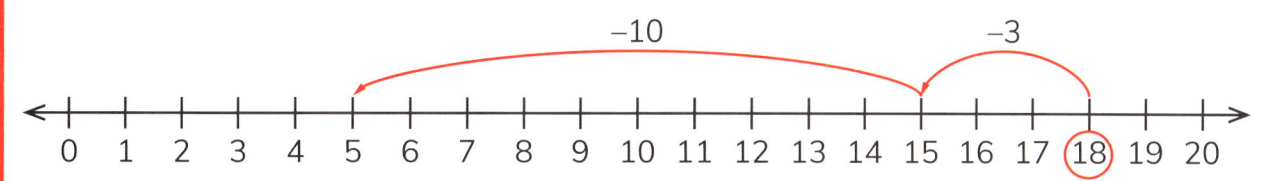

<--|--|--|--|--|--|--|--|--|--|--|--|--|--|--|--|--|--|--|--|-->
0 1 2 3 4 5 6 7 8 9 10 11 12 13 14 15 16 17 (18) 19 20

with jumps −10 (from 15 back to 5) and −3 (from 18 back to 15)

13 is 10 and 3. I counted back 3 first.

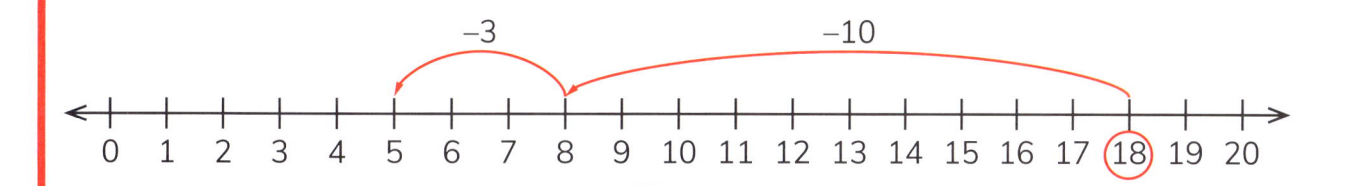

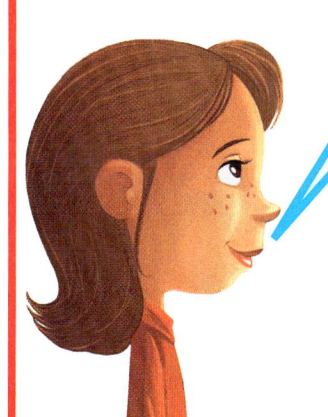

<--|--|--|--|--|--|--|--|--|--|--|--|--|--|--|--|--|--|--|--|-->
0 1 2 3 4 5 6 7 8 9 10 11 12 13 14 15 16 17 (18) 19 20

with jumps −3 (from 8 back to 5) and −10 (from 18 back to 8)

18 is 10 + 8, so it is easy to jump back 10 to 8. Then I subtracted 3. 18 − 13 = 5.

Both methods work.

13 Working with numbers to 20

4   Draw your jumps.

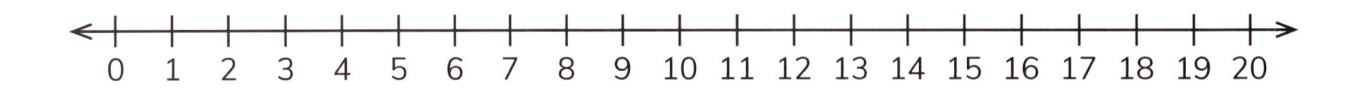

19 − 14 = ☐

```
←─┼──┼──┼──┼──┼──┼──┼──┼──┼──┼──┼──┼──┼──┼──┼──┼──┼──┼──┼──┼─→
  0  1  2  3  4  5  6  7  8  9 10 11 12 13 14 15 16 17 18 19 20
```

Worked example 7

14 − 8 = ☐

Answer: 14 − 8 = 6

> 8 is 4 and 4.
> First I counted back 4 to 10.
> Then I used complements to 10.
> 14 − 8 = 6.

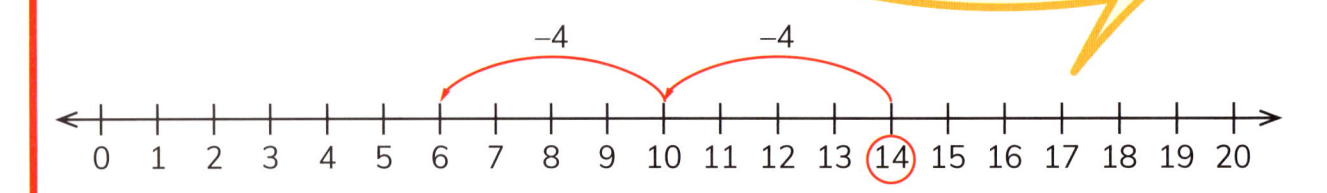

```
                              −4      −4
                            ⌢⌢⌢   ⌢⌢⌢
←─┼──┼──┼──┼──┼──┼──┼──┼──┼──┼──┼──┼──┼──┼──┼──┼──┼──┼──┼──┼─→
  0  1  2  3  4  5  6  7  8  9 10 11 12 13 (14) 15 16 17 18 19 20
```

5   Draw your jumps.

> Remember to check you subtracted the correct amount by adding (regrouping) your jumps together.

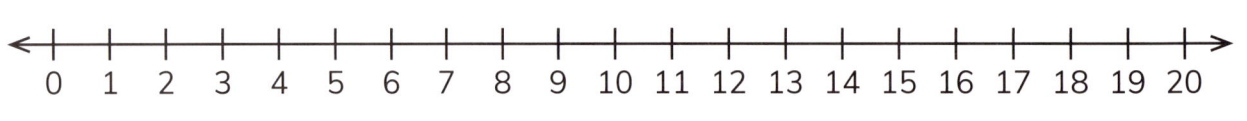

13 − 7 = ☐

```
←─┼──┼──┼──┼──┼──┼──┼──┼──┼──┼──┼──┼──┼──┼──┼──┼──┼──┼──┼──┼─→
  0  1  2  3  4  5  6  7  8  9 10 11 12 13 14 15 16 17 18 19 20
```

13.2 Subtraction by counting back

> **Let's investigate**
>
> What happens when you subtract 0 from a number?
>
> How could you show subtracting 0 on a number line?

6. Choose a number from each circle.

   Subtract the smaller number from the larger number.

   Do this twice. Choose which method to use.

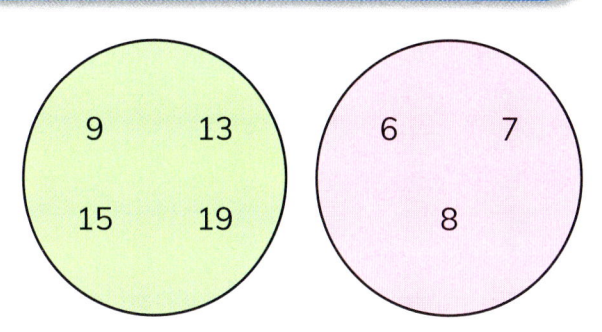

   Write your number sentence.

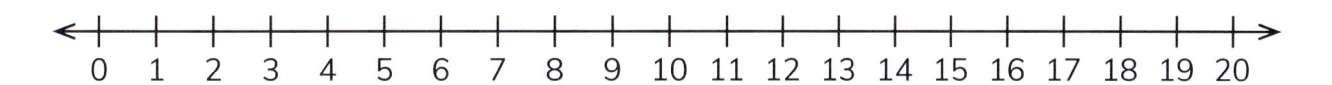

   Green circle: 9, 13, 15, 19

   Pink circle: 6, 7, 8

   ← 0 1 2 3 4 5 6 7 8 9 10 11 12 13 14 15 16 17 18 19 20 →

Share your work on question 6 with your partner.
Did you do the calculations in different ways?
Talk about both of your methods.
Is one method better or more efficient than the other?

13 Working with numbers to 20

7   Find the difference.

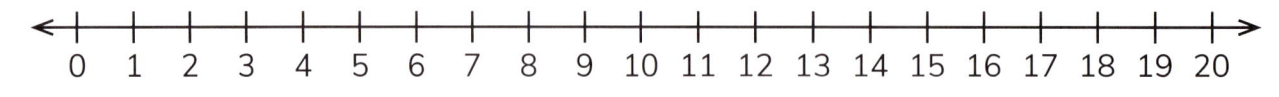

```
←─┼──┼──┼──┼──┼──┼──┼──┼──┼──┼──┼──┼──┼──┼──┼──┼──┼──┼──┼──┼──→
  0  1  2  3  4  5  6  7  8  9 10 11 12 13 14 15 16 17 18 19 20
```

18 − 14 = ☐   9 − 4 = ☐

The difference between 8 and 11 is _____.

The difference between 3 and 9 is _____.

Look what I can do!

- I can subtract by counting back, using a number line to help. ◯ ◯
- I can split numbers into smaller numbers to help with subtraction. ◯ ◯
- I can use complements to 10 to help with subtraction. ◯ ◯

> 13.3 Using the number line

We are going to ...

- use what we know about addition and subtraction to solve word problems
- use what we know about numbers to estimate solutions
- work out doubles up to double 10.

When you use addition and subtraction, it is usually to solve a problem you have. Problems are often in words. You can write a number sentence to help solve word problems.

double   word problem

13.3 Using the number line

Exercise 13.3

1 Solve these calculations.

←—+—→
 0 1 2 3 4 5 6 7 8 9 10 11 12 13 14 15 16 17 18 19 20

8 + 0 = ☐   0 + 3 = ☐   14 + 0 = ☐

8 − 0 = ☐   3 − 0 = ☐   14 − 0 = ☐

2 Your target is 15. Record your own way to get from 0 to 15.

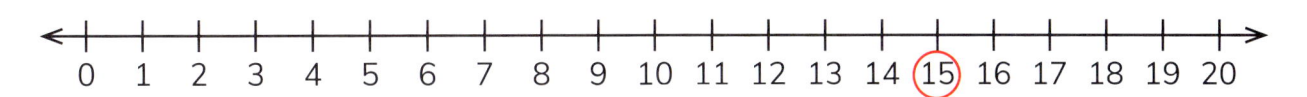

←—+—→
 0 1 2 3 4 5 6 7 8 9 10 11 12 13 14 (15) 16 17 18 19 20

Write your number sentences.

3 Start at 11. Your target is 0.

Record your own way to get from 11 to 0.

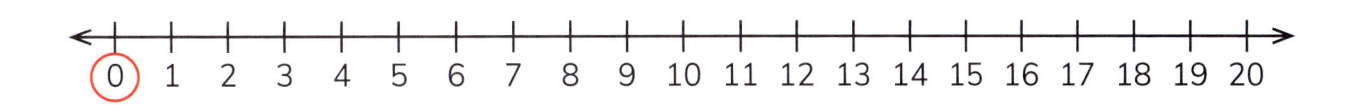

←—+—→
 (0) 1 2 3 4 5 6 7 8 9 10 11 12 13 14 15 16 17 18 19 20

13 Working with numbers to 20

4 Write the number sentence for each word problem.
   Estimate the answer. Then solve your number sentence.

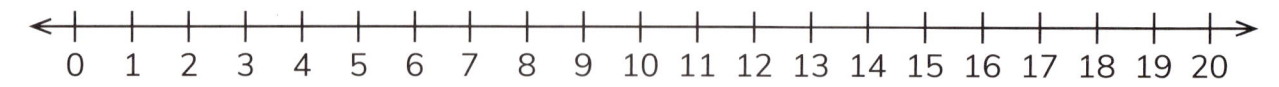

   0 1 2 3 4 5 6 7 8 9 10 11 12 13 14 15 16 17 18 19 20

   There were 3 biscuits in the tin.
   Mum emptied a packet of 10 biscuits into the tin.
   How many biscuits are in the tin now?

   There were 14 socks on the washing line.
   5 socks blew away.

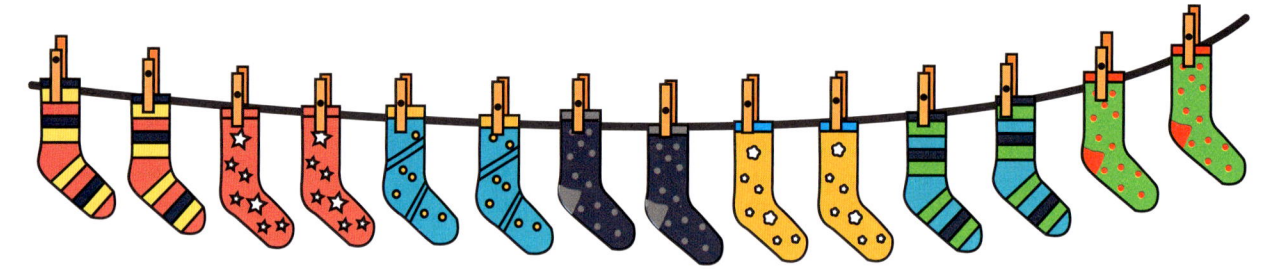

   How many socks are left on the washing line?

13.3 Using the number line

5   Complete the doubles table. What will you use to help you?

Number	0	1	2	3	4	5	6	7	8	9	10
Double						10					

Let's investigate

Aliya says all **doubles** are even numbers.

Is Aliya correct? Explain why.

Do you think using a number line is better than using counting objects?

Explain your thinking to your group or partner.

Look what I can do!

- I can use what I know about addition and subtraction to solve word problems.
- I can use what I know about numbers to estimate solutions.
- I can recall or quickly work out doubles up to double 10.

13 Working with numbers to 20

> 13.4 Money

We are going to …
- look at coins and banknotes
- sort coins in different ways
- use coins in a class shop.

We use money to buy things. You need to recognise which coins or banknotes you have so that you can spend them on the things you want to buy.

banknote   coin   money   price   value

Exercise 13.4

1   Draw a ring around the words or numbers you can see on your coins or banknotes.

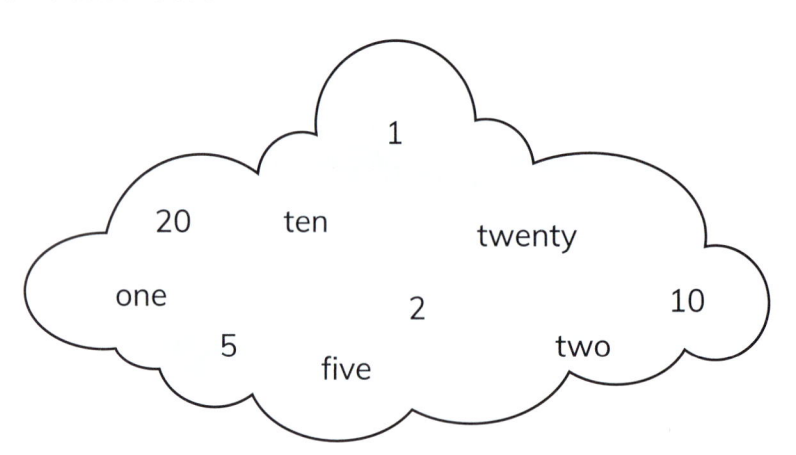

   1
   20   ten   twenty
   one   2   10
      5   five   two

13.4 Money

2 Here are some made-up coins.
   Match each coin to its **value**.

   One   Two   Five   Ten   Twenty

   2   1   20   5   10

Worked example 7

Sort these coins.

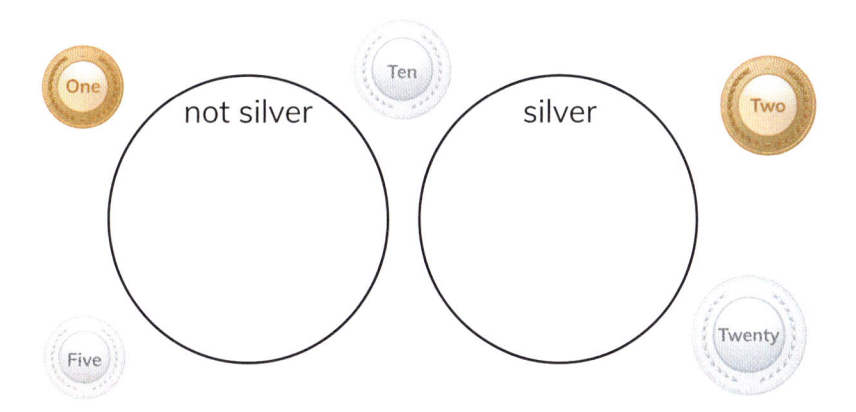

not silver   silver

Answer:

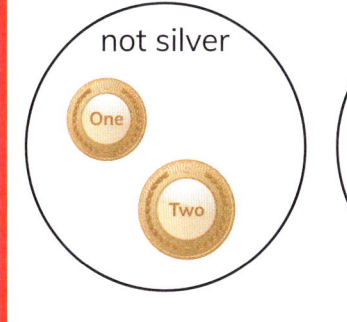

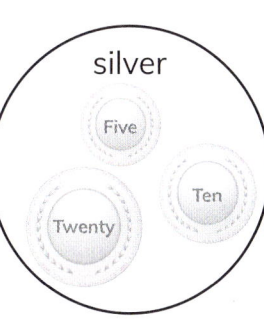

not silver: One, Two

silver: Five, Ten, Twenty

Silver coins in this circle. Not silver coins in the other circle.

199

13 Working with numbers to 20

3 You will need some coins.

Sort the coins. Use 2 or 3 circles.

Draw or rub the coins you put in each circle.

Label each circle.

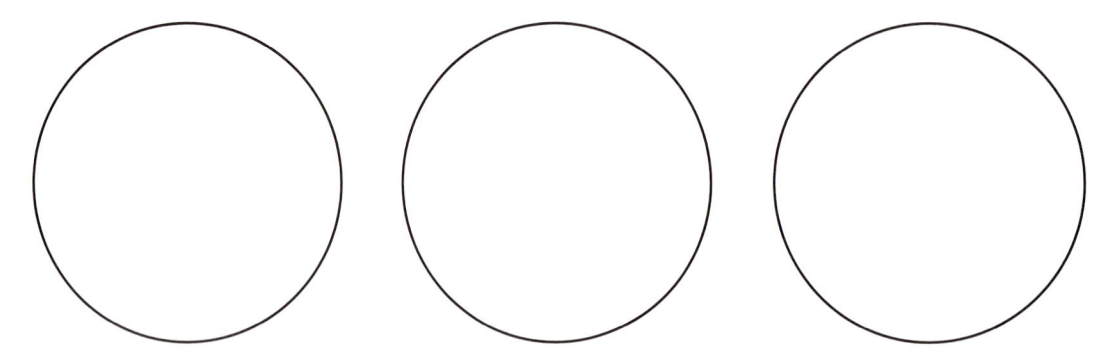

4 Write your own price for the ball.

Which coins and banknotes could you use to pay for it?

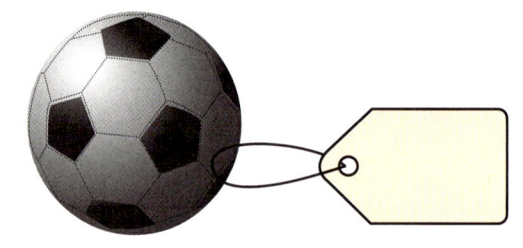

Draw each coin and banknote.
Or you could do a rubbing of each coin.

13.4 Money

Let's investigate

You will need some coins.

Show your partner the side of the coin with no number or number word on it. Can your partner say the value of the coin?

Swap over.

Can you name each of the coins?

Look what I can do!

- I can recognise different coins and banknotes.
- I can sort coins in different ways.
- I can use coins to buy things in our class shop.

Check your progress

1   Add 6 and 9.

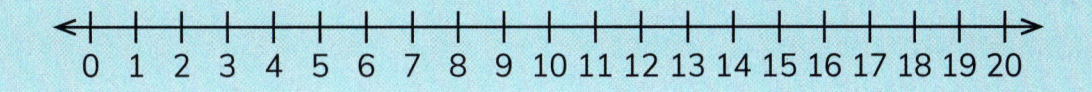

0 1 2 3 4 5 6 7 8 9 10 11 12 13 14 15 16 17 18 19 20

13 Working with numbers to 20

Continued

2   Subtract 7 from 12.

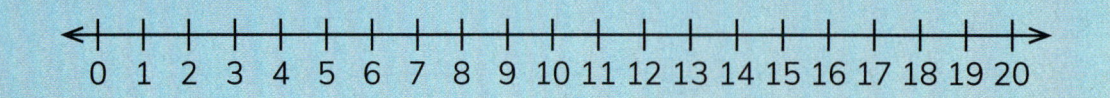

<-+->
  0 1 2 3 4 5 6 7 8 9 10 11 12 13 14 15 16 17 18 19 20

3   Decompose the number you are subtracting.

Draw your jumps.

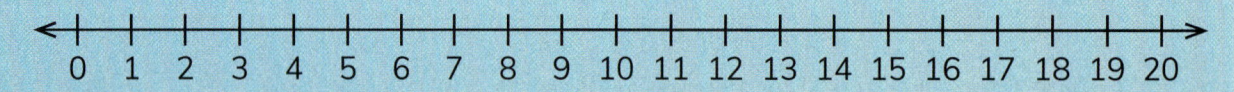

17 − 13 = ☐

<-+->
  0 1 2 3 4 5 6 7 8 9 10 11 12 13 14 15 16 17 18 19 20

4   Write the number sentence for this word problem.

Estimate the answer then solve your number sentence.

There were 16 cookies on a plate.

9 were eaten.

How many cookies were left on the plate?

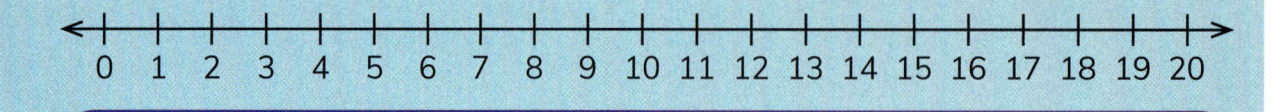

<-+->
  0 1 2 3 4 5 6 7 8 9 10 11 12 13 14 15 16 17 18 19 20

14 Statistics (2)

Getting started

1. What do you think?

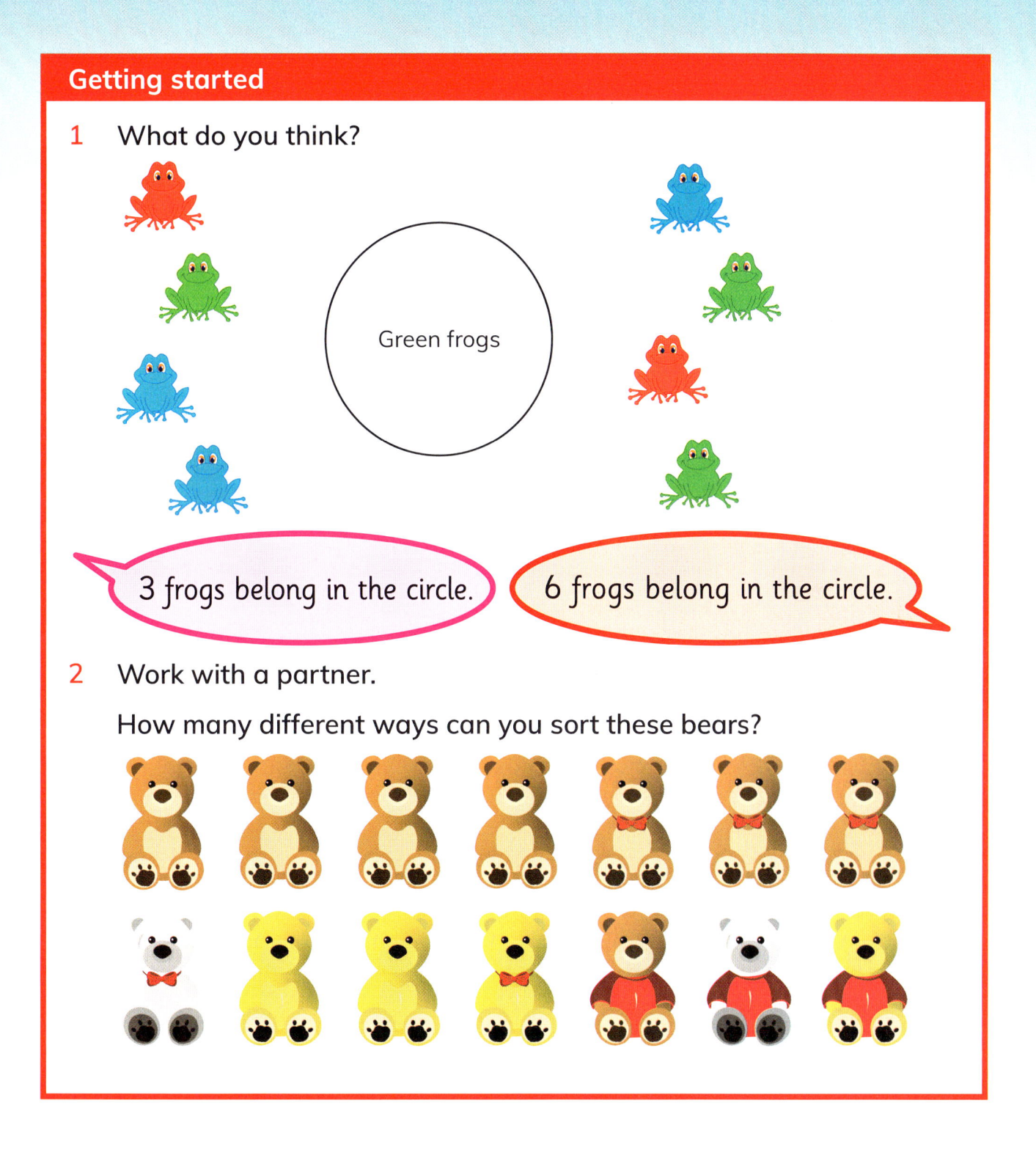

   Green frogs

   3 frogs belong in the circle.

   6 frogs belong in the circle.

2. Work with a partner.

   How many different ways can you sort these bears?

14 Statistics (2)

How do we know how many of each sweet is sold?

What would be the best way to record the sales?

How do we know the favourite thing to buy?

How could we find out?

This unit will show you different ways to sort and show data so that you can choose the best way when you have collected information.

You will revisit Venn diagrams and will learn about pictograms, Carroll diagrams, lists, tables and block graphs.

> 14.1 Venn diagrams, Carroll diagrams and pictograms

We are going to ...

- develop understanding of Venn diagrams
- explore Carroll diagrams and pictograms.

A **pictogram** is a chart that uses pictures to show **data**.

Pictograms use columns or rows of pictures to show the numbers involved.

A pictogram must have a title to show what each picture means.

Sunshine hours   ☀ = 1 hour of sunshine

Friday	☀ ☀ ☀ ☀
Saturday	☀ ☀ ☀ ☀ ☀
Sunday	☀ ☀ ☀ ☀ ☀ ☀ ☀

Carroll diagram   label   pictogram   title

A **Carroll diagram** is used to organise data using a set of rules.

For example, you can sort a set of shapes into shapes with curved sides and shapes with straight sides.

| Has legs and arms | Does not have legs and arms |

14 Statistics (2)

Exercise 14.1

Worked example 1

Where would you put the fruit and vegetables in this Venn diagram?
Write the letters in the correct place on the diagram.

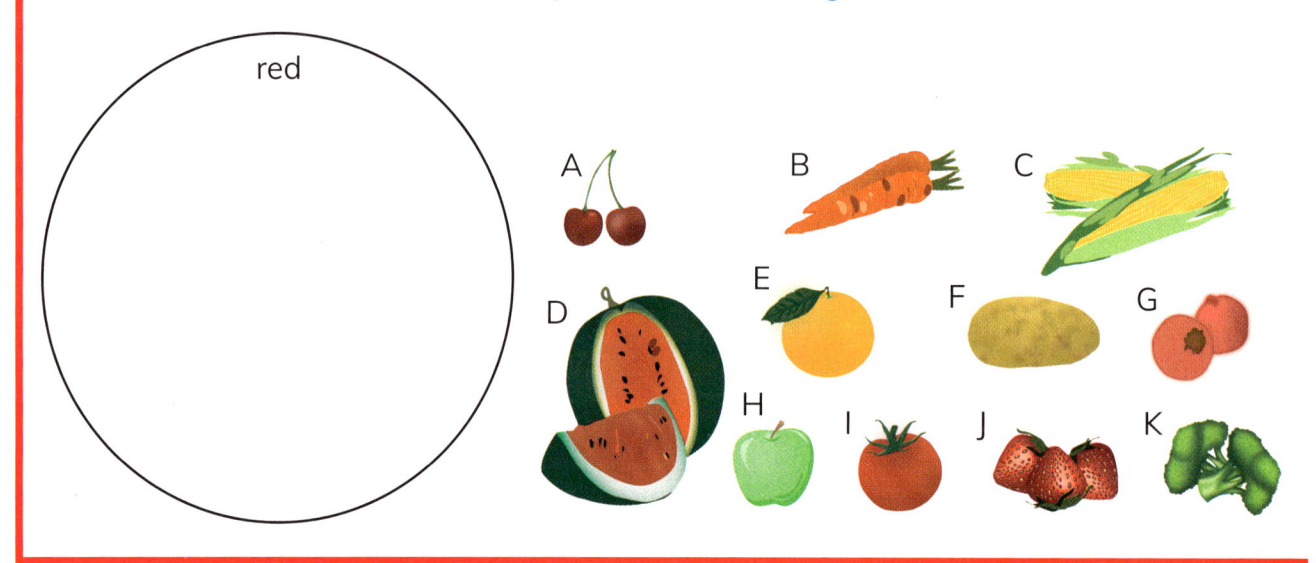

(red circle)

A cherries, B carrot, C corn, D watermelon, E orange, F potato, G peach, H apple, I tomato, J strawberries, K broccoli

Answer:

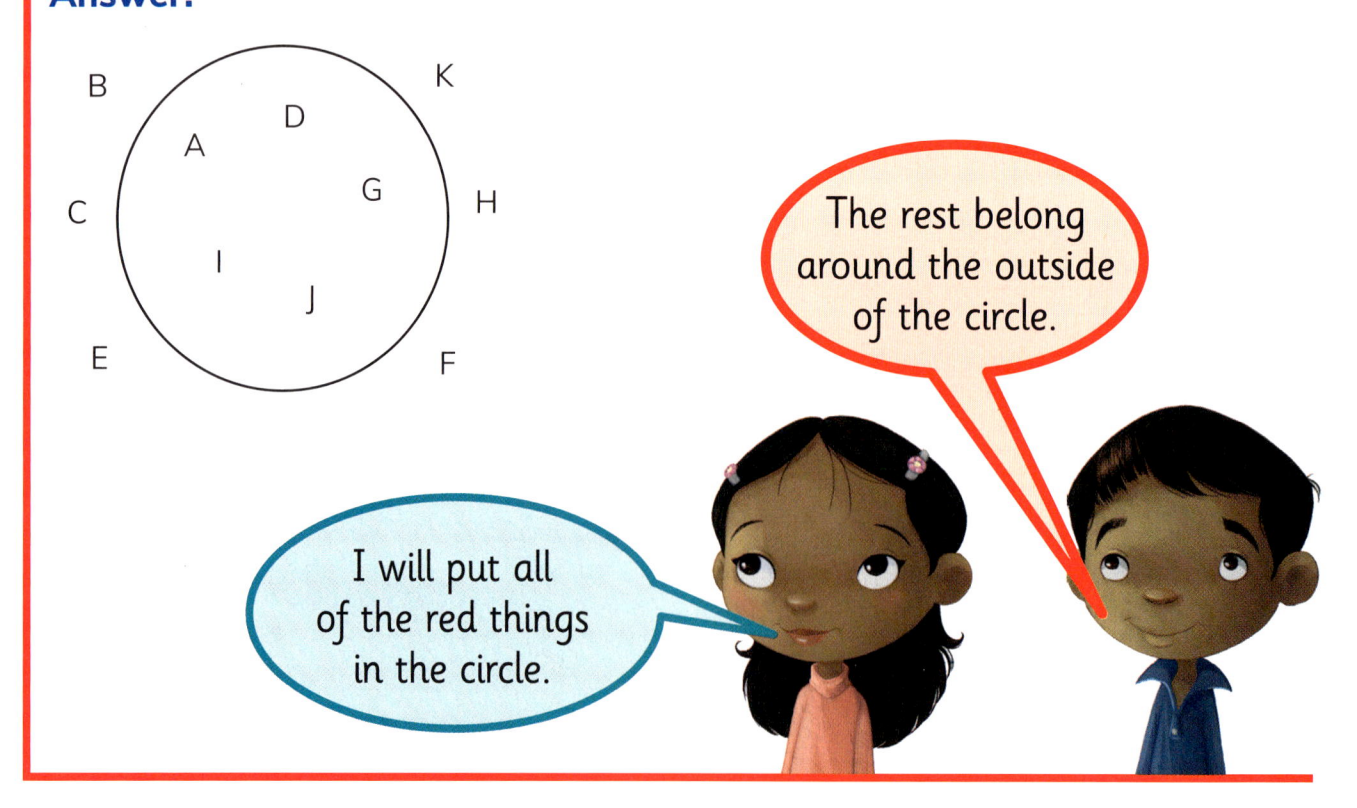

Inside circle (red): A, D, G, H, I, J
Outside circle: B, C, E, F, K

"I will put all of the red things in the circle."

"The rest belong around the outside of the circle."

206

14.1 Venn diagrams, Carroll diagrams and pictograms

1 Talk to your partner.

Where would you put these animals in the Venn diagram?

Write the letters in the correct places in the diagram.

A B C D E F G H

lives in water

14 Statistics (2)

2 Draw lines to sort the pairs of shoes into the circles.

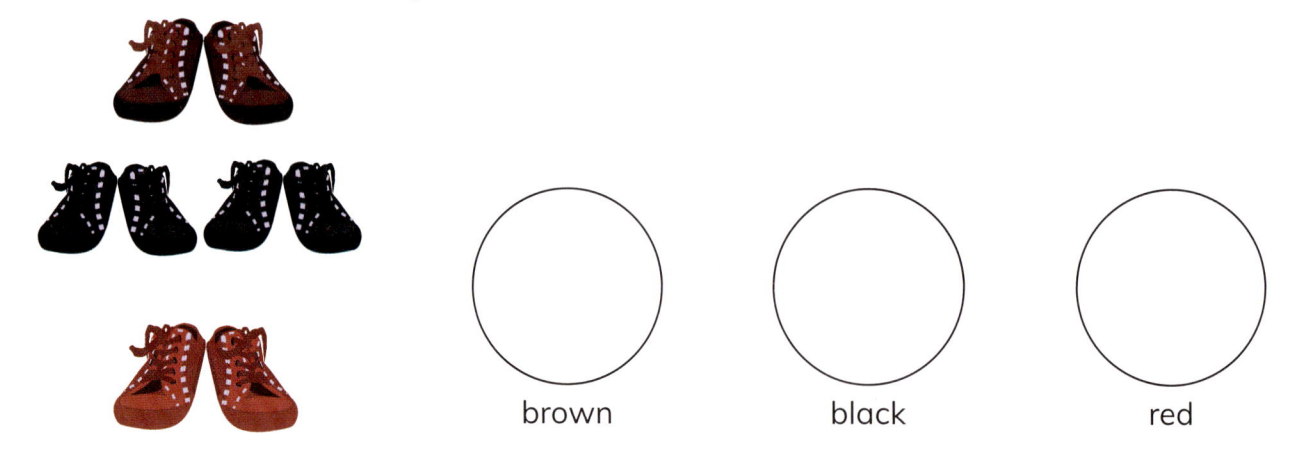

brown   black   red

Complete the pictogram by drawing the pairs of shoes in the table.

brown					
black					
red					

Which colour has the most shoes? _____

3 Draw lines to sort the toys into the correct boxes using the Carroll diagram.

wheels	not wheels

14.1 Venn diagrams, Carroll diagrams and pictograms

4   Work with a partner.

Sort the numbers into odd and not odd.

Write them on the Carroll diagram.

1	odd	not odd	11
2			12
3			13
4			14
5			15
6			16
7			17
8			18
9			19
10			20

5   This pictogram shows favourite sports.

Write 3 things you can see from the pictogram.
Use the words **more**, **less/fewer**, **most** and **least/fewest**.

Favourite sports

Favourite sport	Number of children who chose it
Swimming	🏊 🏊 🏊 🏊 🏊 🏊 🏊 🏊
Riding a horse	🐎 🐎 🐎 🐎 🐎
Archery	🏹 🏹 🏹 🏹 🏹 🏹
Running	🏃 🏃 🏃 🏃

1 picture = 1 child

_____

_____

_____

14 Statistics (2)

6 This Venn diagram shows how shapes have been sorted.

Write 3 things you can see from the Venn diagram.

Use the words **more**, **less/fewer**, **most** and **least/fewest**.

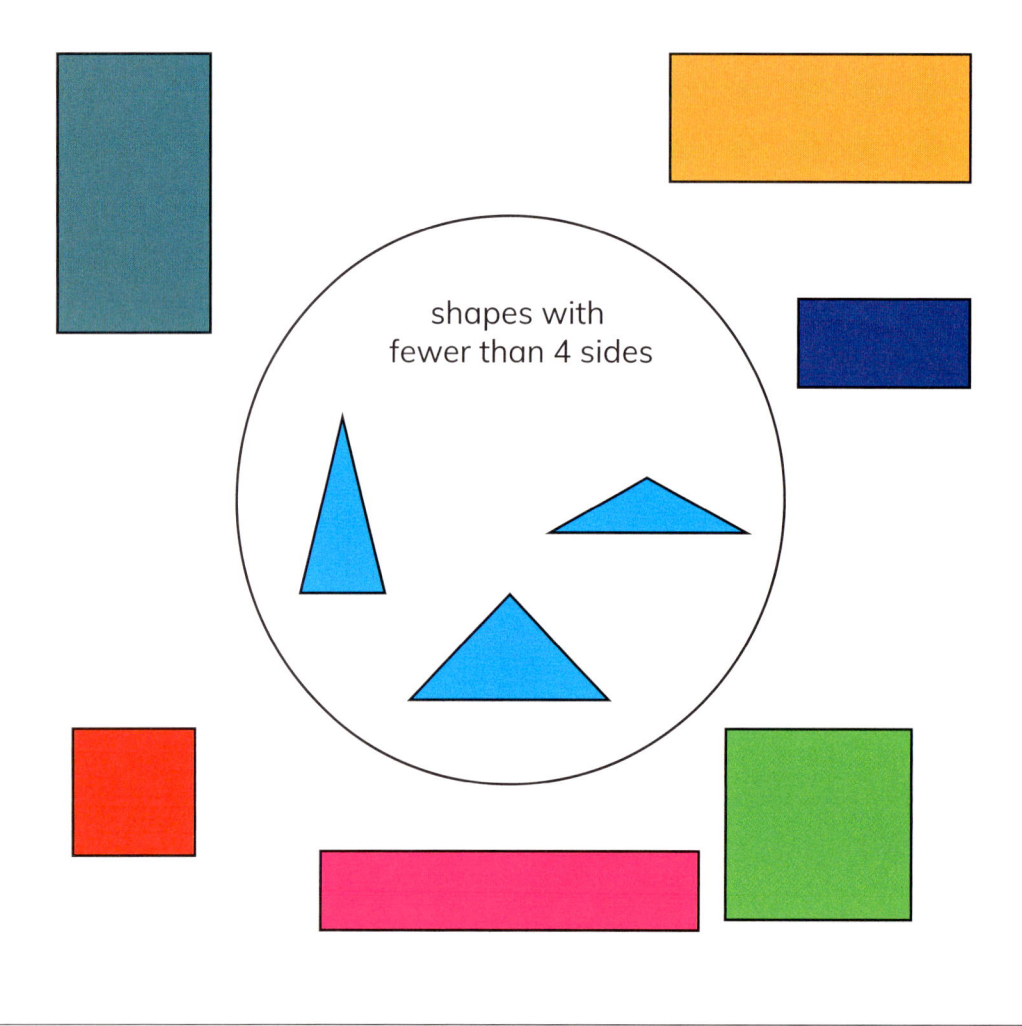

shapes with fewer than 4 sides

_____

_____

_____

14.1 Venn diagrams, Carroll diagrams and pictograms

Let's investigate

Here is an empty pictogram.

It needs a **title**.

Talk to your partner.

What could the title be?

red										
blue										
green										

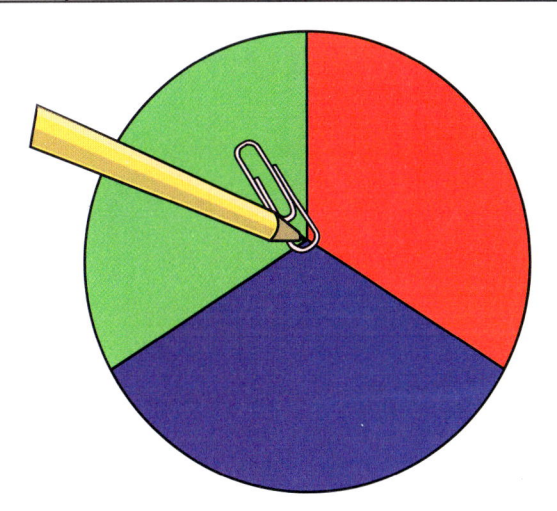

Spin a spinner 5 times each.

After each spin, draw a matching colour ball in a square of your pictogram.

Always start from the left. Do not leave a gap.

Which colour did you spin the most?

Which line is the longest?

14 Statistics (2)

What did the pictogram show you?

If you played the game again, would the pictogram look the same?

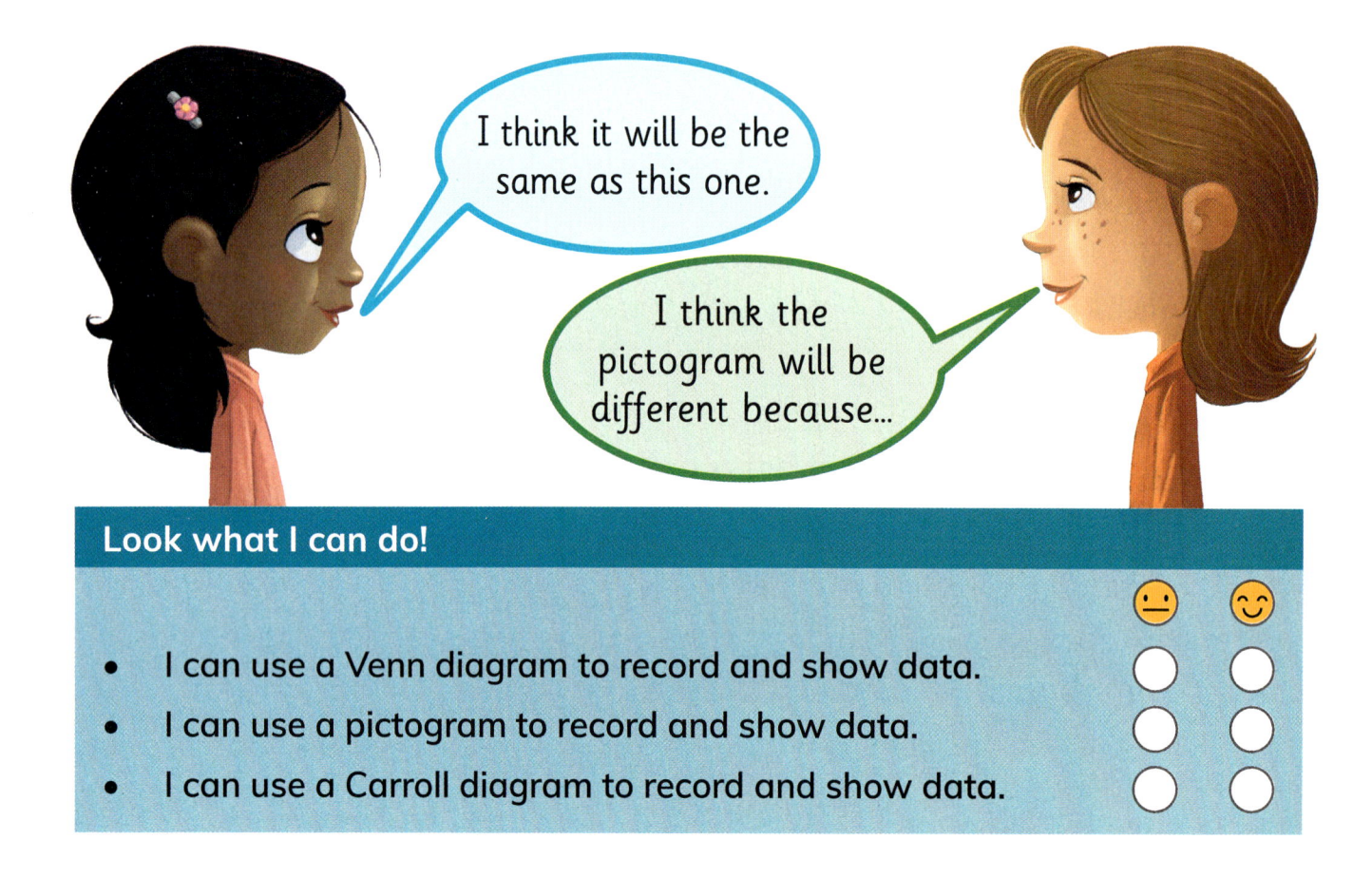

I think it will be the same as this one.

I think the pictogram will be different because…

Look what I can do!

- I can use a Venn diagram to record and show data.
- I can use a pictogram to record and show data.
- I can use a Carroll diagram to record and show data.

> 14.2 Lists, tables and block graphs

> **We are going to…**
> - **learn how to write lists**
> - **learn how to complete and use tables and block graphs**
> - **describe data using lists, tables and block graphs.**

We use **lists** and **tables** to show images rather than use lots of words.

We often use lists to remind ourselves about things we need to buy at the shops.

A list has a heading to tell you what the list is about.

A table is a way of showing data using rows and columns.

A **block graph** uses 1 block for each object or answer.

It is an easy way to find the most, the least, less, more or the same when using data.

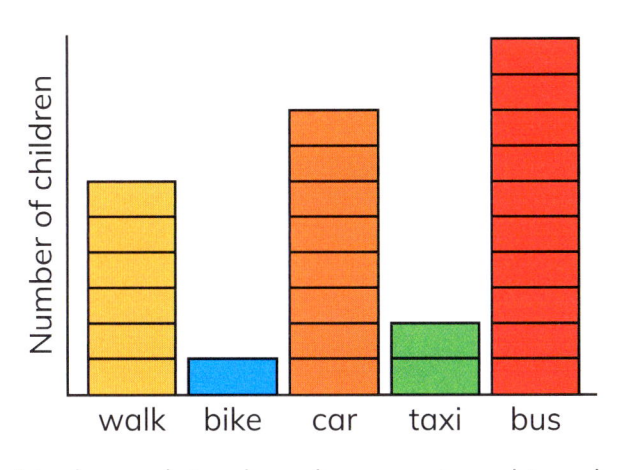

Shopping list

milk
bread
tea
apples
beans
butter
soup
eggs

> block graph   list   table

A block graph to show how we travel to school

14 Statistics (2)

Exercise 14.2

1. Here is a list of ice creams that Sandeep sells.

   Sandeep made a table to show how many ice creams he sold on Monday and Tuesday.

   Ice cream menu

   chocolate   vanilla   strawberry

Flavour	Monday	Tuesday
chocolate	8	4
vanilla	5	8
strawberry	12	6

   How many chocolate ice creams did Sandeep sell on Monday?

   How many strawberry ice creams did he sell on Tuesday?

   How many vanilla ice creams did he sell all together?

2. Make a list of your 3 favourite toys.

   _____

   _____

   _____

   Swap your list with a partner. Do you have any of the same things? How can you find out what toy is liked most by the whole class?

   _____

14.2 Lists, tables and block graphs

3   Here is a pictogram to show the flowers that Izabelle sold on Wednesday.

1 picture = 1 flower

Count the flowers in each row.

Fill in the table to show how many flowers Izabelle sold on Wednesday.

Flower	Wednesday
🌹	5
🌼	
iris	
🌻	
🌼	

Draw a ring around the flower that sold the most.

Draw a cross through the flower that sold the least.

215

14 Statistics (2)

4 This block diagram shows people's favourite animals in the zoo. Use it to fill in the table.

Favourite animals in the zoo	
Zebra	4
Tiger	5
Monkey	6
Elephant	3

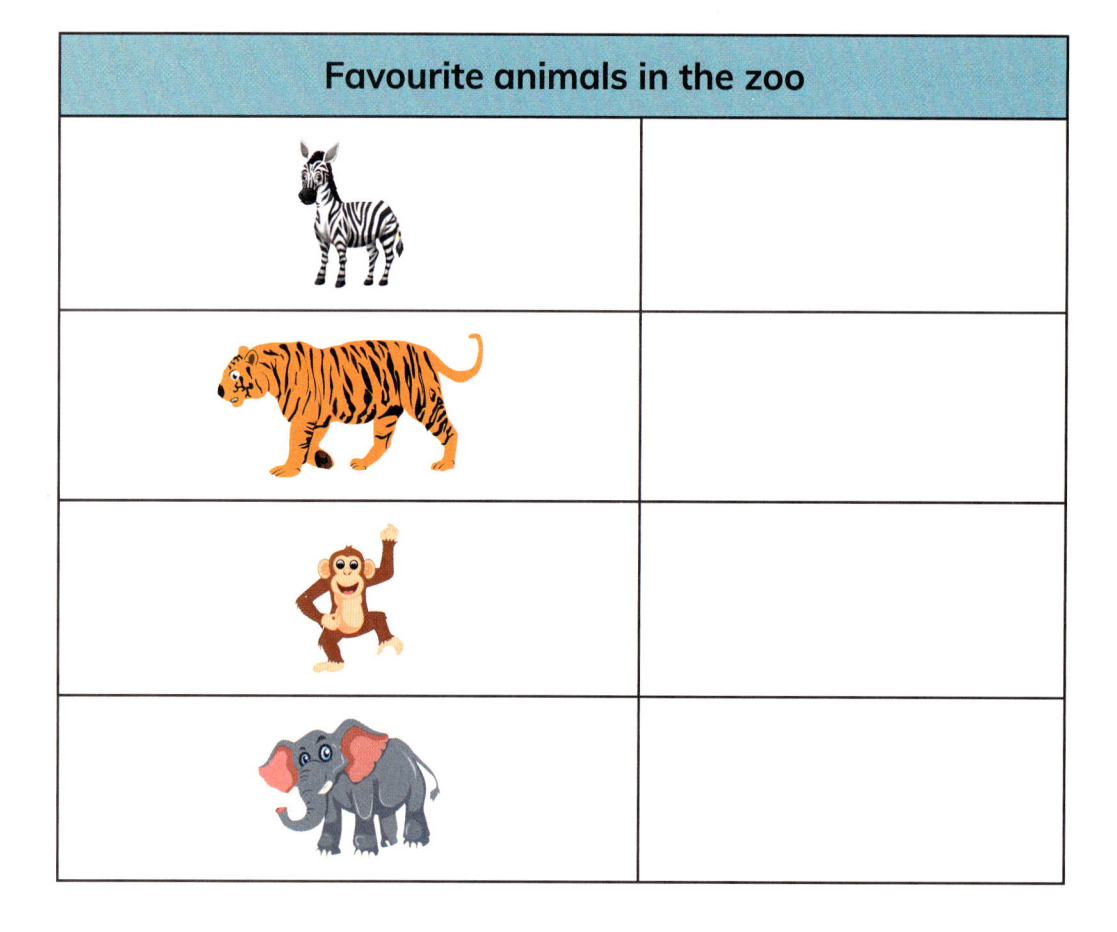

14.2 Lists, tables and block graphs

5 The pet shop has some animals for sale.

Complete the block graph to show how many different pets there are.

Number of pets				
6				
5				
4				
3				
2				
1				
0				
	rabbit	fish	chick	bird

14 Statistics (2)

Let's investigate

Play this game with a partner.

You will need a paper clip for the spinner.

Take turns to spin the spinner twice.

Add the 2 numbers together.

Colour the block with the matching total.

Have 10 turns each.

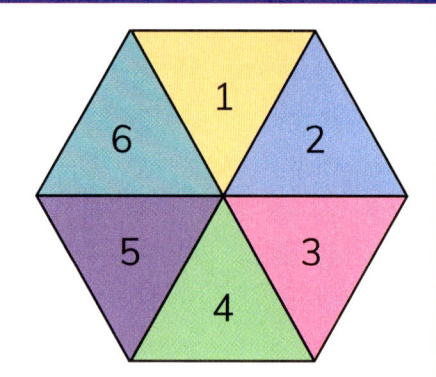

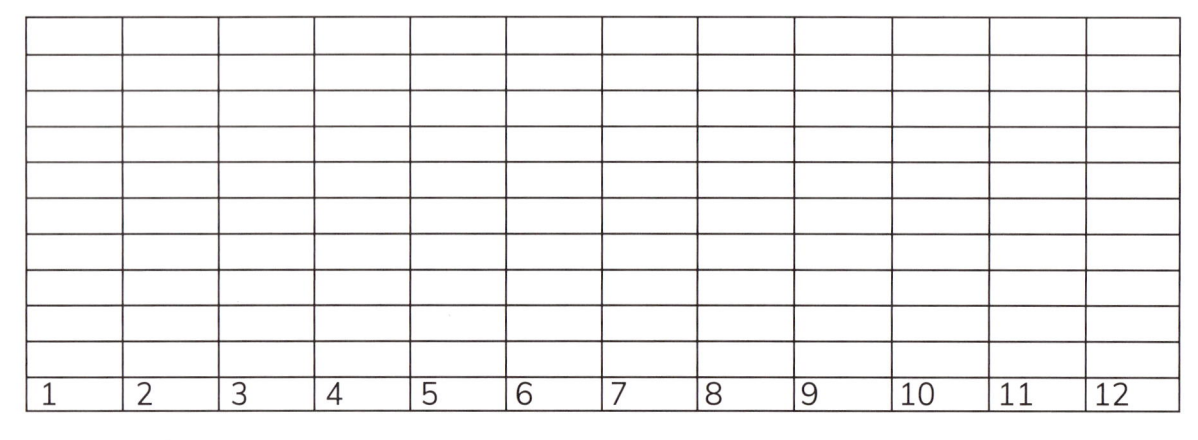

1	2	3	4	5	6	7	8	9	10	11	12

Do you think you will always get the same graph?

Tell your partner why you think that.

Why did number 1 not have any blocks filled in?

Play the game again and see if you can get number 1.

Do you know why?

Look what I can do!

- I can write lists.
- I can complete and use a table.
- I can complete and use a block graph.

14.2 Lists, tables and block graphs

Check your progress

1   Here is a pictogram showing the colour of socks worn by the children in class 1.

Each sock = 1 learner

white socks	🧦	🧦	🧦	🧦	🧦	🧦	🧦	🧦
blue socks	🧦	🧦	🧦	🧦				
red socks	🧦	🧦	🧦	🧦	🧦			

Complete the sentences about the socks.

_____ children wore white socks.

_____ children wore blue socks.

_____ children wore red socks.

_____ more children wore white socks than blue socks.

_____ was the most popular colour of socks.

14 Statistics (2)

Continued

2. Sort the toys into the Carroll diagram.

   Draw lines to join them to the right box.

like	do not like

3. Look at this block graph.

   It shows the favourite colours of 14 children in the class.

   Count the blocks.

   Draw a ring around the correct answer.

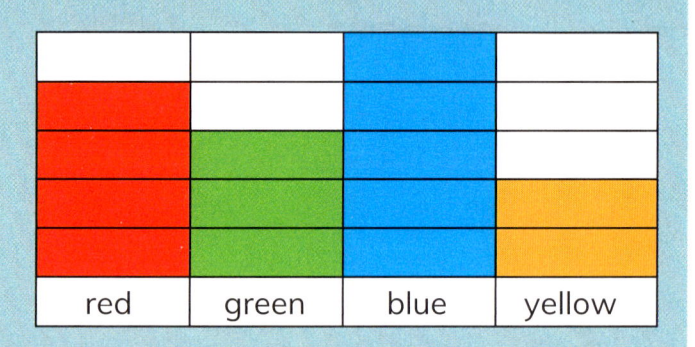

   Most children like: **red / green / blue / yellow**.

   Write how many:

   children like red _____

   children like yellow _____

   children like green. _____

15 Time (2)

Getting started

1 All the days of the week have 'day' at the end of their name.

Write one day of the week in each box.

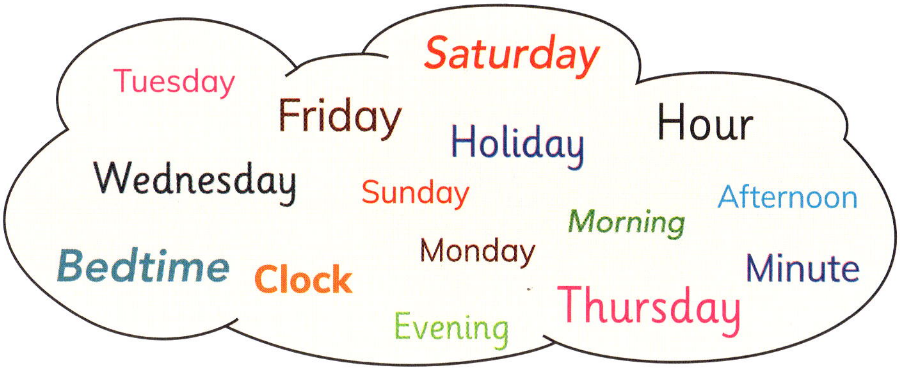
Tuesday
Saturday
Friday
Holiday
Hour
Wednesday
Sunday
Morning
Afternoon
Bedtime
Clock
Monday
Minute
Evening
Thursday

2 What time is it?

12
1
2
3
4
5
6
7
8
9
10
11

12
1
2
3
4
5
6
7
8
9
10
11

12
1
2
3
4
5
6
7
8
9
10
11

______________ ______________ ______________

15 Time (2)

It is very important to be able to tell the time.

You need to be at school, the doctor's, the dentist and many other places at the correct time.

You need to know the order of the days of the week and the months of the year.

You don't want to go to the dentist on the wrong day!

> 15.1 Time

We are going to …

- know the position of the clock hands for o'clock and half past times
- know the days of the week and the months of the year
- recognise and use the repeating patterns of the days of the week and months of the year.

Look more closely at the position of the hands on a clock. Many years ago, clocks only had one hand.

The days of the week and the months of the year always come in the same order, just like numbers.

month   year

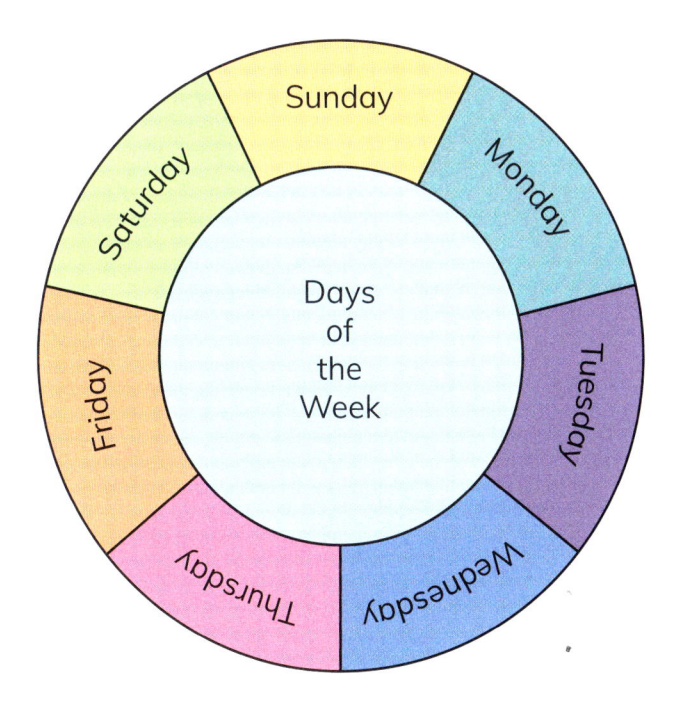

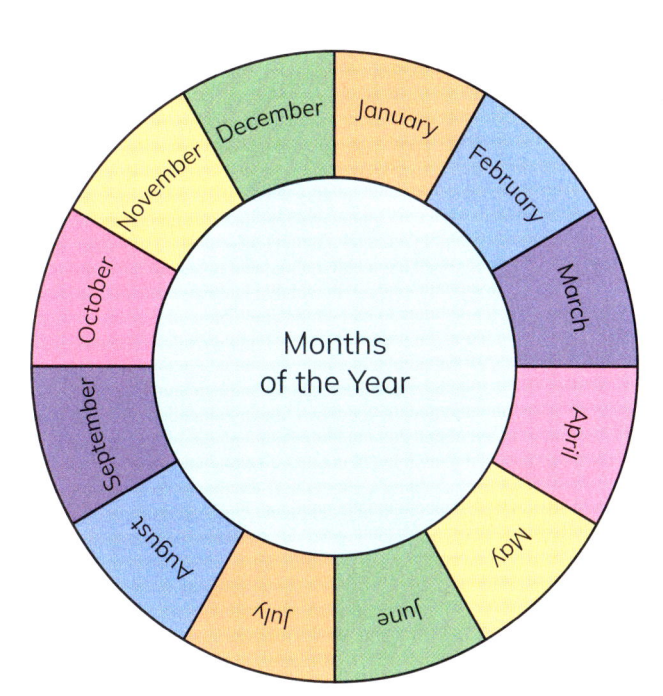

15 Time (2)

Exercise 15.1

1 What time is it?

   Write the time in words below each clock.

   _____   _____   _____

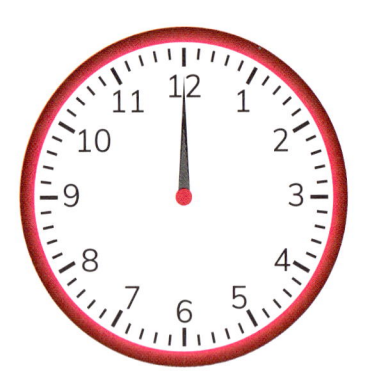

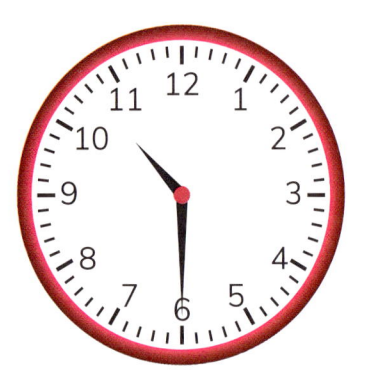

2 What time is it?

   These clocks only have one hand.
   Write the time in words below each clock.

   _____   _____   _____

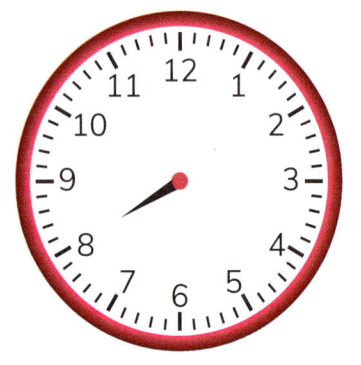

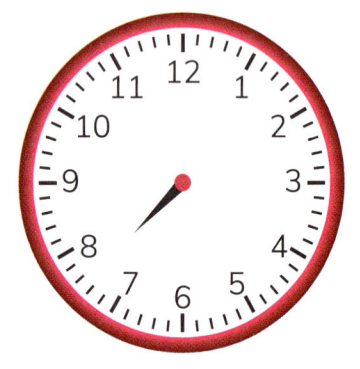

Is it easier to tell the time on a clock with one hand or two hands?

Why do you think that is?

15.1 Time

3 Today is Monday. What day will it be **tomorrow**? _____

Today is Friday. What day was it **yesterday**? _____

Today is Thursday. What day will it be in 2 days' time? _____

Today is Monday. What day was it yesterday? _____

4 Complete these sentences.

There are _____ days in a week.

Two days of the week begin with S.

They are _____ and _____.

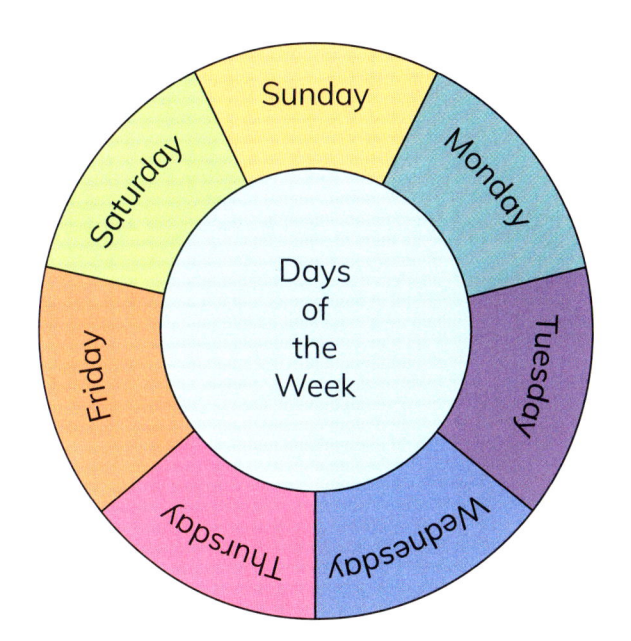

| Worked example 1 |

It is April. Which **month** will it be next?

_____

225

15 Time (2)

Continued

Answer:

It is April now.
The next month will be May.

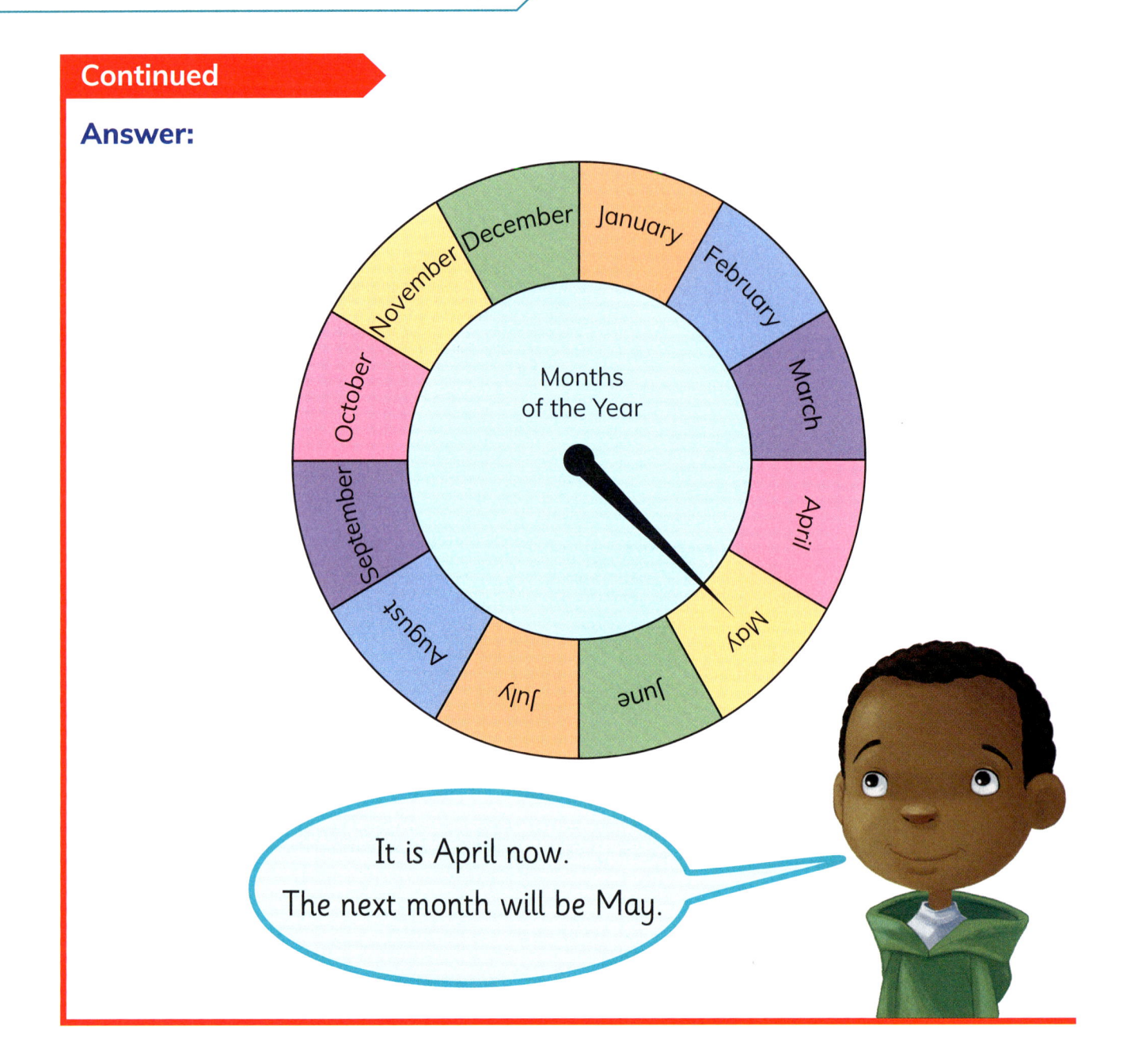

5. It is February.

   What is the next month? _____

   It is August.

   Which month was it last month? _____

   It is October.

   Which month was it last month? _____

15.1 Time

6 Complete these sentences.

There are _____ months in a **year**.

Two months begin with the letter A.

They are _____ and _____.

Let's investigate

What is your age in months and years?

Use your months of the year wheel to help you find out.

Are you older or younger than Zara?

I am 6 years and 3 months old.

Look what I can do!

- I know the positions of the clock hands for o'clock and half past times.
- I know the days of the week and the months of the year.
- I can use a days of the week wheel and a months of the year wheel to help me answer questions.

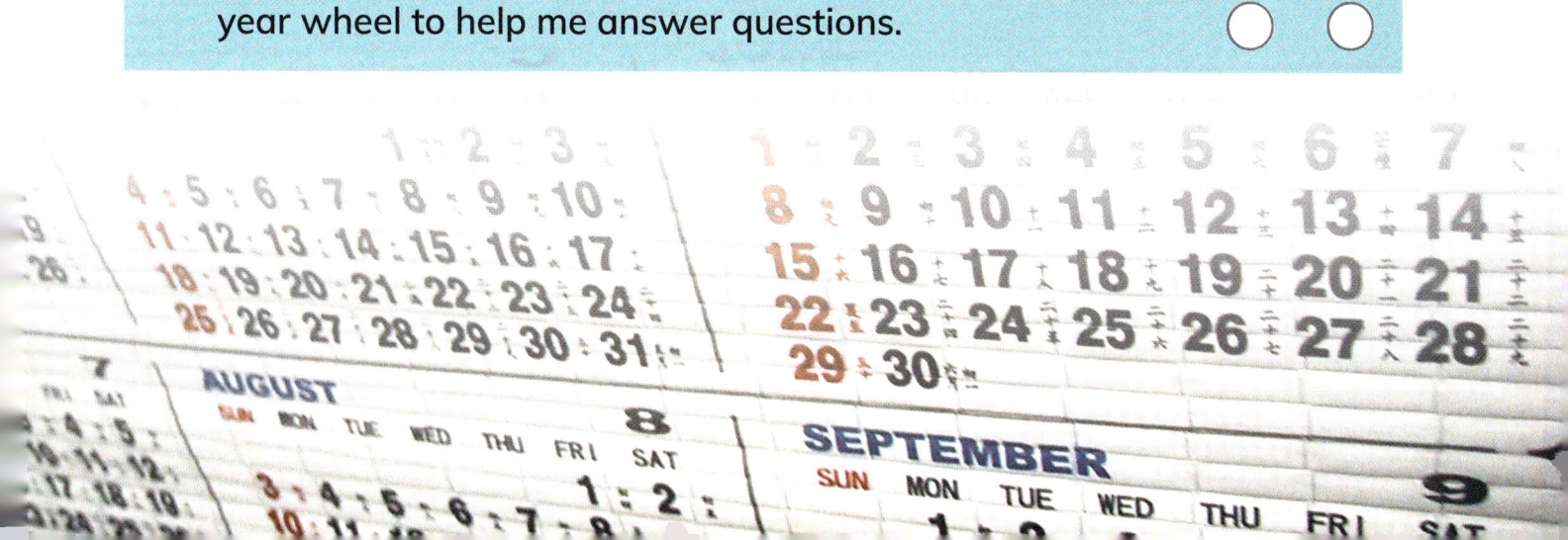

15 Time (2)

Check your progress

1. Draw lines to match the times that are the same.

15.1 Time

Continued

2   Complete the sentences.

Today is Tuesday.
Yesterday was _____ and tomorrow will be _____.

Today is Friday.
Yesterday was _____ and tomorrow will be _____.

3   Here are the days of the week and the months of the year.
Find the 12 months of the year.
Draw a ring around each month.

July   Tuesday

Sunday   November

June   January   May

September   Thursday

Monday   March

Wednesday

August   Saturday

April

February   Friday   December

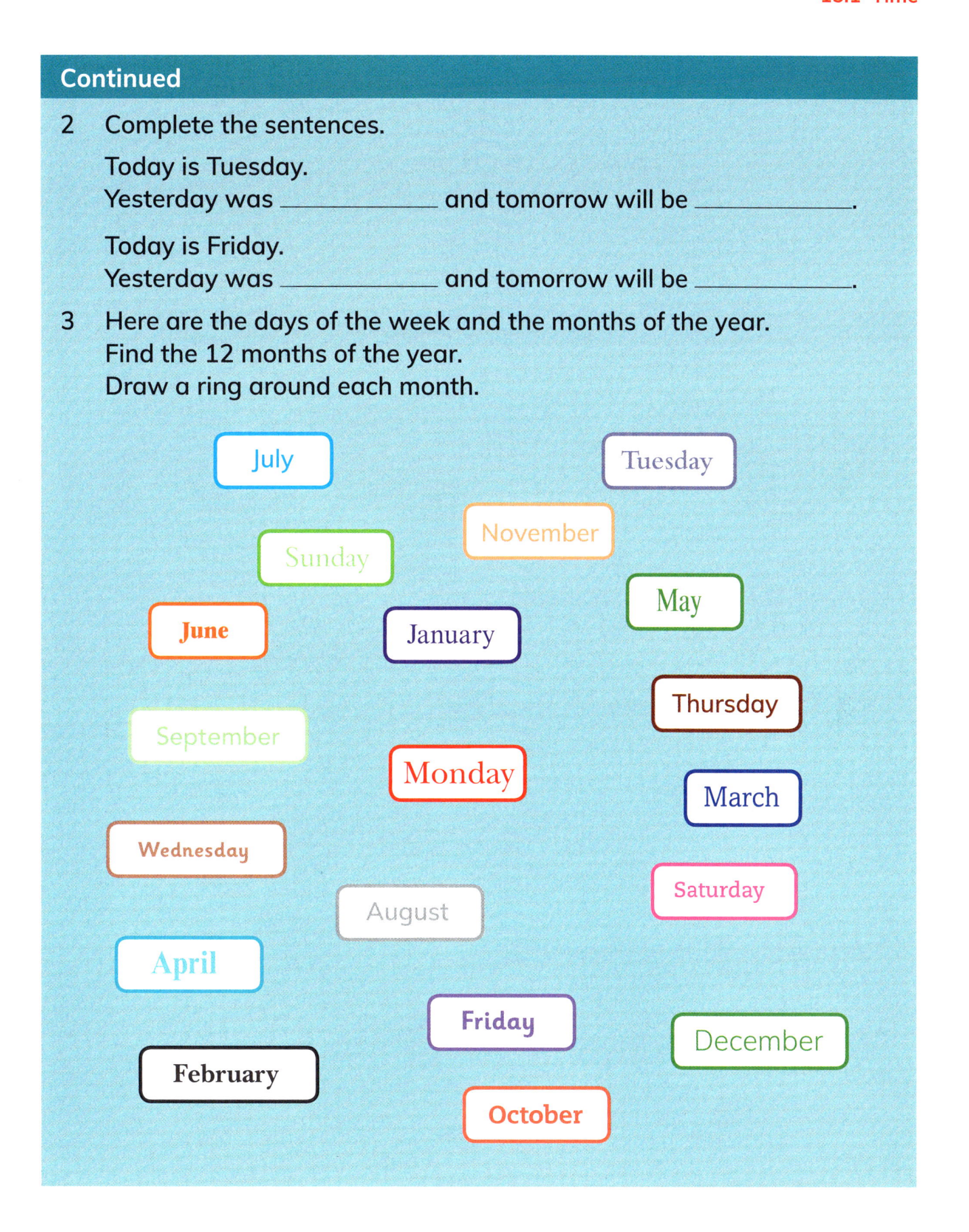

October

16 > Position, direction and patterns

Getting started

Where is the 🐘 in the queue? _____

Who is between the 🦓 and the 🐊? _____

Where is the 🐊 in the queue? _____

Who is between the 🐒 and the 🦓? _____

Where is the 🐒 in the queue? _____

Who is between the 🦁 and the 🐘? _____

Where is the 🦜 in the queue? _____

16 Position, direction and patterns

How do I get to the train station from school?

Walk to the shop then turn left.

Walk to the park, then turn right.

You are learning about position, pattern and direction so that you can use them during your everyday life.

You need to be able to find your school, the shops or the park.

If you don't know when to turn left or right you will walk a straight line forever!

16 Position, direction and pattern

> 16.1 Position, direction and patterns

We are going to …
- **use words to describe and continue patterns**
- **use words and actions to describe direction**
- **use words to describe position.**

A sequence is a list of objects or numbers that are in a special order.

This order could be going forwards or backwards.

A sequence has a rule.

Sometimes it can have two rules.

Sequences and patterns have rules that we need to understand so we know what comes next.

Patterns are everywhere.

We see them on our clothes, on our walls, on our buildings and on flowers and trees.

We see lots of patterns in maths too.

> left   right   sequence

> 1, 2, 3, 4, 5 is a sequence of numbers.

> So is 5, 4, 3, 2, 1.

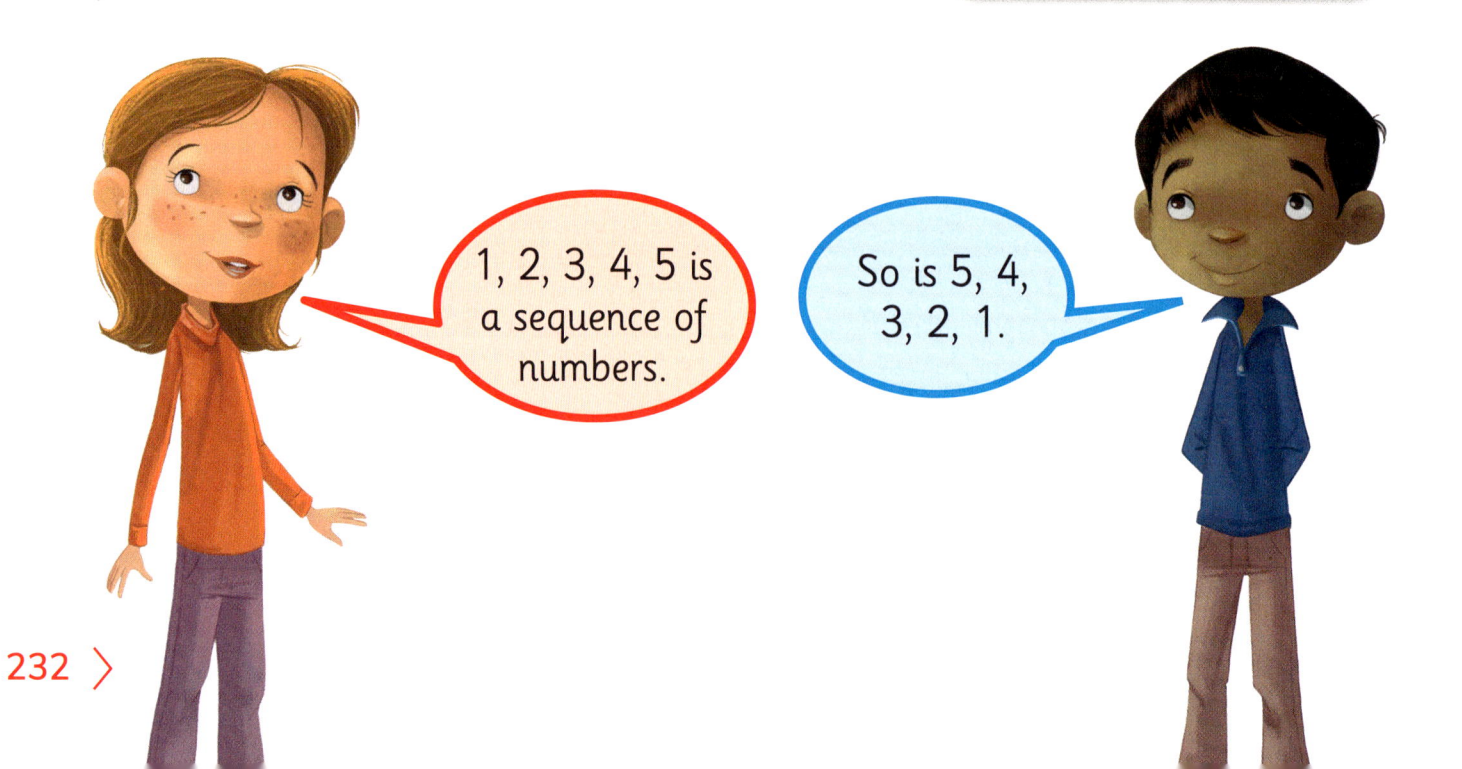

16.1 Position, direction and patterns

Exercise 16.1

1 Describe the pattern that you can see.

   Draw a repeating pattern of your own. Describe it to a partner.

2 Look at the row of learners.

   Draw the next 2 learners at the end of the row.

   Keep the pattern of their arms the same.

   Make your own pattern using arms.

233

16 Position, direction and pattern

3 Draw and colour your own pattern.
Use shapes or objects.

Worked example 1

Use the clues to colour each shape.
1. Red is next to green.
2. Green is above yellow.
3. Blue is between yellow and purple.
4. Purple is below orange.

Answer:
Red is **next to** green.

It could be this   or this   or something else.

I'm going to use this one.

I'm going to use this one.

16.1 Position, direction and patterns

Continued

Green is **above** yellow.

Blue is **between** yellow and purple.

Purple is **below** orange.

We've used the same colours and we've followed the same rules, but our pictures look different.

16 Position, direction and pattern

4   Work with a partner.
    Solve the clues to colour the squares.
    Orange is below green.
    Yellow is between green and purple.
    Yellow is above blue.
    Red is next to blue.

5   Work with a partner.
    Fill in the missing words.

    next to   above   below   between

    The green square is _____ the red square.

    The blue square is _____ the yellow square.

    The yellow square is _____ the blue square.

6   Make your own coloured squares puzzle.

    Ask your partner some questions about your puzzle.

16.1 Position, direction and patterns

7   Look at this arrangement of shapes.

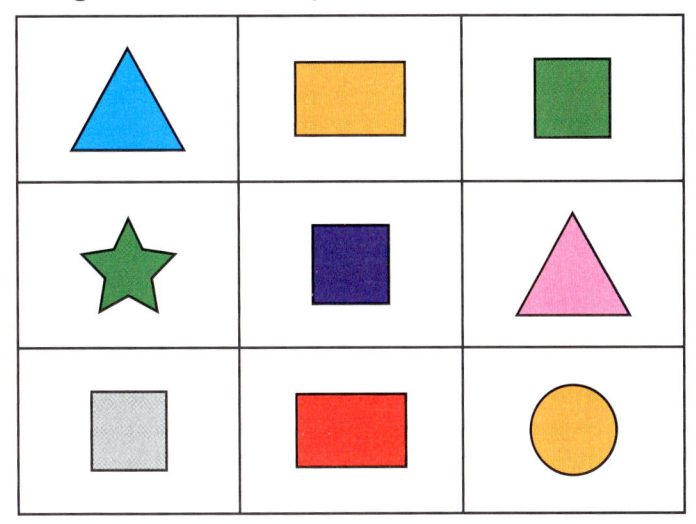

    Draw the shape that is:

    above the grey square

    next to the yellow circle

    below the green square

    above the green star

    between the blue triangle
    and the green square

8   Give directions to your partner to
    get from the start to the finish.

    Each section is a step.

    Start by taking 2 steps forward
    and then turn right.

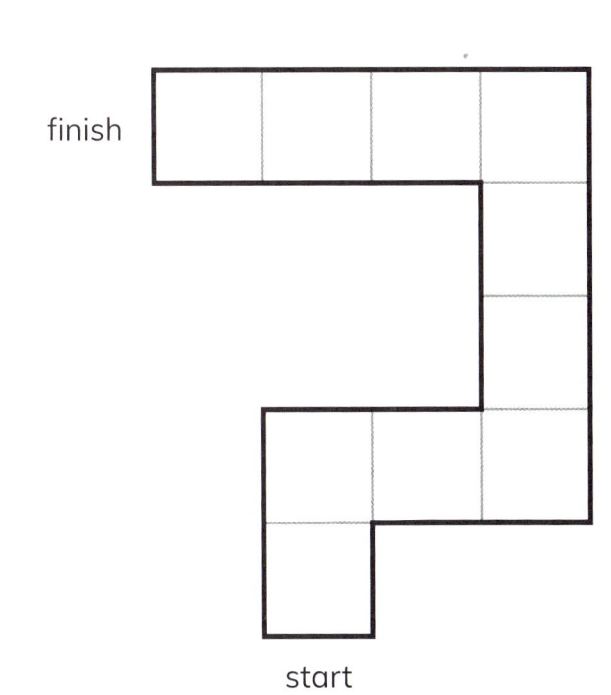

    finish

    start

    237

16 Position, direction and pattern

9

Colour her **left** hand **red**.

Colour her **right** hand **blue**.

Colour her left shoe **green**.

Colour her right shoe **yellow**.

Colour the left flower **red**.

Colour the right flower **yellow**.

16.1 Position, direction and patterns

10 Work with a partner.

Colour the path Aisha takes to get to her house without bumping into objects.

The path has been started for you.

Find 2 other ways she could take.

Colour one green.

Colour the other one blue.

start

Can you tell someone else about the path to the house?
Can you use words like left and right?
What could help you to remember?

Look what I can do!

- I can describe position using objects.
- I can describe direction using left and right.
- I can use language to describe patterns such as next to, between and beside.

16 Position, direction and pattern

Check your progress

1. Give directions to your partner to get from the start to the finish. Use a small car to help you.

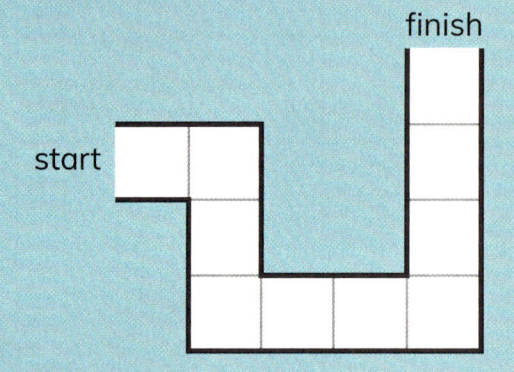

2. Where is Jack?

   Follow the directions to take Jack on a journey.
   Forward 2. Turn left.
   Forward 1. Turn left.
   Forward 2. Turn left.
   Forward 2. Turn left.
   Forward 2. Turn left.
   Forward 1. Turn left.
   Forward 2.
   Where is Jack?
   Draw a picture of Jack at the end of his journey.

> Project 6

Finding drawers

Look at the drawers in this picture

Each drawer is labelled with what is inside of it.

Which drawer is the coloured paper in? _____

Can you describe the position of this drawer?
_____

Where are the toy cars kept? _____

Where is this drawer compared to the drawer of paintbrushes?
_____

Talk to your partner and describe where some of the other drawers are.

Glossary

$\frac{1}{2}$	the mathematical symbol for half	158
2D	a flat shape, such as a square	37
3D	a shape that isn't flat, such as a cube	37
above	over the top of something else – the chicken is **above** the box	89
add	put amounts together to find how many altogether	68

altogether	the total	68
balance scales	an instrument used to measure mass	168
banknote	paper or plastic notes used as money	198
behind	the chicken is **behind** the box	89
below	the chicken is **below** the box	89
beside	next to something – the chicken is **beside** the box	89

between	in the middle – the chicken is **between** the boxes	19
block graph	a graph that is made using blocks, each block represents the same amount of something	204
calculation	using mathematics to work something out, on paper or in your head	76
	I know 9 and 1 is 10, so 9 and 4 is more than that...	
capacity	the amount that something can hold – the jug has a bigger capacity than the cup	167

| **Carroll diagram** | a diagram that sorts objects into two groups | 204 |

Has legs and arms	Does not have legs and arms

circle — a round 2D shape — 42

clock — an object that shows the time — 111

coin — thin metal disc used as money — 27

compare — check whether two things are the same or different — 22

complement — complements to 10 are the same as number bonds, or number pairs that total 10. 7 and 3 are complements to 10 because 7 + 3 = 10 — 180

compose	put parts of a number together to make the whole	188
count	say the number names in the correct order, often to find out how many objects	10
counting back	counting down from a larger number to a smaller number 12, 11, 10, 9, 8…	132
counting on	counting forwards from any number 12, 13, 14, 15…	132
cube	a 3D shape with square faces	32
cuboid	a 3D shape with rectangular faces	140
curved	not straight – a circle has curved sides	38

cylinder	a 3D shape with 2 circular faces and a curved surface	38
data	facts, for example, the heights of everyone in your class	98
decompose	separate a number into its parts, usually tens and ones	188
digit	0, 1, 2, 3, 4, 5, 6, 7, 8, 9 are all digits	123
double	two lots of the same amount, for example double 4 is 8	194

edge	where two surfaces meet	38
empty	an object with nothing inside	168
equal	the same as – these glasses contain an equal amount of juice	22
estimate	a sensible guess, using what you know	12
even	when a number of objects can be grouped in twos, that number is an **even** number	31
face	a flat surface on a 3D shape	38

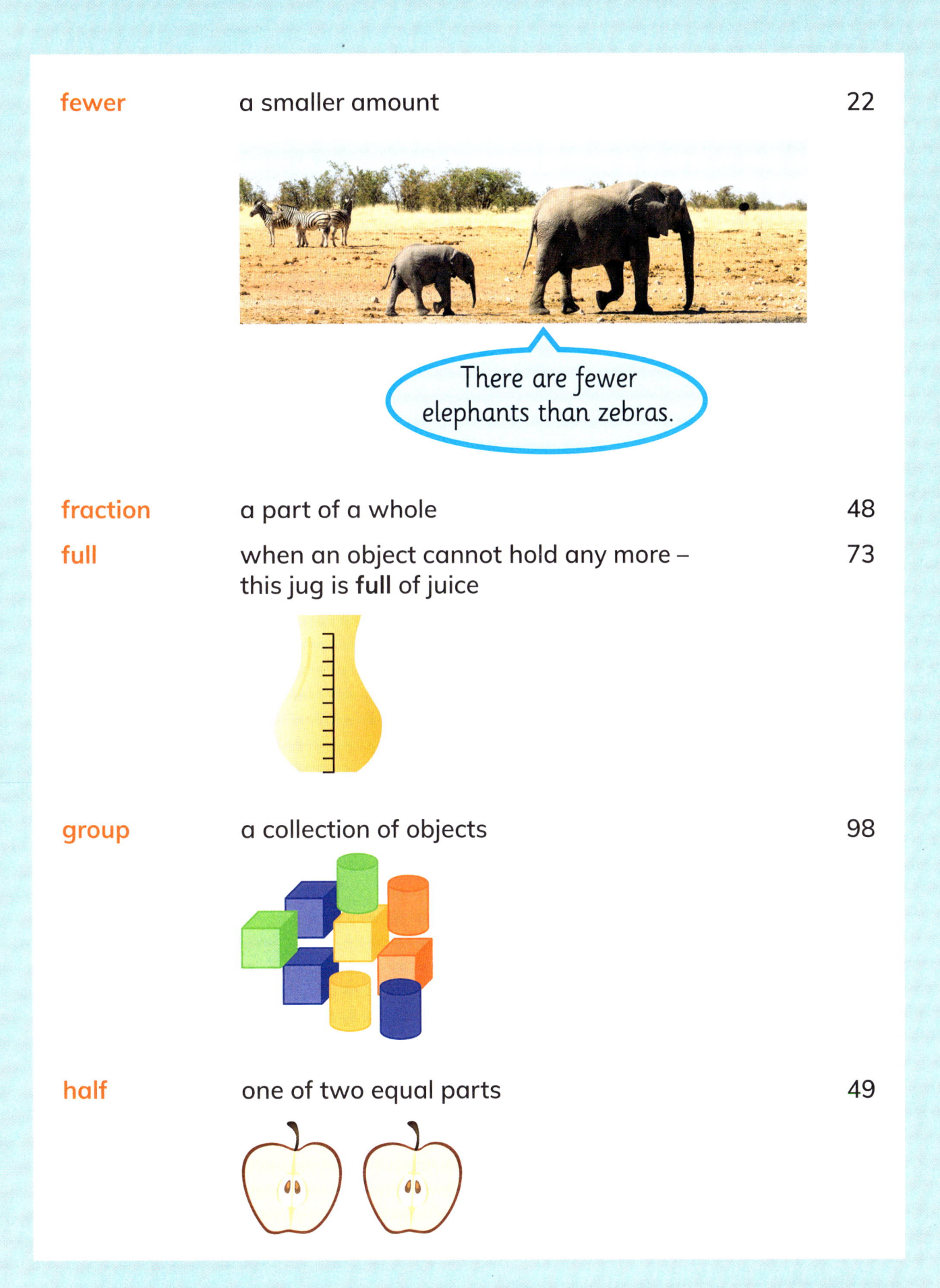

fewer	a smaller amount	22

There are fewer elephants than zebras.

fraction	a part of a whole	48
full	when an object cannot hold any more – this jug is **full** of juice	73
group	a collection of objects	98
half	one of two equal parts	49

half past	30 minutes past the hour – this clock shows half past 7	111
halve	to cut a whole into two equal parts	158
hands	a clock has two hands which show the time, an hour hand and a minute hand	111
heavy	weighs a lot – an elephant is heavy	167
hexagon	a 6-sided shape	147
hour	60 minutes	111

how many?	a question asking you to find out the number of objects	12
in front of	the chicken is **in front of** the box	89
label	writing showing what something is	11
left	the shoe is to the **left** of the duck	231
length	how long something is	56
less	a smaller amount	22
light	weighs very little – a feather is light	168

251

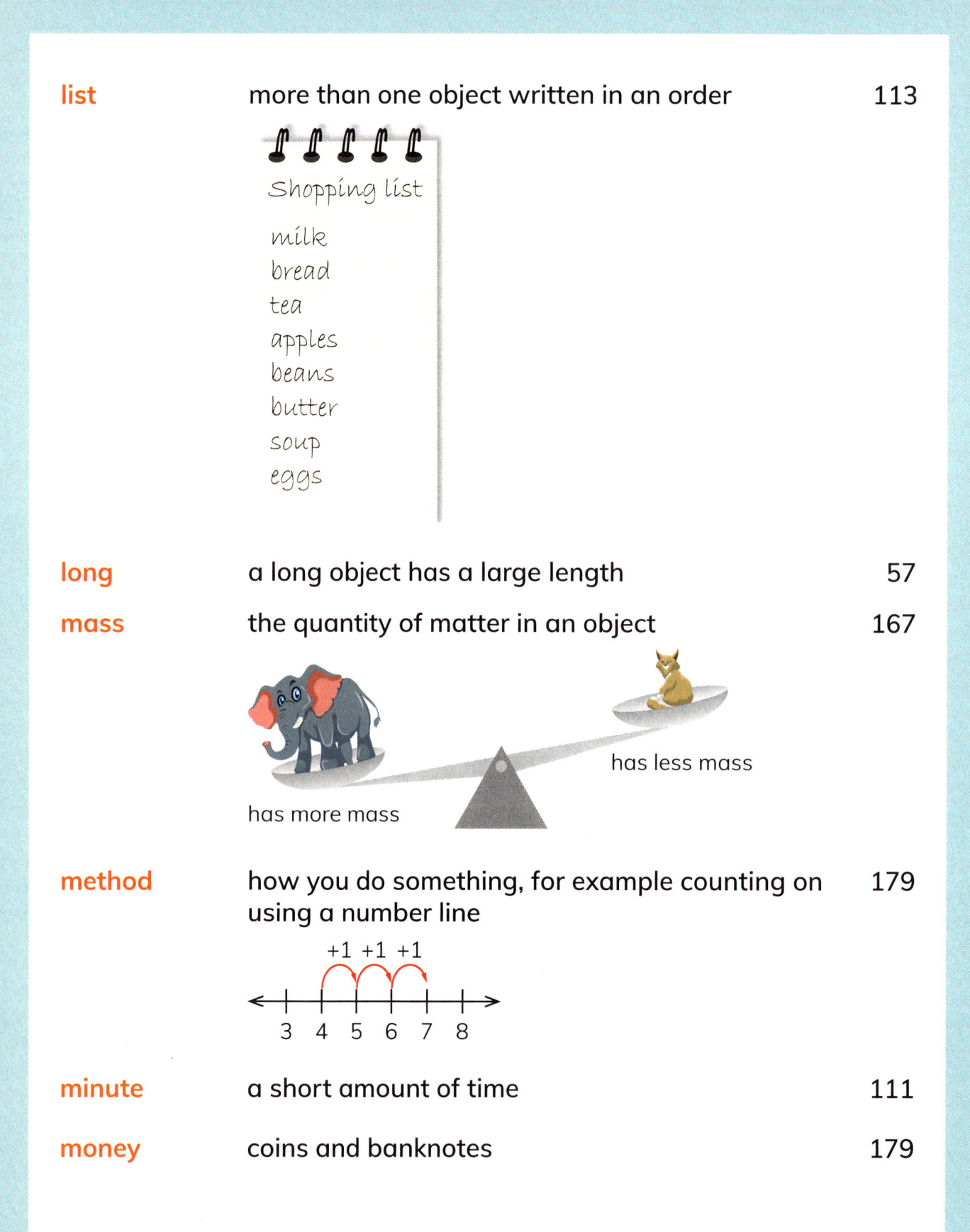

list	more than one object written in an order	113

Shopping list
milk
bread
tea
apples
beans
butter
soup
eggs

long	a long object has a large length	57
mass	the quantity of matter in an object	167

has more mass — has less mass

method	how you do something, for example counting on using a number line	179
minute	a short amount of time	111
money	coins and banknotes	179

month	one of the 12 parts of the year	222
more	a bigger amount	22

There are more zebras than elephants.

next to	beside – the chicken is **next to** the box	56
number	a count, label or measure	10
number bond		69

5 + 1 = 6 is a number bond for 6.

253

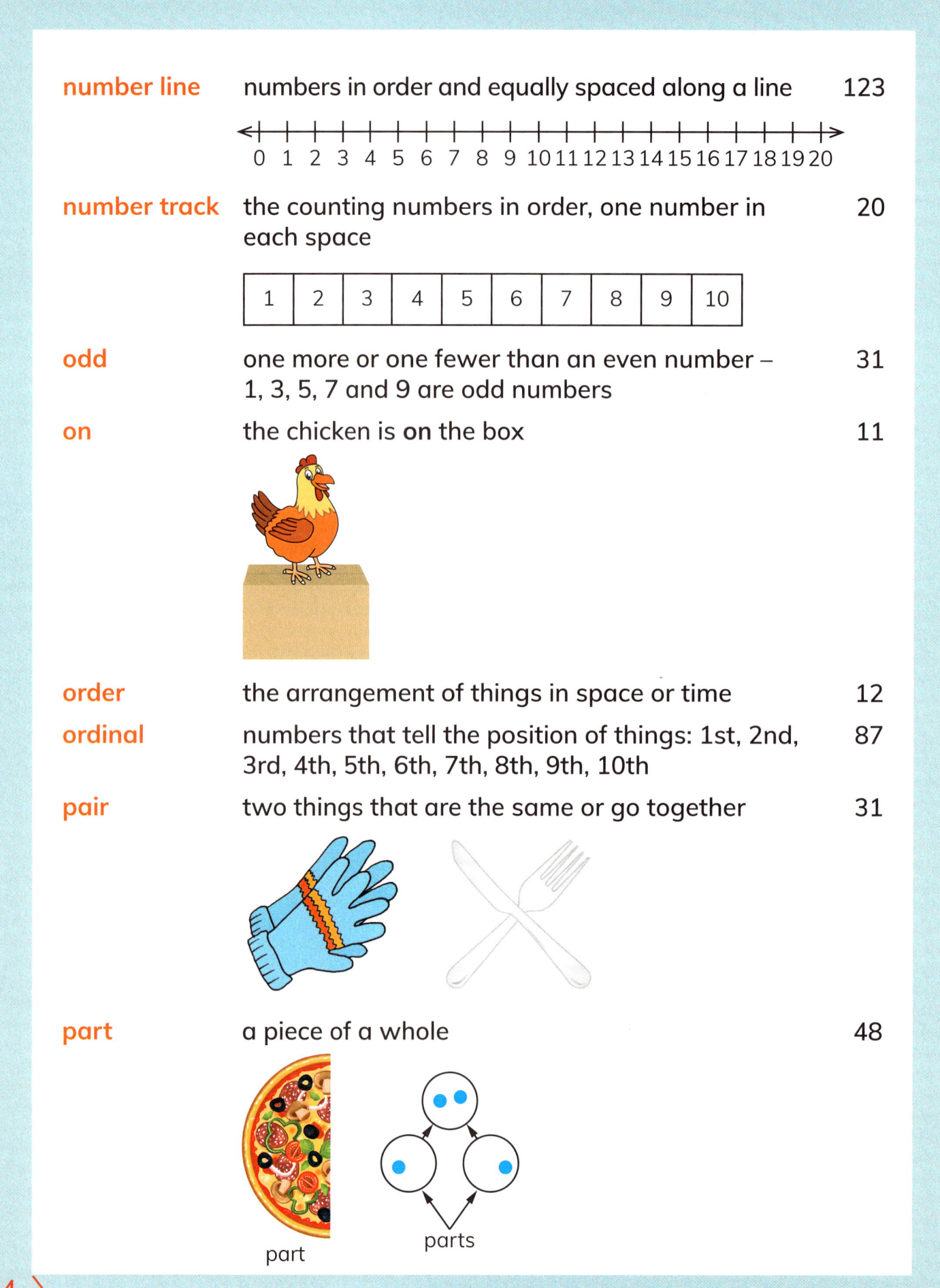

number line	numbers in order and equally spaced along a line	123

```
0 1 2 3 4 5 6 7 8 9 10 11 12 13 14 15 16 17 18 19 20
```

number track	the counting numbers in order, one number in each space	20

1	2	3	4	5	6	7	8	9	10

odd	one more or one fewer than an even number – 1, 3, 5, 7 and 9 are odd numbers	31
on	the chicken is **on** the box	11
order	the arrangement of things in space or time	12
ordinal	numbers that tell the position of things: 1st, 2nd, 3rd, 4th, 5th, 6th, 7th, 8th, 9th, 10th	87
pair	two things that are the same or go together	31
part	a piece of a whole	48

part

parts

pattern	a regular arrangement, often repeated	31
pentagon	a shape with 5 sides	147
pictogram	a graph that is made using pictures, each picture represents the same amount of something	204

Sunshine hours ☀ = 1 hour of sunshine

Friday	☀ ☀ ☀ ☀
Saturday	☀ ☀ ☀ ☀ ☀
Sunday	☀ ☀ ☀ ☀ ☀ ☀ ☀

place value cards	cards used to show the value of each digit in a number	119
point	put a finger on or towards something	19
position	where something is	87

price	how much you need to pay to buy an item	198
pyramid	a 3D shape where the sides are triangles which meet at the top and the base is a flat shape	140
rectangle	a 2D shape with 4 sides, the opposite sides are equal in length	42
regroup	separate a number into different parts. 5 can be regrouped into 2 + 3, 4 + 1, 1 + 2 + 2 and so on.	180
right	the duck is to the **right** of the shoe	19
rotate	to turn around a fixed point	147
same	when we compare sets or numbers, both sets are equal in size, shape or value	14
sequence	a list of objects or numbers in a special order	232
set	a collection of objects that have something that is the same – here is a set of animals that all have spots or stripes	10

short	a short object has a small length or height	56
side	the line joining each vertex to the next vertex on a 2D shape	42

←— side

solve	work out the answer to a calculation, for example 2 + 3 = 5, 10 − 2 = 8	172
sort	to arrange a group in a special way	38

Green   Not green

sphere	a 3D shape with no straight edges	38
square	a flat shape with 4 straight sides the same length	42
straight	not curved or bending	42
subtract	take a number or amount from another number or amount. Methods of subtraction include take away and counting back.	78

| table | an arrangement of facts and numbers in rows or blocks | 146 |

Flavour	Monday	Tuesday
chocolate	8	4
vanilla	5	8
strawberry	12	6

take away	remove one or more things from a set	78
tall	a **tall** object has a large height	56
teen numbers	the numbers 11, 12, 13, 14, 15, 16, 17, 18, 19	119
temperature	a measured amount of heat	167
thermometer	an instrument used to measure temperature	173

| thin | a **thin** object has a small width | 57 |
| title | the name of a graph, chart, diagram or book | 205 |

title ⟶ Sunshine hours   ☀ = 1 hour of sunshine

Friday	☀ ☀ ☀ ☀
Saturday	☀ ☀ ☀ ☀ ☀
Sunday	☀ ☀ ☀ ☀ ☀ ☀ ☀ ☀

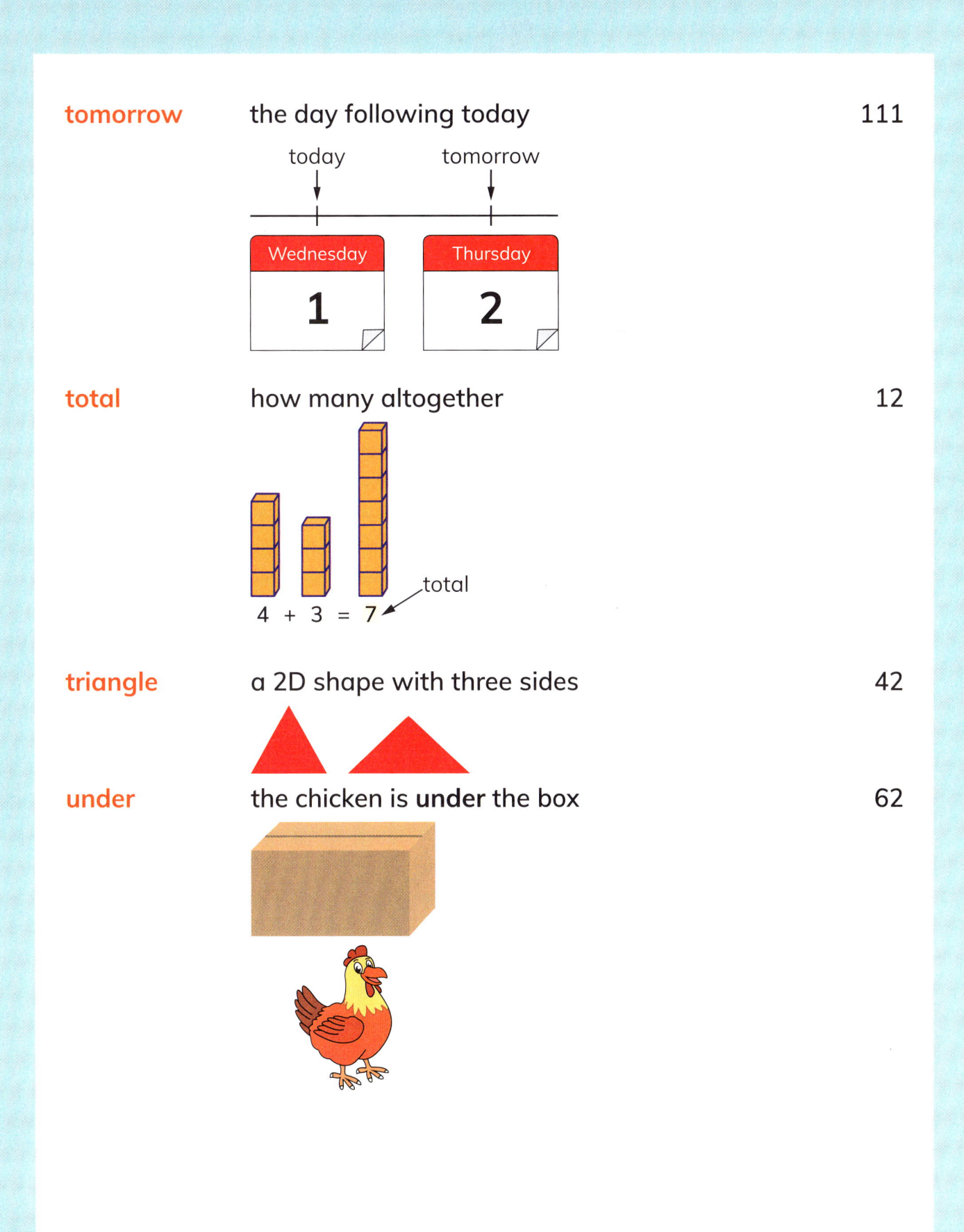

tomorrow	the day following today	111
total	how many altogether	12
	4 + 3 = 7 total	
triangle	a 2D shape with three sides	42
under	the chicken is **under** the box	62

value	the amount marked on a coin or banknote is its value – the value of this banknote is $10	198
Venn diagram	a diagram used for sorting – here is an example of a Venn diagram that sorts fruits and vegetables into red and not-red sets	97
week	seven days: Monday, Tuesday, Wednesday, Thursday, Friday, Saturday, Sunday	111
whole	all the parts of something	33
wide	a **wide** object has a large length from side to side	57
word problem	a problem written in words rather than in a number sentence	194
year	12 months	222

yesterday	the day before today	111

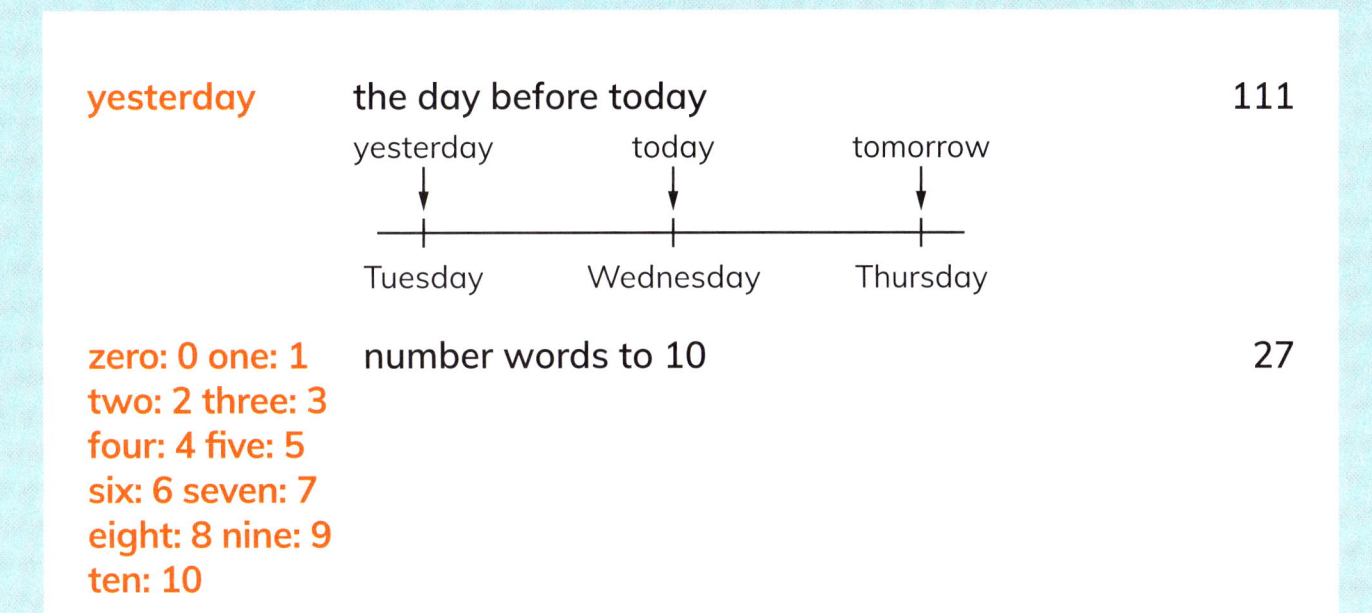

yesterday — Tuesday
today — Wednesday
tomorrow — Thursday

zero: 0 one: 1 two: 2 three: 3 four: 4 five: 5 six: 6 seven: 7 eight: 8 nine: 9 ten: 10	number words to 10	27

Acknowledgements

It takes an extraordinary number of people to put together a new series of resources and their comments, support and encouragement have been really important to us. We would like to thank the following people: Philip Rees and Veronica Wastell for the support they have given the authors; Lynne McClure for her feedback and comments on early sections of the manuscript; Thomas Carter, Caroline Walton, Laura Collins, Charlotte Griggs, Gabby Martin, Elizabeth Scurfield, Berenice Howard-Smith, Zohir Naciri, Emma McCrea and Eddie Rippeth as part of the team at Cambridge preparing the resources. We would also like to particularly thank all of the anonymous reviewers for their time and comments on the manuscript and as part of the endorsement process.

The authors and publishers acknowledge the following sources of copyright material and are grateful for the permissions granted. While every effort has been made, it has not always been possible to identify the sources of all the material used, or to trace all copyright holders. If any omissions are brought to our notice, we will be happy to include the appropriate acknowledgements on reprinting.

Thanks to the following for permission to reproduce images:

Cover by Omar Aranda (Beehive Illustration); *Inside* Yih Chang Chew/GI; ntmw/GI; Carol Yepes/GI; SMXRF/Star Max/GI; Westend61/GI; Nenov/GI; Westend61/GI; Suelen Tu Han Lee/GI; Jenny Dettrick/GI; SCIEPRO/SCIENCE PHOTO LIBRARY/GI; Chris Clor/GI; ROBERT BROOK/SCIENCE PHOTO LIBRARY/GI; bortonia/GI; Peter Cade/GI; Flavio Coelho/GI; Richard Drury/GI; ThomasVogel/GI; Peter Dazeley/GI; Jessica Lee Photography/GI; fotograzia/GI; Poh Kim Yeoh/GI; itsme23/GI; Francesco Riccardo Iacomino/GI.

GI=Getty Images